Mysticism East and West

Cover art by *Jane A. Evans*

Rudolf Otto

Mysticism
East and West

A Comparative Analysis of
The Nature of Mysticism

This publication made possible with
the assistance of the Kern Foundation

The Theosophical Publishing House
Wheaton, Ill. U.S.A.
Madras, India / London, England

First Quest edition, 1987.
A publication of the Theosophical Publishing House, a department of the Theosophical Society in America.

Library of Congress Cataloging in Publication Data.

Otto, Rudolf, 1869-1937.
  Mysticism East & West.

  (A Quest book)
  Translation of: West-östliche Mystik.
  Reprint. Originally published: New York: Collier Books, 1962, c1960.
  Includes bibliographical references.
  1. Mysticism—Comparative studies. 2. Philosophy and religion.
3. Eckhart, Meister, d. 1327. 4. Saṅkarācārya. I. Title. II. Title:
Mysticism East and West.
BL625.0713 1987   291.4'2   86-30016
ISBN 0-8356-0619-8 (pbk.)

Printed in the United States of America

Contents

Transition from Part A to Part B

Part B/The Differences.
Eckhart versus Sankara

Appendices

Foreword

This book attempts to penetrate the nature of that strange spiritual phenomenon which we call mysticism by comparing the two principal classic types of Eastern and Western mystical experience. By means of this comparison, and by explaining the individual features of one type of those or the other, the nature of mysticism itself becomes gradually more comprehensible.

At the same time, in the spiritual development of these two types there is revealed from the earliest days of ancient Indian mystical speculation right on to the modern speculative system of Fichte, an astonishing conformity in the deepest impulses of human spiritual experience, which—because it is almost entirely independent of race, clime and age—points to an ultimate inward hidden similarity of the human spirit, and justifies us in speaking of a uniform nature of mysticism. But we are immediately confronted with the equally important task of showing the possibilities of manifold singularities occurring within this uniform nature, and thereby of meeting the erroneous assumption that mysticism is "one and ever the same." Only thus is it possible to comprehend such great spiritual phenomena as, for instance, the German Meister Eckhart, the Indian Sankara, the Greek Plotinus, the mystics of the Buddhist Mahayana School, in all their characteristic individuality, instead of allowing them to disappear into the shadowy night of "general mysticism." The nature of mysticism only becomes clear in the fullness of its possible variations.

In the winter of 1923 to 1924 I was invited to Oberlin College, Oberlin, Ohio, to give the Haskell Lectures on the subject of Western mysticism compared with the mysticism of the East, with special reference to the types represented on the one hand by Eckhart, and on the other by Sankara. I gave these lectures in the autumn of 1924, and have since published several of them, some in outline and others in more detail, in various journals. In this book I have collected, completed and expanded them so that it repeats my Haskell Lectures in an enlarged form. In publishing these I look back with sincere gratitude to the hospitality and the willing help extended to me in my work in the States, particularly by my colleagues and friends, Dr. Fullerton and Dr. Foster. My thoughts turn also in gratitude to the time which I was able to spend in Japan and India fourteen years ago, and to the men who helped me there to gain an insight into the strange world of Eastern mysticism. My thanks are especially due to that venerable figure, the Reverend Dr. Johnson of Benares, a truly Christian missionary and a loving and careful investigator into the thought world of India, with whom I made my journeys to the sages and saints of the Indian schools, and to the centers of their learning and worship. Here for the first time in actuality I saw opening out before me the curious parallels between the feeling and experience of the Eastern and Western worlds. But I also recognized their intimate peculiarities and dissimilarities. This book will deal with Eastern and Western mysticism viewed under both aspects.

It will be obvious to the reader that the book has grown out of separate lectures and addresses. I have collected them into one volume, but have purposely left to the various sections the relatively independent form which they already possessed. This has led to a number of repetitions, particularly in the section connecting the parts A and B. But as I have said in the notes to that section, such occasional repetitions seemed useful especially when dealing with particular points less easily understood and of greater subtlety. It will also be obvious that this work presupposes the inquiry which I made in my book *Das Heilige (The Idea of the Holy)*, and that it links up with certain chapters of my work: *Das Gefühl des Überweltlichen* partly translated in *Religious Essays*.

Separate chapters of this book have been translated into English previously by my friends Dr. Kemper Fullerton, Dr. Foster, and Dr. Cumming Hall. The whole work has now been translated afresh by B. L. Bracey and R. C. Payne. I extend to them all my warmest thanks.

Throughout the book in quoting Meister Eckhart where the reference is given as Evans, the translation of his works by C. de B. Evans has been used *(The Work of Meister Eckhart).*[1] In all other cases the translation has been made direct from the editions of Pfeifer, Büttner or Lehmann.

The quotations from Plotinus are taken from Stephen McKenna's English translation of the *Enneads* with the exception of the extract from the *Sixth Ennead* on p. 194.

[1]Watkins. England.

About the Author

Rudolf Otto (1869-1937), German theologian and philosopher, was nurtured in the Lutheran faith. After serving as professor of theology of Göttingen and at Breslau, in 1917 he became professor of systematic theology at the University of Marburg, where he remained until his death. He published many books and essays, mainly on the history and psychology of religion.

While visiting North Africa and Japan in 1911-12, Otto gained an appreciation of oriental faiths and later became an influential interpreter of Hinduism. Among his important studies in this area are the present work, *Mysticism East and West* (1926), and *India's Religion of Grace and Christianity* (1930). His last work was a series of German translations and commentaries on the Bhagavad Gita and the Katha Upanishad.

Otto's major work, *The Idea of the Holy* (1917), established him as a significant figure in theological circles. It is considered one of the most important religious books of the first half of this century. In the work he combines an analysis of the depth of religious experience with a creative synthesis of modern German theology.

Otto contributed to the devotional life of the Lutheran Church and worked to develop a vital worship service that reflected his conviction that a profound mystery lies at the heart of religion. He helped prepare material for church service, schools, and private worship. The major emphases in all his work were on the numinous quality of religious experience, on individual intuitive insight, and on the importance of religious autonomy.

Introduction

> *...East is east, and west is west,*
> *And never the twain shall meet...*

so writes the English poet, Rudyard Kipling. Is that true? Are the thought worlds of East and West so different and incomparable that they can never meet and therefore at bottom never understand each other?

For this question and its answer there is no more fitting sphere in the spiritual life of man that that of mysticism and mystical speculation, for these rise from the very depths of the human spirit. Here, therefore, will be shown most clearly what is peculiar and incomparable in any spiritual type. If there are any incomprehensible and fundamentally divisive differences between them they will be strongest in this region. Indeed, it has often enough been maintained by Orientals that no Westerner could ever penetrate the inmost nature of Indian mystic thought or comprehend the secrets of the Chinese Dhyana-mysticism of a Bodhidharma or a Hui-Neng; and similarly by the West that no Oriental can ever experience in its depth and reality the motives of the great Western speculative philosophy beginning with Aristotle and going on to Kant and Fichte, to Darwin and Gauss. In complete contrast to such statements it is often claimed that mysticism is *the same* in all ages and in all places, that timeless and independent of history it has always been identical. East and West and other differences

1

vanish here. Whether the flower of mysticism bloom in India or in China, in Persia or on the Rhine and in Erfurt its fruit is one. Whether it clothe itself in the delicate Persian verse of a Jelaled-din Rumi or in the beautiful middle German of a Meister Eckhart; in the scholarly Sanskrit of the Indian Sankara, or in the laconic riddles of the Sino-Japanese Zen School, these forms could always be exchanged one for the other. For one and the same experience speaks here, only by chance in varying dialects. "East is west, and west is east."

In the following pages we shall briefly compare Western and Eastern mysticism; and in doing so we shall be guided by the two points of view expressed above. But we wish to anticipate and set out beforehand our results. We maintain that in mysticism there are indeed strong primal impulses working in the human soul which as such are completely unaffected by differences of climate, of geographical position or of race. These show in their similarity an inner relationship of types of human experience and spiritual life which is truly astonishing. Secondly, we contend that it is false to maintain that mysticism is always just mysticism, is always and everywhere one and the same quantity. Rather, there are within mysticism many varieties of expression which are just as great as the variations in any other sphere of spiritual life, be it in religion generally, or in ethics, or in art. Thirdly, we affirm that these varia-tions as such are not determined by race, or geographical situa-tion, but that they may appear side by side, indeed that they may arise in sharp contrast to one another, within the same circle of race and culture.

For this comparison of East and West we select two men who have been the greatest representatives and interpreters of that which is understood by Eastern and Western mysticism, and who are often set side by side: from the East the great Indian Acharya Sankara, and from the West the great German Meister Eckhart. With a little skill it would be possible so to weigh up and present their fundamental teachings that the words of the one would read like a translation into Latin or German from the Sanskrit of the other, and vice versa. That is certainly not mere accident, for words and names are themselves not things of chance but arise of neces-sity out of the subject-matter itself and give it expression. In their resemblance or even their identity is mirrored the resemblance or identity of the matter which they have to express.

The analogy between these two masters—(for Acharya also means "master" as does "Meister")—is in yet other respects re-remarkable. Neither is a chance phenomenon in his own age. As their respective epochs themselves show striking general similarities, so these two men correspond in the positions which they hold in and toward their own time. Both are to the same extent expressions and focusing points of great and more general tendencies and movements with which their age and environment were filled. Both, in a similar fashion, have roots in the heritage of past ages and great traditions, which they expand and build up anew. Each of them is at the same time theologian and philosopher and works with all the theological and philosophical conceptions of his day. Both are men of abstract, soaring and yet subtle speculation. Both are mystic and scholastic in one person, and attempt to express the content of their mysticism through the medium of their highly developed technique. Both present their teachings in the form of commentaries to the ancient holy Scriptures of their religious communities. Sankara does this by commenting on the Upanishads and in particular the sacred Bhagavad Gita; Eckhart by expounding the books of the Bible. Both use the same method of exposition: they force the old texts into the service of their own doctrines. Then they gather up their teaching into one great speculative work: Sankara in his Bhashya to the Brahma-sutra's, Eckhart in his *Opus Tripartitum*. In fact, as has already been indicated, they are "contemporaries," although Sankara lived and flourished about 800 A.D. and Eckhart lived from 1250 to 1327. For contemporaries in the deeper sense are not those who happen to be born in the same decade, but those who stand at corresponding points in the parallel development of their environments.[1]

But still more remarkable than these outward analogies is the resemblance of their attitude to mystical experience, of the speculation which springs from it, and of the impulses which guide this speculation. In the first main section of this book we shall be dealing with these similarities, and shall see in them the deep-rooted kinship which unquestionably exists between the souls of Oriental and Occidental.

[1] In this sense for example the Japanese Honen and Shinran are not only of spiritual kinship with Luther, but actually his contemporaries.

PART A

Conformity

1

Similarity in Metaphysical Speculation

1. Sankara is the classic teacher and interpreter of "Advaita" in its most strict and subtle form. Advaita means non-duality or "secondlessness," and the doctrine of "secondlessness." (The usual translation is monism but non-dualism is more exact.) This monistic doctrine can be summed up in general terms as follows: "True Being is Sat alone, Being itself, the eternal Brahman, unchanging and unchanged, undivided and without parts, Ekam eva advitiyam." That is (a) the multiplicity of things exists only through "Maya" (which is usually translated as "mere appearance").—Sat itself is the One only, ekam eva; (b) in itself Brahman or Being is absolutely and immutably "One only," without parts, without any multiplicity, and therefore without the multiplicity of differences and delimitations. Hence it is necessarily without any distinctions at all: nirgunam, nirvisesham. Therefore it is "advitiyam," non-dual, both outwardly and inwardly, and is opposed also to all alteration (vikara) and to all change:

> Change rests simply upon a word.
> It is a mere name.

Thence it is also opposed to all beginning (utpada) and becoming (sambhava).

This Eternal One in its uniform nature is wholly and purely Atman or spirit (chit and chaitanyam), pure consciousness (jnana), pure knowledge. Similarly, because it is without division, this spirit or consciousness or knowledge is beyond the three antitheses of Knower, Known, and the act of Knowing.[1] Thus it is at once "anantam," without end, and beyond space and time.

The soul of man, the "inward Atman," is nothing less than this one, eternal, unchangeable, homogeneous Brahman itself. Through the enigmatic power of Maya there arises in the soul "advidya"—not-knowing (or, better; false knowing). Maya "superimposes" (adhyaropa) upon the reality of the One Being the deceptive multiplicity of the world. So Being, which is One only, appears to the soul as world, as manifoldness, as many seprate objects (prapancha), and the soul beholds itself as a separate soul, entangled in samsara, the course of this changing world, caught in the chain of birth and rebirth. When however the true and complete Knowledge (samyagdarsanam) comes to it, the illusion of variety and multiplicity disappears. The soul sees and knows itself as the eternal Brahman.

Knowledge thus summarized is the true knowledge. The common thought of the people in popular conception or scientific form, in mythology or theology, is "mithyajnana"—false knowledge—an illusion far below the level of knowing.

2. It would be possible to treat Eckhart just as we have here dealt with Sankara. Expressions from his writings could be gathered together which were exactly, or almost exactly, equivalent to those quoted above. Sentences could be taken unchanged from his works, or others could be formed in line with his thought, exactly corresponding to those of Sankara. An almost identical metaphysic could be built up from them in this way. More astonishing still, both mystics express themselves in a metaphysic which seems to be essentially "ontological," essentially a speculation as to the nature of Being, using methods which are startlingly alike, and a still more similar terminology. (a) Eckhart might have chosen the same text as the starting point of his speculation which Sankara takes, namely the *Great Saying* from Chhandogya, 6, 2, 1:

---

[1]In our language it is not so much unconsciousness as supraconsciousness, not so much the lack of consciousness as the identification of the Known with the Knower.

Sat eva idam agre asit, ekam eva advitiyam:
Being only was this in the beginning, one only, secondless.

Out of the mists of primitive mythology and mythical cosmology
had dawned in India that "intuitus mysticus" of which we shall
speak later. From mystical intuition ontology was born in India
(and perhaps the same may be said of Greek ontology and philosophy). The intuition arose from and was stimulated by the multiplicity of the things of this world; "Idam," "this here," that is
to say the manifold world is its object. But now the seer beholds
this multiplicity in "unity," as one, and as "the One," which
suffers no second. This One is esse and ens, "Being," is that
which is—absolutely and purely (eva). Further, in the "beginning" (Latin, "in principio") was this One only. What the intuitive mind sees as an essential and ontological relationship of the
One and the many, the naïve mind apprehends and symbolizes
as a temporal relationship,[2] as the "primordial" which was at the
beginning of all time. The developed mind afterwards corrects
such a mistake, yet the old naïve terminology is retained, for
"principium," principle, still implies literally a temporal beginning. Both Sankara and Eckhart are thinking not of a temporal
but of a metaphysical or ontological relationship of the One to the
Many. Yet Eckhart still retains the old term "in principio," and
together with "Being"(esse) it is the very shibboleth of his position. "To see things in principio, in their origin or their principle," is to see them in God, in the eternal oneness of their
primary essence, where all "idam," all "this and that," all "hic
et nunc," all multiplicity and duality is eternal Unity.

(b) Now, this unity is Esse, is "That which is," is Being itself.

---

[2]Thus I interpret the puzzling Aristotelian formula: το τι ην ειναι. This formula
is meant to indicate what the definition of an object should be, viz. to show the
nature of an object in answer to the question, "What was it?" That appears to
me to mean that the definition must indicate what the object itself was *a priori*,
quite apart from the details, accidents and incompleteness of its occurrence, and
purely in conception before it appears in the singularity or manifoldness of its
concrete realization. A primary relation of the *conceptual* existence of an object
to its realization "in concreto," that is a logical and not a temporal relation, is
here expressed by a preterite. A similar expedient is to be found also in our term
a priori which in its form expresses a relationship in *time*, while purely logical
and metaphysical relationships are meant.

The last definition is also contained in the Indian word Sat, because Sat is the identification of the subject and the function of being, as, conversely, Eckhart's "Esse" [to be] includes both existence and the existing subject.

Not only mysticism but personalistic Scholasticism also defines God as Being, regarding this as the expression of His essential nature. At the same time it stated: Deus *est* suum esse, that is, He does not *have* being as other things have their being, so that they come under the category of being. But He *is* His own being, and is also that which in the highest sense can alone be called Being. Eckhart, however, goes a step further still: "Esse est Deus." Being here is not predicated of God, but conversely, God is predicated of Being; Esse is thereby logically the first conception of speculation. Not a certain being, not an individual being, not a person (however superior) to whom one can point in distinction from other persons, but Being itself is God. This is also analogous to the speculation of the Chhandogya. For here also, *after* the conception of Being has been established, it is confessed that: Sa Atma (It, the One and the Sat, is Atman).

This Being, as also in Sankara, is "Esse absolutum, simpliciter nullo addito," Being through and through and nothing other than Being, without any addition (sad eva, without any upadhi)

> cuius quidditas est sua anitas, nec habet quidditatem praeter solam anitatem, quam esse significat.[3]

As pure Being (esse) God is completely "fashionless," without "How" or mode of being, neither this nor that, neither thus nor otherwise, just as Brahman is pure Being, is "nirgunam" and "neti, neti," absolutely "One." Therefore it is already as esse purum and simplex above all conceptions and conceptual differentiations, and so beyond all comprehending and apprehending (akaranagocharam, avagmanogocharam). For our comprehension is bound up with distinctions, with genus and differentia specifica.

(c) Now, these expressions, which are derived from logic with

---

[3] " . . . whose essence is its existence, and which has no essence except this existence alone, which Being signifies."

its limitations, are for both masters alike only the starting point for higher flights of speculation, which leave mere logical difficulties behind. The pure "Godhead" becomes incomprehensible and inexpressible, so that every predicate which could be used would veil and upset the very conception, and as Eckhart says, would make of God "an idol." The Godhead becomes therefore a Not-God, a Not-Spirit, a pure silence, a soundless void, yea, a sheer "Nothing."

(d) "And this pure Nothing is to be the highest, the end of all longing and desire!" the reader may cry indignantly. For here likewise it is the same with the two masters—their halting attempts to describe by negations and contrasts with the here and now an eternal, positive but unnamable One, are taken in all seriousness for mere negations and abstractions, in spite of Eckhart's assurances that such negation is only meant to be negatio negationis, limitationis, privationis. Both teachers end their speculations with similar warnings. "Wouldst thou be perfect, do not yelp about God," says Eckhart. "This Atman is silent," says Sankara.

(e) There are further curious similarities between the two in the relationship which they postulate of this entirely supra-personal Godhead to the personal God. Sankara formulates the relation as that between the higher and lower Brahman, identifying the latter with Isvara, the personal God. Eckhart contrasts the "Deitas" with "Deus," the Godhead with God. God is for him the conscious, personal, tripersonal God of Church doctrine.[4] This self-knowing, thinking, self-contrasting, and as such, strictly personal God, is "God." But, "God becomes and disbecomes," says Eckhart. High above Him stands the pure Godhead. Out of the Godhead comes God: Godhead is the ground of His possibility, and He is enfolded again within the Godhead in the course

---

[4]Like Augustine, Eckhart tries to support and to use the doctrine of the Church, for he interprets the Son as the self-thought of God—the knowledge with which the Father knows Himself and is conscious of Himself and of His own fullness of Being. The Son is the eternal Word, namely the "Word" as thought or knowledge, and indeed as the divine Self-Knowing (which it is vain to make into a separate Person).

of the "God process." The seer has to pass beyond "God" into
the silent void[5] of the Godhead itself. That is the highest vision,
and whoever still has "a God" has not yet reached to the highest
and the last. He stands only at the verge of eternity, but not yet
within it. This highest Godhead is, like the Brahman, the absolute "One," and the word becomes for Eckhart as for Sankara
an expression of the numinous character of the highest Being. It
is not only beyond being, beyond goodness, but the "supra-
Being" and the "supra-Good"—it is the "mirum" which even
the terms of greatest exaltation cannot embrace on account of its
absolute "otherness."[6] Like Brahman, it is neither conscious nor
self-conscious. As in the case of the Brahman, it is beyond the
contrast of subject and object, knower and known, yet it is above
and not below this contrast.

3. In order to give more concrete examples of the parallels in
the speculative systems of Eckhart and Sankara we quote here a
series of passages from Eckhart, to which are added the corresponding Sanskrit words in brackets.

(a) As Sankara, in the sixth Prapathaka of the Chhandogya-
upanishad,[7] Section 1, puts Sat at the beginning of all things and
thereby considers it as the principle of all things, similarly Eckhart in his prologue to the *Opus Tripartitum*, page 535, states that
"ipsum esse" (Being itself) is not a dependent and added
delimitation of separate things or of things in general:

> Non enim supervenit ipsum esse rebus tanquam posterius, sed
> est prius (agre asit) omnibus rebus. Ipsum esse non accipit, quod
> sit, in liquo nec ab aliquo nec per aliquid, nec advenit aut super-
> venit alicui, sed praevenit et prius est omnium.[8]

---

[5]The word translated here as "void" appears as "Wüste" in the German text.
It is used to imply the vastness of ultimate mystical experience, which has passed
beyond the disturbance of thought to a silence as of the desert. TRANS-
LATOR'S NOTE.

[6]For "mirum" and the "Wholly Other" the reader may compare Rudolph Otto's *The Idea of the Holy*, p. 25.

[7]Chhandogya-upanishad with Sankara's Commentary, anandasramagran-
thavali*h*, 14.

[8]Being itself is not added to things as if it came after them, but it is before all
things. Being itself does not receive anything either from anything nor by anything, neither is it appended to nor does it follow anything, but it precedes and
is prior to all things.

Everything which is separate (so long as it is still viewed as separate) has being only from this ipsum esse which precedes everything as the causa prima and the causa universalis (Sat as Karana):

Ab ipso igitur esse et per ipsum et in ipso sunt omnia.[9]

And this Being is evidently "secondless" (advitiyam), for:

Quod enim aliud est ab esse (sato 'nyad), nihil est.[10]

Just as evidently is it eternal (nityam) and beyond space and time (kaladesa-animittam)

mensuratus eternitate, nequaquam tempore (page 536).[11]

It is absolutely "unum," not only in comparison with others but in itself (ekam, advitiyam, nirvisesham)

manens indivisim...in uno nulla est distantia, nihil inferius altero, nulla prorsus distinctio figurae, ordinis aut actus (page 537).[12]

This eternal one, undivided, non-multiple Being is for Eckhart, God, as for Sankara the Sat is the Brahman:

Esse est Deus (page 537).—Deus igitur et Esse idem.[13]

Such Being is opposed to all becoming and therefore to all change (avikriyam):

Deus autem, utpote esse, initium est et principium et finis. Quod enim est, non fit nec fieri potest.[14]

(b) It is, however, esse purum et simplex (Sat eva). For

[9]Therefore from Being itself, and by and in it are all things.
[10]For what is other than Being is nothing.
[11]It is measured by eternity, not by time at all.
[12]"...remaining undivided...in the One there is no distance (as between separate objects), nothing inferior to the other, absolutely no distinction of form or condition or activity."
[13]"Being is God...Therefore God and Being are the same." In support of this Eckhart appeals to Exodus 3:14: "Ego sum qui sum," " 'I am that I am"; and, "Qui est, misit me," " 'I am' hath sent me."
[14]"But God, that is Being, is the beginning and the principle and the end. For that which is, does not become, nor can it become."

sicut album solam qualitatem significat, sic ens solum esse[15]
(page 542).

It is the One (unum) as without distinction (nirvisesham) and opposed therefore to the many (multum, nanatva) and to all inequal-
ity (ekarasa)—the formless fashionless Godhead as Eckhart so
often says in German. It is infinitum (ananta) because it is at the
same time indefinitum (anirvachaniya) and immensum because it
cannot be measured by any standard.

It is not being this or that, it is esse absolutum, simpliciter
nullo addito (absolute Being, simple and without addition), the
purum esse et nudum esse (the pure and naked Being) (p. 560).
Thus Eckhart comments on the personal "I" of Exodus 3:14:

> I AM THAT I AM—Li ego pronomen est primae personae,
> cuius quidditas est sua anitas, nec habet quidditatem praeter
> solam anitatem, quam esse significat.—Discretum pronomen
> autem meram substantiam signat: meram autem sine omni acci-
> dente (uphadi), sine omni alieno (anyad), substantiam sine quali-
> tate (nirguna) et sine forma (amurta, without namarupe) hac aut
> illa (na iti na iti). Haec autem Deo et ipsi soli congruunt qui est
> super accidens, super speciem, super genus—ipsi inquam soli.[16]

Does that not sound like a translation from the Sanskrit when
Sankara, in his Commentary on the Gita, writes:

> The purpose of all words is to illuminate the meaning of an ob-
> ject. When they are heard they should enable the hearer to under-

---

[15] "As white signifies quality alone, so 'ens' signifies Being alone."

[16] 'I am that I am'—the 'I' is the pronoun of the first person whose existence
is His essence and Who has no essence beyond this existence which Being signifies. . . . But the pronoun by itself signifies unmixed Being, without accidents
(uphadi) without anything foreign to its nature (anyad), substance without quality (nirguna) and without form (amurta, without namarupe) without this or that
(na iti, na iti). All these (negative) attributes are to be ascribed to God and to
Him alone, Who is above accidents, above species, above genus—to Him alone,
I say."

Deus non est in genere, nec genus habens nec speciem. (God is without any
genus, having neither genus nor species).

Li ego non substantiam signat; quae sit in *genere* substantiae, sed quid altius
et per consequens purius, includens perfectiones omnium generum. Since Ego
(I) does not signify being in a genus of being, but signifies what is above that
and in consequence purer than that, at the same time including the perfections
of all genus.

stand this meaning (presupposing that speaker and hearer agree in their understanding of words), and this according to the four categories of substance, of activity, of quality and of relationship. For example, cow or horse belongs to the category of "substance." Or "he cooks, he prays" belongs to the category of activity. White, black, belong to the category of quality. Having money, possessing cows, belong to the category of relationship. Now there is no class of "substances" to which the Brahman belongs, no genus commune. It cannot therefore be denoted by words, which, like "being" in the usual sense signify a category of things. Nor can it be denoted by quality, for it is without qualities; nor yet by activity, because it is without activity according to the Scriptures, "at rest, without parts or activity." Neither can it be denoted by relationship, for it is "secondless," is not the object of anything, but is its own self. It is therefore true that it cannot be defined by word or idea; it is the One as the Scripture says: "Before whom words recoil."[17]

Eckhart proceeds:

His simple nature is regarding forms, formless, regarding being, beingless, regarding becoming, becoming not, regarding things, thingless, and therefore He escapes from things of becoming, and all such things there come to an end.

And in another passage he says:

He is the purely One without the admission (uphadi) even in thought (na manag api) of anything quantitative or differentiated, above everything which suffers even in thought or name the faintest shadow of difference (bheda), in whom all delimitation and qualification is lost.

Or:

For in God there is not this nor that which we could subtract from Him or which we could isolate and retain by differentiation. There is nothing in Him but One, He Himself.

[17]Note here particularly how Sankara immediately continues: "If it now be falsely supposed that because the Brahman cannot be denoted as being, it is to be described as Not-Being," our text, in order to exclude this supposition (which makes Brahman a non-entity) teaches the "astitvam" of Brahman (what Eckhart calls "is-ness" "Istigkeit"), figuratively attributing to the Brahman all the organs of the living: "Hand, foot, hearing, etc.,"

Therefore, in order to avoid the error of attributing non-entity to the Brahman, it is designated as that which is to be regarded as "Not-Being and not Non-Being."

Or:

> God is neither this nor that (na iti, na iti) like these manifold things. God is One.

(c) Eckhart also says of this One That Is:

> God is the same One that I am (tat tvam asi).

Or occasionally he can speak of

> ...the clothed Godhead, clad with difference, multiplicity and incompleteness, all which, together with similarity (instead of identity) is foreign to God Himself.
> With Him we are one, not only as united, but in an absolute At-one-ment.

And:

> As the Godhead is nameless and all naming is alien to Him, so the soul also is nameless. (Cf. the corresponding relation between Brahman and atman). For it is here the same as God (Identification).

This relationship like that of the Brahman and the atman, is primary and essential:

> I have maintained ere this and I still maintain that I already possess (nitya-siddha) all that is granted to me in eternity. For God in the fullness of His Godhead dwells eternally in His image (the soul itself).

But this eternal, primary relationship is obscured through lack of knowledge (avidya):

> It is hidden from the soul, as the Prophet says: "Lord thou art a hidden God." This treasure of the Kingdom of God has been hidden by time and multiplicity and the soul's own works (karma) or briefly by its creaturely nature, (tirodhana through nanatva). But in the measure that the soul can separate itself from this multiplicity, to that extent it reveals in itself the Kingdom of God (the satyasya satyam). Here the soul and the Godhead are one (ekata).

Indeed, here the soul as a separate unit is "dead and buried in the Godhead."

Where there is such unity there is no longer mere equality or similarity, no distinction of subject and object:

> Where they (the soul and God) are one in essence they are not equal, for equality coexists always with difference. Therefore the soul must put off equality with God in order to realize identity with God.

And:

> So long as something is still the *object* (vishaya) of our attention we are not yet one with the One. For where there is nothing but the One, nothing is seen.

And:

> The Knower and the Known are One! Simple people imagine that they should see God, as if He stood there and they here. That is not so. God and I, we are one in knowledge.

(d) The Godhead standing high above God as the Brahman above Isvara, is, like the Brahman, not only free from all fashioning, but also from all works:

> Not the Godhead made this or that (akartritvam), but God (Isvara) first creates all things. Where God is the creator, there He is manifold and knows multiplicity. But where He is One, there He is free from all works, and knows in such oneness (of Knower, Known and Knowing) nothing beyond what He is Himself (svayamprakasatva of the akartri-brahman).

For evidently: as Godhead and primal unity it is "knowledge" (jnana) and Supreme Spirit (parama-atman):

> The Godhead is by its nature Reason. Or: The living (chit) essential (satya) absolutely real (nishpanna) Reason (chaitanya), which is itself its own object, and is itself ever the same, lives and is only in itself. Here I have given no definition of Him,[18] but I have stripped Him of all definition as He Himself is the only determination of indetermination, and lives (chit) and is blessed (ananda), (solely) because He *is* (sanmatra).

---

[18] As in Sankara the predicates sat, chit, chaitanyam, nityam, anantam, svayamprakasata, ananda are not to be regarded as viseshana.

> God is abstract being, pure perception, which is perceiving
> itself in itself. (Evans, 377)
> A living essential rationality which comprehends itself and is
> and lives in itself, and is the very same.

This absolute essence is indeed spirit, but in its absolute oneness
is not to be compared with any other spirit still remaining in the
distinction of subject and object. It is Knowledge (jnana) but, like
the Jnana which is Brahman, without subject and object:

> a pure knowledge, living and moving in itself.

(e) This eternal, primary One is not "God," though Eckhart
often so terms it, but it is the "Godhead." Herein lies the most
extraordinary analogy between Eckhart and Sankara: high above
God and the personal Lord abides the "Godhead," having an
almost identical relationship to God as that of Brahman to Isvara.
This relationship had already been formulated in an abstract,
purely academic form in Scholasticism before Eckhart, and to
that extent, even in this most curious doctrine, Eckhart is still a
Schoolman. But what had been previously an academic question
for the doctors became in him a penetrating and inspiring vision:
a flame leaping within him, to the kindling of which that doctrine
was merely the chance historic spark. He knows that he has
something unheard of to say:

> Meanwhile consider, I beseech you, by the eternal and imper-
> ishable truth, and by my soul: grasp the unheard-of. God and
> Godhead are as distinct as heaven and earth. Heaven stands a
> thousand miles above the earth, and so the Godhead is above
> God. God becomes and disbecomes—Whoso understandeth this
> preaching him I wish well. But had no-one been here I must have
> preached this to the collection-box.

(f) The personal God of India, Isvara, issues from the Brahman
simultaneously with the atman, the soul, and both appear
together as simultaneous and mutually determined occurrences.
It is the same in Eckhart's teaching. Only with and for the soul,
with and for the creature, is God, God as person, as subject and
as conscious of objects.

> Only as I (i.e. the individual soul) flowed out of the abyss, out
> of the source and stream of the Godhead did all the creatures pro-
> claim God.

This teaching of Eckhart's is summed up and expressed in words which could equally well be used as the confession of Sankara:

> When I came out of God, that is, into multiplicity, then all things proclaimed: "There is a God" (the personal God, creator of things). Now this cannot make me blessed, for hereby I realise myself as creature (karya, kaladesa-nimitta). But in the breaking through (i.e. through all limitations, in samyagdarsanam) I am more than all creatures, I am neither God nor creature: I am that which I was and shall remain, now and for evermore, (the atman as nitya-mukta and nitya-siddha). There I receive a thrust which carries me above all angels (as the mukta is above all devas and their heavens). By this sudden thrust I become so rich that God (Isvara) is not sufficient for me, so far as he is only God and in all his divine works. For in thus breaking through I perceive what God and I are *in common*. There I am what I was. There I neither increase nor decrease. For there I am the immovable (achala), which moves all things. Here man has won again what he *is* eternally (what he is in principio, agre) and ever shall be. Here God is received into the soul.

Thus we have set two metaphysical systems side by side, which in general and in detail appear strikingly similar. They are, in truth, alike. But above all they resemble each other most in the fact that they are *not* "metaphysical" at all but something wholly other.

2

Not Metaphysics but a Doctrine of Salvation

1. Sankara is usually regarded as the greatest philosopher of India, and Meister Eckhart in the history of philosophy as the creator of an original philosophical system. Yet both are at bottom alike in that they are not so much philosophers as theologians. They are indeed metaphysicians, but not in the sense of the metaphysics of Aristotle or of the philosophical schools. Their impelling interest is not "science" as a theoretical explanation of the world. "We do not explain the world. We explain it away"—as a follower of Sankara said to me, and here he touched upon the core of the matter. Neither of them is concerned for "knowledge" out of curiosity to explain the world, but each is impelled by a longing for "salvation." This is somewhat obscured in Sankara's works, and also in Eckhart in his Latin writings, where the speculative groundwork of his doctrine of salvation is stressed. But in his German writings it is almost impossible to isolate his metaphysical sentences as such. Even in the quotations given above, it was necessary to force the sayings out of their context, because they are at once involved with soteriological applications and associations.

2. Both men, it is true, are searching for a "knowledge of Being," and it is this question which calls forth their most weighty utterances. But it is knowledge of Being as knowledge of blissful Being. This means that their compelling interest is not a scientific interest in the ultimate—in the Absolute and its relation to the

world, resulting in some extraordinary statements about the "Soul" and its metaphysical relationships—but that both are guided by their interest in something which lies outside scientific or metaphysical speculation. This idea measured by these or any other rational standards must appear utterly fantastic and completely "irrational": it is the idea of "salus," of salvation, of sreyas, of Heil, and of how this is to be won.[1]

This conception which is found in the teaching of both Sankara and Eckhart gives their "metaphysical" phrases and terms a meaning which they would not otherwise possess. It is this which makes the two men first truly mystics and colors all their concepts with mysticism. The "Being" of which they speak is to be a "salvation." That that Being is one, without a second, that it is undivided, without apposition or predicate, without "How" or fashion, these are not merely metaphysical facts but at the same time "saving" actualities. That the soul is eternally one with the Eternal is not a scientifically interesting statement, but is that fact upon which the salvation of the soul depends. All affirmations and arguments in proof of the absolute unity, the complete simplicity, and the perfect identity of the soul with God, all the evidence and declamation against multiplicity, separateness, division and manifoldness—however much they may sound like rational ontology—are for both of them only ultimately significant because they are "saving." "Where there is distinction even for a moment, there is *danger,* there is great *need.*"

3. Truly, from the standpoint of our present-day ontology it is almost impossible to understand how men could be interested in these lifeless assertions about an undivided Being, a "sanmatra," a pure Being, which is nothing but Being, an Esse purum et simplex, a modeless Being, the "neti, neti" that is neither this nor that. The surrender and loss of self in this pure Being would seem entirely meaningless for us: and to dwell within it would be both tedious and valueless. But that both Eckhart and Sankara had this curious interest, and were indeed im-

---

[1] This was implied by the very meaning of "Being" for Sankara as well as for Eckhart. The Sanskrit word Sat (Being) as used in ordinary speech already connotes the true and the good. And the Latin "Esse" according to the old teaching of the schools is convertible with Verum (true) and Bonum (good).

pelled by it, must make us examine the matter more closely to find out what they both really meant.

4. The Being of which they speak was evidently for both the truly *valuable,* the sole and absolute value from which all values are derived. For that reason only is it the object of their interest. This Being however becomes truly valuable as it is contrasted with a certain antithesis, of which we do not immediately think in these days. And this occurs in two grades or stages which the masters do not consciously distinguish but which can be clearly described as follows:

(a) Being has its value in a clearly conceivable, rational form—(a) so far as it is contrasted with "becoming" and the "change" inherent in becoming. Thus the Mandukya-upanishad says (4, 71):

> *This is the highest saving truth*
> *That there is no becoming anywhere.*

We today are not used to such antitheses. When we speak of Being we think chiefly of simply "existing," and usually we do not contrast this with "becoming," for even that which is in process of becoming exists. And a process of becoming, e.g. a process of growth exists—it exists as growth. Therefore, Being, as existence, has for us no real opposite, save the simple negation of itself. But not so, say, for the Eleatics or Plato, and especially for Eckhart and Sankara. For them "Becoming" stands in direct antithesis to "Being."

> *Quod enim est, non fit nec fieri potest*[2] (540).

Becoming, however, is a curious intermediate state between Being and Not-being, between Sat and Asat, something which (as Sankara says of the Avidya) is "not determinable by Sat nor by Asat" (sadasadbhyam anirvachaniyam).

With Becoming appears change (vikara, vikriya) the Anityam, the not-steadfast, the fleeting and transitory, as opposed to Being. Vice versa, Being is opposed to all change and thereby to all transitoriness. Therefore Sat is at the same time "satyam" the true, and the sole *reality* compared with which all Becoming

---

[2] For that which is, does not become, nor can it become.

sinks to mere appearance. Being, as imperishable reality, is at the same time the "Perfect" and "Complete," and this even more as it is wholly and purely Being itself (sat eva), esse purum et simplex; as it is without any admixture or addition, without upadhi or accidens (accident), without guna or qualitas (quality). All these pronouncements on Being are indeed "ontological" expressions, but they are at the same time in the highest degree expressions of *value*. They contain and declare a "salvation" for him who feels and suffers from the instability of Becoming, who, enmeshed in the ceaseless change of becoming and "wandering," is under the painful ban of multiplicity, who, like Nachiketas in the Kathaka-upanishad,

> *Knowing there that which does not die nor grow old*
> *Finds himself here growing old, dying...*

and who knows that he will be set free from this cycle when he has reached and become "that which is," or Being itself. Without this valuation of Being the teaching of both men would be mere abstruse ontology. But, again, without this valuation, neither would have written a line. A few examples may be cited here. The one among them which shows most clearly the motive of speculation as to Being is the one in which the concept of "Being" is not used at all: Brihadarany. 2, 1ff. The old sage Yajnavalkya gives up house and home in order to follow the way of salvation. He leaves his possessions to his two wives. But his wife Maitreyi refuses these and all the riches of the world with the words:

> *Yena na amrita syam, kim tena kuryam!*
> *If I am not thereby free from death, what are these to me!*

To be free from death and the world of death and from the transitory, *that* is to reach the true, immortal Being. And so Being is surrounded by continually recurring synonyms which interpret its meaning:

> Here [in this world] nothing is eternal. All activity only helps
> that which is perishable. But I am a seeker after perfection, which
> is eternal, undying, fearless, unchanging, unmoving and constant. (Sankara on Mund. 2. 21)

This perfection however is:

> Brahman, without beginning, without end, imperishable,
> deathless, quenching fear, pure and transparent and nothing but
> Being. (Sankara on Mund. 2. 10)

It may neither begin nor cease for then it would not be eternal
(Mand. 597). It must be wholly one, without parts, for otherwise
it would be transitory. For

> Decay consists in loss of parts. Witness the body. No decay is
> possible in that which has no parts. (Sankara on Mund. 6)

It must be absolutely without division, for

> were there division that which is eternal would become mortal.
> (Sankara on Mund. 3. 19)

The synonyms for Being which show most profoundly its
soteriological meaning are found in the ancient verses of the
Brihadarany: 1, 3, 28, which belong to the daily prayers of the
devout Hindu:

> *From Non-Being lead me to Being.*
> *From darkness lead me to light.*
> *From death lead me to deathlessness.*

And what of Eckhart? He says with the Indian:

> In that which has distinctions man finds neither Unity nor Be-
> ing, nor God, neither Rest, nor Blessedness nor Perfection.

> Defect means lack of being. Our whole life ought to be being.
> So far as our life is being so far it is in God. (Evans 206)

> Thus ought we to be taken away from the inconstancy and from
> the storm of the earthly flux.[3]

> God is unchangeable. So he is the most desirable. (Evans 242)

(b) We here come to a further point, which is clearly expressed
in Eckhart and is implied in Sankara: pure Being which is only
Being is at the same time fullness of Being—the immeasurable
richness of Being.

> Nihil entitatis universaliter negari potest ipsi enti.[4]

---

[3] That is almost "samsara."
[4] No kind of reality can be denied to Being itself.

says Eckhart (546), and Sankara affirms the same in his explanation of Gita 13, 13. For Eckhart this thought is the rational outcome of his logic. Being is the general concept to which all other concepts are subsidiary and within which they are all contained. To be sure, for us today the most general concept is the widest in compass but the poorest in content. But that is not the opinion of Eckhart and his logic. For him the more general concept contains the subordinate ideas within it in such a way that it includes all their essential content. For example, color would not be for him emptier or poorer in content than blue, red, or green, but incomparably richer than each separate color, since it has in it the possibility of all known colors and not only of these but of all possible colors.

> Quanto res est perfectior in esse et simplicior, tanto est copiosior secundum rationes (555).[5]

> Includens perfectiones omnium generum (567).[6]

And:

> The nobler a thing is the more general it is.

Or:

> Quanto quid est simplicius et unicius tanto est portentius et virtuosius, plura potens.[7]

Thus for Eckhart, Being is not, as for us, the most void but the immeasurably rich, is "dives per se."[8] And whoever reaches Being enters into all the essential richness of Being. Thus Eckhart says:

> God is a sole good in which all separate goods are contained.

> That is the fulfillment, the full enjoyment of Godhead; that is oneness. (Evans 182)

---

[5] The more perfect and simple a thing is in its being the more copious it is regarding its content.
[6] Including the perfections of all genera.
[7] The simpler and more unique this is the more portentous and virtuous, commanding more.
[8] Rich in itself

All things are to God as a drop to the ocean. The soul imbibing God turns into God as the drop becomes the ocean. (Evans 242)

In Deo non cadit privatio nec negatio, cum sit plenitudo esse.[9]

This fullness, particularly the fullness of value, increases in conception the more that Being is *simply* Being, is one only, and the further removed it is from determination, manifoldness and difference:

He who would grasp it aright must estrange himself also from the "Good," and "True," and from all, which even in thought or name still has any suggestion or shade of difference. He trusts alone in the One, free from all manifoldness and difference, in which all distinction and attribute is lost and is one. This One makes us blessed.

Or again he says:

We conceive essence as naked and pure Being as it is in itself. For (precisely in its purity of being) Essence is higher than knowledge and life, for insofar as it is essence it has both knowledge and life.—If the soul knows God in His creatures, that is only evening light: If it knows His creatures in God that is morning light: but if it know God as He who alone is Being, that is the clear light of midday. Therefore man ought to desire, to behold with an almost insane passion that Essence is thus noble.

Or:

As long as I am this or that, have this or that, I am not all things nor have I all things. Purify till thou nor art nor hast, not either this nor that, then thou art omnipresent, and being neither this nor that thou art all things. (Evans 127)

Both in Indian logic and in Sankara these conceptual relationships are touched upon, it is true, but they play no part in his theological speculation. Nevertheless, we can still feel in his work the influence of the ancient Upanishad teaching that Brahman is

> *sarvam idam,*
> *yatkimcha jagatyam jagat.*
> *(All that which ever is in all the world).*

---

[9] In God there occurs no want nor negation since He is being in fullness.

The comparison which is often made with the Esse of Western mysticism also holds good for the Sat of Sankara: that it is like the mother-lye which in itself is completely simple and homogeneous (ekarasa) and "only one," yet contains dissolved and suspended in it the fullness of reality. This comparison is nowhere more fittingly applied than to the fundamental doctrine of Sankara in the passage on the sixth Prapathaka of the Chhandogya-upanishad. It is his purpose here to show how the one "Sat" is the matrix of the entire fullness of Being. His parable of the honey has exactly the same meaning as the simile of the homogeneous mother-lye. Thus also the introduction to the Isa says:

> Full is that. Full is this. Fullness is drawn from the full. Take fullness from the full: it remains always full.

Or again:

> *Incompleteness is the one place,*
> *Fullness the other.*

Sankara's method in dealing with the Brahma-sutra's (I, 1, 12-3, 13) is particularly instructive, bearing in mind this superabundant fullness of the Brahman. Brahman here is to be sought in meditation in ever higher and higher things of this world. It is true that all these things and their multiplicity are only upadhi's (fictitiously superimposed). But still they are the rungs of a ladder by which man may climb "higher and higher" to the All Highest Himself; to the most exalted, eternal, uniform Atman, whose all-surpassing Being in its fullness and richness is revealed ever more clearly step by step through such "distinctive powers of Divinity." These feelings of expansion and enlargement are also characteristic of Sankara's mysticism, through which the mystic believes he will reach the unending fullness of Being when he arrives at Being itself. "Sarvam eva avisanti," says the Mundaka-upanishad (3, 2, 15). And Sankara adds: "He who has reached the all-penetrating Atman," enters into the All. ("He becomes all things," says Eckhart.)

  (b) All these preceding valuations could be considered as in a certain measure rational, but it soon becomes obvious that for both masters there rises beyond them a still higher scale of values, which leads to a completely non-rational, or as we should say, a "numinous" value. From this viewpoint it becomes clear that for Eckhart as for Sankara the whole scheme of speculation about Being is in itself only a preliminary task, undertaken in the service of another and higher idea. In the light of this, Being itself takes on a new aspect. It is removed from the rational sphere to which it unquestionably belonged at first, and becomes simply an ideogram of the "Wholly Other," of the "Anyad," the alienum, the dissimile, of which we spoke in the *Idea of the Holy*, page 25ff. Thus Eckhart says:

> For that is God's attribute and His nature, that He is unlike to anything and alike to nothing.

This "Wholly Other" attribute of Being is quickly discernible in Eckhart's works, when as the real, the true Being it is contrasted with that which is generally meant by the term Being, the empirical Being, as we might say. And this higher stage and its non-rational nature becomes still clearer when, after he has for long enough made Esse (Being) the definition of the nature of the Godhead, Eckhart finally declares that God is above Being:

> Great masters teach indeed that God is unconditioned Being. (He has taught the same himself a hundred times!) But that is not so: He stands as high above Being as an angel above a gnat. It is as wrong to call God Being as to call the sun pale or black.

And again:

> Therefore one should press forward into the truth: to the pure Unity which is God Himself. Thus one comes to strange wonders, and one should stand still in these wonders for human sense cannot penetrate to the ground of it.
>
> But what is exalted above the spirit that is the One itself, an incomprehensible wonder.

Therefore God is much more a "naught" which is yet an incomprehensible "aught":

> Everything which has being, hangs (is suspended) in the Naught. And that same naught is such an incomprehensible aught that all the spirits in Heaven and upon earth cannot comprehend it nor sound it.

And:

> When I say further: "God is Being"—that is not true. He is something quite transcendent (atisaya). He is a Not-Being above Being (sat-asat-param).

But that clearly means Being as the entirely non-rational in the sense in which I have tried to define this word and its use elsewhere *(The Idea of the Holy,* page 60).

> Had I a God, whom I could understand, I would no longer hold him for God.

The nature of this non-rational element Eckhart himself describes with acute precision:

> Now you will ask: How does God work without an image in the depth and essence of the soul? That I cannot know, for the soul has only power to conceive in images, and since the images come always from without, God's work remains hidden to it.— That is most wholesome for the soul, for the inconceivable tempts her as to something wonderful and makes her pursue it. For she feels indeed that it is, but does not conceive what it is.
> Therefore a Master has said: "In the middle of the night, when all things were hushed in a deep stillness, there was spoken to me a 'hidden' word. It came like a thief stealing in." What does he mean by that? A word that was yet hidden? Is it not in the nature of words to reveal what is hidden? "But it opened itself and shone before me as though it would reveal something to me, and gave me (in feeling, without distinct ideas) tidings of God. Therefore it is (rightly) called a word. But what it was, was hidden from me" (an inconceivable idea). Therefore it is said: "It came in a whisper, in a silence, to reveal itself." It appeared and was yet hidden.
> When St. Paul was caught up into the third heaven, where God should be made known to him, and then returned to earth, he forgot nothing. Only it was so deep within him (in ineradicable feeling) that his reason was not sufficient for it. It was hidden from him.

This superconceptual but at the same time most certain comprehension, Eckhart calls the "unknowing knowing."

In Indian thought also how far "That which is" lies on the border, indeed, beyond the border of the conceptual and in the

region of the non-conceptual, is expressed in the very words of
the Kathaka 6, 12, which yet strive to designate the eternal by
the idea of Being alone:

> *Not by speech, not by thought,*
> *Not by sight does one grasp Him.*
> *He is: by this word and not otherwise*
> *Is He comprehended.*

Were Brahman really grasped through this "He is" he would be
comprehended through speech. Therefore this "He is" is itself
really beyond speech. And so Sankara himself says in commenting on the Gita 11, 37:

> In the deepest sense of the highest truth is that which Vedins
> call the inexhaustible, beyond Being as beyond non-being. It is
> reality alone, nothing else.

Above all he expresses the entirely non-rational nature of this Sat
by the assertion that it is Brahman, which with its brihattvam
(majesty) and its gambhiratvam (depth) is completely atisayam,
passing all comprehension. From ancient times it is the mysterious, wonderful, entirely suprarational essence, the "yaksha,"
which completely disclaims all thought and expression. It is deep
and more than deep (atigamibhira). It is as difficult to plumb as
the mighty ocean, (dushpravesyam mahasamudravad, the Mandukya-upanishad 4, 100), its path is as little to be traced as that
of the birds in the sky. For as the scripture says:

> *He who is the self of all beings and the salvation of all beings,*
> *About whose path even the heavenly powers are in confusion,*
> *Seeking the track of the trackless,*
> *As one cannot find the path of the birds in the air.*
>
> (Mandukya-upanishad, 4, 95)

Though often testified to in the text of the Vedas and by the
Masters of Hinduism, yet it cannot be known, for:

> *He is proclaimed by a miracle,*
> *He who attains Him is wondrously favored by Fortune.*
>
> (Mand. 4, 82)

5. In the writings of both Masters it is clear that the idea of
pure Being (in spite of their own assertions) is nevertheless mere-

ly the utmost which concept or "ratio" can offer in the approach
to the highest of all things. But it still falls short of the summit
itself, and finally reveals itself as only a rational "schema"
(model) of something which is fundamentally transcendent—
something numinous.

"Sa atma. Tat tvam asi." "Brahmasmi": that is palpably
something more and something "wholly other" than the rational
expression: "I have become pure Being, I am Being itself." And
it is precisely the same when Eckhart speaks of "homo nobilis"
as "deified man." This also is more than a man who has arrived
at true Esse (Being). Every concept fails utterly here. In speaking
of this experience Eckhart departs often enough from mere definition of Being. He can, indeed, entirely forget it. He is then no
longer in the sphere of Being: he is purely and absolutely in the
sphere of "wonder" (as he himself calls it), in the region of a
purely numinous and non-rational valuation. When on these
heights he still uses the word "Esse" and "collatio esse," this
esse has become in very fact a sheer "wonder," which is completely incomprehensible and fantastic to the ontologist and the
metaphysician, but quite familiar to the theologian. It is the same
with the original conception of Brahman. Eckhart uses the word
"wonder" while the Upanishad-tradition uses ascharya and
yaksha, and ultimately the Brahman becomes this also for
Sankara. However much he struggles to confine it in the concepts
of sanmatra, chit, chaitanya, jnana, he has to leave it finally as
that which is: namely as that

> before which words recoil, and to which no understanding has
> ever attained.

6. In any case, when we put (a) and (b) together, as sat eva or
esse purum et simplex, and as that which in truth is above sat and
esse, as the still rational and as the wholly suprarational—then
Brahman for Sankara and God and Godhead for Eckhart, as including both these elements, is the One who saves, and is the
superabounding value and salvation itself. It is for this reason
alone that Sankara proclaims his Brahmajijnasa and Eckhart his
metaphysic of Being and supra-Being. For this alone they spend
themselves in thought and create their doctrine and attempt to
destroy opposing doctrines. "For," says Sankara,

to accept the opposing doctrines without consideration might injure one's blessedness and lead one into evil. Therefore the study of the Brahman is to be recommended as the means to blessedness.

Brahmabhavo mokshah, To be Brahma means to be saved.

Eckhart says even more profoundly:

God is the only value.

Or:

Sum—that is as much as to say a thing which contains all good in itself.

3

The Way of Knowledge

1. Both Sankara and Eckhart are teachers of a salvation—in that lies their most fundamental point of agreement. But a further congruity between these masters of the East and of the West is found in the fact that for both the way to salvation is "knowledge."

For even more than in the content of their speculation and in the goal of salvation as unity with the Divine itself these mystics resemble each other in their *method* of reaching, or possessing salvation. Their method is the same, it consists in this—that in reality they have none! All that we usually term "mystical method," all purposeful self-training for "mystical experiences," all soul-direction, schooling, exercising, the technique for attaining a spiritual state, artificial exaltation of the self—this is far removed from them and lies aside from their path. Their mysticism is no mysticism in the usual sense of the term. Or rather, it is a type of mysticism which by its attitude is further removed from other types of mystical experience than from many forms of non-mystical piety.

Sankara, it is true recognizes the old Indian tradition with regard to the "eightfold Yoga," but he is no Yogin, and the samyagdarsanam is not to be won through Yoga. At most Yoga is a preparation for it, and it can be entered through a knowledge of the "Great words" "Tat tvam asi" without Yoga. Similarly, Eckhart on occasion recognizes the old traditional "methodus mystica,'' the via purgativa, illuminativa, unitiva. But his own method has nothing to do with it.[1] Indeed, it is a contradiction of his fundamental thought. For the "works" of the via purgativa according to his assumption can only be performed when the Eternal has been found and attained. Before that they are lifeless, effect nothing, and lead to creatureliness, not to God. (Similarly Luther speaks of "works" apart from and prior to faith.) In the same way both masters are far removed from illuminism, from mystical-occult visions and apparitions, from the magic and semimagic of trance conditions, from physical ecstasies and seizures, from conditions of nervous stimulation and overstimulation, and from all that is visionary.

2. Further, both are equally opposed to a rival system which appeared in their respective epochs. This was what we in the West usually call "voluntaristic mysticism," a very misleading term. For what it is really meant to denote is not voluntas as will but as excited emotionalism, and mysticism as an intoxicated eroticism. This includes seeking and striving after "sensations" and "experiences," after the emotional excitement and consolation of ebbing and flowing rapturous states, half or wholly sensual; a striving after the bliss of the secret intercourse of the "bridal chamber," and a general overemphasis of personal feelings and moods. In the East of Sankara's time and environment the rise of emotional Bhakti, the bhaktimarga in place of the jnana-marga, corresponded exactly to this emotional element in Western mysticism. It is true that bhakti and bhakti-marga could also be used as a name for the "way" of simple love of God and of personal relationship to Him, as for instance, with Ramanuja, who here resembles Luther. But for the most part it was just this "voluntaristic mysticism": a strongly sensual and often sexually determined emotional life, which, particularly in Krishna eroticism, has its parallels to Western "bride mysticism." It is peculiar to this "bhakti mysticism" as to our "voluntaristic mysticism," that it seeks to attain unity with the Highest through coalescence by an emotional exaggeration and glow of feeling.

---

[1] He does occasionally cite mystical method, as, for instance, in one place the four stages of ecstasy (raptus). But this passage is a scholarly quotation. He himself is never the follower of a method in any technical sense.

And even the Highest is thought of as responding to amorous longings. In contrast to this Sankara's outlook is cool and clear-sighted, serene and pure. In his writings at least we find nothing of this attitude. The path which he prescribes is in complete opposition to it, and equally so is the way of Eckhart.

3. The special character of the mysticism of both masters is that of an intellectual and not of an emotional mysticism. And because both are seekers after a knowledge, jnana, vidya, samyag-darsanam, they are not content to remain in a state of mystical premonition, of mere sentiment, or of inexpressible emotion. No one could be further removed than they from the supposedly fundamental confession of the "mystic": "Feeling is everything, words are smoke and sound." On the contrary, theirs is a knowledge which is to be translated into a comprehensible doctrine with all the aids of proof, scholarly presentation and keen dialectic. Indeed we are confronted with an almost unbelievable spectacle: both these heralds of the absolutely non-rational, inconceivable, and incomprehensible Godhead which escapes all definition and before which "words and understanding recoil," become the most critical theorists, the strictest of scholastics, and create a language and dogma of rigid formulas.[2]

"God is a silence rather than speech." "This atman is silent." "The most beautiful thing which man can say of God is that, knowing His inner riches he becomes silent. Therefore prate not of God," say Eckhart and Sankara. And yet both do say a great deal, penetrate into the inexpressible, proclaim its inmost state and try by the most definite doctrine to communicate to their pupils what they believe themselves to possess as explicable knowledge.

Nowhere does doctrine play a greater part than with these two

[2] The school of Sankara afterwards retained and exaggerated this tendency, and became rationalistic and dialectic. It confines the unspeakable within such close limits, forces the non-rational into such stiff formulas, and develops such stereotyped and unyielding technical language, that feeling is almost crushed out; the glimmer of the mystery almost disappears, and a hair-splitting dialectical system replaces the deeply significant language of the mysteries of the Upanishad-tradition.

In this sense the relation of the later Sankara school is similar to that of the later Eleatics, and their dialectic.

mystics. Thereby they represent in common a special type of mysticism to be distinguished from other "mysticisms": a teaching mysticism differing from a mysticism which speaks through song or through symbols only, or from a cult,[3] or a completely silent mysticism.

4. But one thing is certain, every word of instruction and all knowledge which comes from such teaching is still not the knowledge which matters: the real knowledge of the object itself to which teaching can only point the way. It is true that at first sight in Sankara's works, where one would soonest assume this recognition, it appears to be otherwise. According to him, knowledge of salvation is knowledge on the basis of authority, and the acceptance of a doctrine. All knowledge of the Brahman and of unity with the Brahman, he says, rests upon the authority of the Sruti, the Scripture, particularly on its Great words: "tat tvam asi," "That art thou" (viz. the Brahman). He claims to be a "scripture-theologian," a theologian of authority, for he only resorts to reasoning and proofs of his own in so far as he can refute the attacks of his opponents by their aid. But the real purpose of this affirmation on his part is principally to reject all human "anumana," all mere reasoning of "tarka," as powerless to find Brahman. And this assertion that no common logical or scientific consideration, no conclusions drawn, no proofs offered, in short, no power of the ordinary understanding could reach the highest knowledge, he makes in common with Eckhart. The latter expresses his conviction in a "doctrine of faculties." He distinguishes a particular faculty for the transcendental, the "intellectus" which is not in the least what we ordinarily call intellect, but is above all "ratio" or mere faculty of discursive, conceptual understanding which proves facts and draws conclusions, and functions quite differently from "ratio" as "ratio pura."[4]

---

[3] As in the book *De ecclesiastica Hierarchia of* Dionysius Areopagitica.

[4] Compare Coleridge's differentiation of "understanding" and "reason," or Kant's "Verstand" and "Vernunft." Here "understanding" as ordinary discursive faculty is "tarka." Coleridge's "reason" and Kant's "ratio pura" as a faculty of idea and of the "intelligibilia" agree with Eckhart's "intellectus" as opposed to mere "ratio discursiva."

Eckhart combines this teaching with the traditional conception of the "intel-

These latter teachings have again their exact parallels in the mysticism of India and even in its terminology: "atmani, atmanam, atmana": "Know the Atman in the atman alone through the atman." *Alone through the atman*—that means not by the power of the indriyani or of the manas or the buddhi, not through the senses, or by common sense or by the activity of the discursive understanding, but dispensing with all these organs and mediators, directly through *the atman* itself. *The Atman:* means the Atman-Brahman. *"In the atman":* is in the depth of man's own atman.

Another parallel is the passage in which Sankara says: "Atman is not capable of proof nor does it need any." It is "svasiddha." It is "self-proven." For, itself inconceivable, it is the ground of every possibility of conceiving, of every thought, of every act of knowledge. And even he who denies it, in so far as he thereby thinks, considers, and asserts, presupposes it.

But above all Sankara holds that knowledge based on the scriptures is merely the finger which points to the object and which disappears when it is itself looked upon. The real knowledge is that which he calls "one's own vision"—darsanam. This vision for him, as knowledge for Eckhart, is not a matter of "having visions." It is rather an awareness of identity with Brahman, and that as an "intuitus," a dawning of insight, our own clear-sighted realization of that which the scriptures taught. This awareness cannot be "produced," we cannot reason it out. It is not a "work." It comes or does not come independently of our will. It must be seen. The way may be prepared by the words of the Vedas and by meditation (pratyaya) on them, but in the end it must be our own vision. It dawns like an aperçu (Goethe) and

lectus passivus" and the "intellectus agens," substituting God himself or the eternal Word for the latter, which "informs" the "intellectus passivus" and thus gives it knowledge. This teaching is for him one with his mystical doctrine of the birth (Eingeburt) of "the Son," who is indeed the eternal "Word," or the birth of God Himself in the depths of the soul. In a less precise form, however, he teaches that God is known, not in conclusions or proofs of the "ratio," but as the soul, standing clear of all concepts, enters into itself and its own depth. Within itself as in the mirror of the Godhead, in the place where God Himself goes in and out, and which is indeed divine—is God—it attains knowledge.

as soon as it is perceived the Vedas become superfluous. Study and reflection then cease:

> Only for him to whom this awareness does not come as with one stroke (on hearing the Great words: Tat tvam asi) is repeated pratyaya (reflection) on the words of the Vedas necessary.

Or in Sankara's comment on the Bhagavad Gita 11, 54:

> He is able to know Me not only from the scriptures, but also to see me truly and directly.

Such vision is finally not scripture knowledge but inward realization (atmani) and knowledge through the self (atmana). Thus in commenting on the Gita 6, 20, Sankara says:

> When the confusing play of ideas (chittam) has come to rest, and he thus through himself (without the senses) through the purified "inward organ" apprehends the Highest, which is wholly spirit, essentially light, then he wins through to joy.

Compare also Gita 9, 2:

> The royal knowledge, the kingly secret is here knowledge of Brahman. And this is not scripture knowledge, but pratyakshagamanam: an immediate self-knowledge: "just as one feels one's own weal or woe," i.e. in immediate self-perception.

Eckhart deals with the matter likewise, nor could the "knowledge" which he too signifies be more exactly described. Only with him this knowledge has something more restful about it. It does not break out suddenly, or burst forth in a particular act. It is rather an enduring function of the whole personality, a finely distributed element in the life of the soul. Nowhere in his writings therefore is there so precise a theory of knowledge as in this passage from Sankara. Nevertheless, Eckhart also occasionally notices the aperçu-nature of the deeper knowledge, realizing itself in individual acts of the empirical consciousness, and he describes it by a quotation from Augustine:

> In ipso primo ictu, quo velut corruscatione perstringeris, cum dicitur "veritas," mane, si potes.[5]

---

[5] In this first flash when thou art as if struck by lightning, when thou hearest inwardly the affirmation "TRUTH"! there remain if thou canst.

And as Augustine here indicates that the realization of the significance of the concept "Truth" comes as a flash of lightning, so Eckhart from time to time implies the same with regard to the knowledge that God is one's own Being. He describes as follows its character of pure, immediate self-intuition so utterly incomparable to mere reflection and to mediated thought:

> Let him who does not understand this discourse not trouble his heart about it. For so long as a man is not equal to this truth, he will not understand. For it is not a truth to be attained by reasoning thought, but comes directly from the heart of God.

5. The resemblance between the experiences of the two mystics goes still further. For the ultimate significance of Sankara's teaching is that Vidya (knowledge) itself is not of time. It is the Jnana which is eternal, uncreated, imperishable, and inseparable from the atman itself. It is only cloaked by the Avidya (the non-knowing), (what we should call empirical knowledge) which also for Sankara follows the laws of perception and the syllogism. The same is true again for Eckhart:

> The soul has something within it, a spark of supersensual knowledge that is never quenched. But there is also another knowledge in our souls, which is directed toward outward objects: namely knowledge of the senses and the understanding: this hides that other knowledge from us. The intuitive, higher knowledge is timeless and spaceless, without any here and now.[6]

6. Such a fundamental "intuitus mysticus" as we said, lies at the basis of the teaching both of Eckhart and Sankara, and is the real source of their strange assertions and their deep pathos. This intuition is not a result of dialectic but a first-hand and immediate fact and possession of the mystical mind. Another parallel occurs here between the two masters: both veil this fact by their dialectic. Sankara, or at least his pupils, makes every effort to derive this teaching dialectically. They try for example to *prove* that consciousness apprehends only Being and not any form of Being, that difference and change are logically incomprehensible, that the jnana, always uniform and identical, is at the same time with-

---

[6] Both the Jnana and this knowledge are not empirical acts of consciousness, but a hidden, general "consciousness."

out beginning and imperishable. Like the pupils of the Eleatics
they support their own teaching of the One, the Undivided and
Unlimited by oppressing their opponents with the difficulties and
antinomies of perception and thought. Eckhart, on the other
hand, supports his teaching so largely by the dialectic of
Scholasticism, using the Platonic elements of his tradition in
order to establish his "ipsum esse" scientifically, and thence to
reach many of his mystical pronouncements by reason, that one
is easily led astray and does not see the wood for the trees. But
his mysticism is not the result of his Scholasticism, nor of the un-
lucky fact that—as one scholar has contended—he misunderstood
St. Thomas and mixed pure Scholasticism with Platonism. A
peculiar "mysticus intuitus" springing from the depths of his
own mind is fundamental to him, and in his environment it quite
naturally assumed certain Platonic forms of thought and conception, of logic and realism in its doctrine of knowledge and of being, and used them as instruments of dialectic, though often
enough they are more cloaks and disguises to his thought than
real explanations of it. Without these questionable aids his purpose would undoubtedly have created its own symbols, and probably they would have been much more illuminating. And indeed
it has created them. They continually cut across the Scholastic
terminology with their imaginative force and daring imagery,
and it is quite wrong to see in this imagery only the trimmings
of his thought or the poetical expression of his "scientific"
terms. Quite the reverse: the latter are themselves only the ra-
tionalizations and artificial transmutations of something entirely
his own, welling up from a hidden deep, independent of the terminology of scholarly speculation. It is just this personal element
which speaks most directly to the reader, and is understood of itself without explanation. His whole "scientific" speculation (as
is often the case) is merely his "idea" reduced to sterile "concepts."

7. It would be possible to separate the real content of the
mystical intuition in both Eckhart and Sankara from their
technical terms, which belong to the schools of their day and may
seem abstruse to us. With Eckhart it would be easier, for here
the true content is recognizable by anyone capable of a certain
amount of sympathetic understanding, and in his German writ-

ings it bursts the bonds of his Scholastic terminology. In Sankara it is not nearly so obvious since he is not, like Eckhart, a preacher and a poet with the magic gift of causing the truths proclaimed to blossom in the very soul of the reader through the creative power of his language. With Sankara one has first to break through the dry husk of his speculative system and disclose, embedded in his Brahman and Atman, the living features of ancient Indian mysticism as it survives in the Upanishads and the Puranas. It will be our task in the next chapter to pursue this mystical intuition and to describe it in our own terms.

4

The Two Ways: The Mysticism of Introspection and the Mysticism of Unifying Vision

Religion in the higher sense dawns in India as longing for the salvation of Amrita—for freedom from death. The story of Yajnavalkya and his wife Maitreyi which we cited earlier marks its first breaking forth. In this story there still vibrates the consciousness that knowledge of salvation which is "freedom from death" is not the result of a mere transformation of ideas, nor of a simple "evolution" in the ordinary sense of the word. It is, rather, a discovery—a revealing intuition. The positive form of the negative Amrita, "freedom from death," would be "life." This discovery of the eternal Amrita, removed from time and Samsara, thus runs parallel to the ideas of life and the bestowal of life by the eternal Living One Himself, as we have it in our own religious tradition. Maitreyi is also a seeker after "life." Therefore she speaks contemptuously of the goods of this world, and demands something more. This Amrita, this life, however, is more than "immortality," than the mere continuance of our empirical existence into infinity. There is a quivering light of mysticism about it. Maitreyi did not need to seek an empirical immortality. Of that, according to Indian ideas, she had experienced only too much, for death did not extinguish empirical existence, which rolled on from birth to birth unendingly. It was from just this mere "immortality" that the Indian seeker after salvation longed for release. He sought freedom from this whole world of death, and it is only the superficial who believe that religion is born of a longing for mere "immortality." It would be more correct to say "a longing for life" if we remember that this life even in the lower stages of the development of the idea, is not merely natural, empirical life, but something wholly magical, and in its higher stages wholly transcendent.

The search for salvation, for Amrita, as we have said, is clearly the motive prompting speculation about the one, eternal Sat. Sat is only a different expression for the *summum bonum* of Amrita, and often enough in India it bears the old name, Amrita, as in the West the word "being" has the connotation of "life." On occasion, Eckhart can forget all his ontology and say:

> When it [the soul] is wholly united with God and baptised in the divine nature, it loses all hindrances and sickness and inconstancy and is at once renewed in a divine life.

At the same time, this Amrita-idea is filled with that mysterious content of which we have spoken. Yajnavalkya answers the question as to the salvation of Amrita by the teaching of the mystical atman in the depths of our own being, and atman-mysticism blends itself with the mysticism of the eternal Sat-Brahman. Both are combined—Sa atma, just as with Eckhart the search for "life" and being becomes the teaching of the blessed miracle in the depths of the human soul, and of the modeless Godhead as pure Being. And both in Eckhart are similarly inextricably interwoven.

Thus we have in the East as well as in the West two types of mystical experience originally separate, now closely linked together, which it would be possible to separate again from each other, and of which each has its own motive and origin. Both are mystical, but the one is the mysticism of *introspection* and the other the mysticism of *unifying vision*. It will be necessary to speak in more detail of their differences and their interpenetration.

In spite of much formal agreement, mystical experience is capable of great diversity. Its content can be curiously varied. The moods and feelings which it arouses can differ from one another even to the extent of being diametrically opposed. The variety of different types of mystical experience can result in estrangement and conflict. It was the mystics who warred against the mystic Hussein ibn Mansur al Hallaj, and helped to bring him to the cross, while he himself from the standpoint of another type of experience, fought against the mysticism of his day. We shall speak later of differences of quality in mysticism. But what interests us here is that even the form of mysticism, its particular attitude toward its object, the path to its achievement, and thereby the fundamental attitude of the mystic himself, can be of entirely different types. They often combine, and may even help one another occasionally toward completion and fulfillment. Perhaps only in their combination do they represent the ideal of mystical experience. It may be that between them there exists a secret affinity which the mystic himself recognizes and considers natural. But to the non-mystic their extreme difference is striking. The differences here referred to relate to the types of mystical intuition which are indicated in the heading of the chapter. We may call them "the inward way" and "the outward way."

In considering the similarity between Eckhart and Sankara it is interesting to see how both these forms of mystical intuition are found in each of them, and how deeply they interpenetrate. Indeed, the resemblance between the two masters lies here in the way in which two clearly distinct methods of the mystical act itself penetrate and interpenetrate one another. It will be the exacting task of the present chapter, for the purpose of clearer recognition, to separate and tear apart what in the mystic himself is so often closely blended and intermingled.

I. The Inward Way

The maxim of the first type of intuition is: "The secret way leads *inward.*" Withdrawal from all outward things, retreat into the ground of one's own soul, knowledge of a secret depth and of the possibility of turning in upon one's self, is peculiar to the first type—mysticism as introspection. This means sinking down into the self in order to reach intuition, and here in the inmost depth of the self to find the Infinite, or God, or Brahman: atmani atmanam atmana. Here one looks not upon the world but only into the self. For the final vision there is no need of the world; only God and the soul hold true. This intuition would flourish were there no world given, would, indeed, then thrive the more easily.

The word of Augustine applies here: "Deum et animam! Nihil aliud? Nihil omnino."

In Plotinus also both types of mysticism intermingle. The first is clearly expressed by him in a passage of the *Sixth Ennead:*

> Often when I awake from the slumber of the body and come to myself, and step out of the outward world in order to turn in upon myself, I behold a wonderful beauty. Then I believe unshakeably that I belong to a better world; most glorious life works strongly in me and I am become one with the Godhead. Transferred into this I have reached that vital energy and have raised myself above all intellectual things. When I then climb down from this rest in the lap of the Godhead to intellectual understanding I ask myself how there can possibly be a sinking back out of that condition.

This intuition leads to "self-knowledge," to research of the soul, to "psychology," and becomes interwoven with the "theory of knowledge," or resolves into one or other of these. Reduced to "scientific" terms its ideas become the concepts of "inborn knowledge," "knowledge a priori," or even the concept of "general consciousness." In the history of philosophy it is easy to follow the gradual process of this reduction of mystical ideas, and their transference to "science."

II. The Way of Unity

But compare this passage with the following extract from the *Fifth Ennead,* 8:

> They see all not in process of becoming but in Being, and they see themselves in the other. Each Being contains within itself the whole intelligible world. Therefore all is everywhere. Each is there all and all is each.
> Man as he now is has ceased to be the All. But when he ceases to be an individual he raises himself again and penetrates the whole world. Then, become one with the All, he creates the All.

The contrast between the foregoing passages is palpable. Against the introspective intuition of the first type there is set an intuition of a clearly different nature. The mystical intuition of this second way is often so closely bound up with that of the first, that its peculiarity is not immediately noticeable. Nevertheless, there is not only a great difference between the two, but a direct antithesis. The second can be described under the terms: ekatvam anupasyati, ekata-drishti, the unifying vision as opposed to the multiplicity of the object. It knows nothing of "inwardness." While the first form necessarily has its own doctrine of the soul, drawing it into the region of the mystical, and so arriving at a particular soul-mysticism, whence it advances to a higher experience yet always remains largely a mysticism of the soul, the second form has no need of such a doctrine. It looks upon the world of things in its multiplicity, and in contrast to this leaps to an "intuition" or a "knowledge" of its own most peculiar kind, which we, according to our scale of values, may consider either a strange fantasy or a glimpse into the eternal relationships of things.

2. Such vision and the men who possess it are not merely affairs of the past. They are possible at all times, even today. These men are not so far removed from us that we cannot realize their experience to some extent. It was from such glimpses that speculation arose in India, and it was the second type of vision and not the first which gave it birth. Even as early as the Rig-Veda we find this strange feeling for the "Ekam," the "One," while the search for the atman only sets in later, as an addition to this earlier experience, and combines with it from a possible inner necessity which we shall consider elsewhere. Very likely such vision was the beginning of speculative thought not only in India but also in Hellas, and what we call Greek science was maybe the offspring of something which in its inception was mystical intuition. In any case it is not dependent upon doctrine, nor born of rational considerations, nor of the search after causality, nor of a hunger for a scientific explanation of the world. It is born as a revealing experience where there was a predisposition for such insight—where the "eye of heaven" was opened.

3. Sat eva idam agre asit, ekam advitiyam.

So runs the "Great word." "Idam" namely, this manifold world of objects, was Being only, One only, without a second. Intuition arises out of the "idam"—this manifold world. Its multiplicity is taken away, and only "that which is," only the One is beheld. There is more emphasis on the "One only" than on the "being."

This vision we must call "unifying vision" or "vision of a unity," for unity is its watchword—not soul, nor inward man, nor atman, nor Brahman, nor deitas, neither sat nor esse, but "Unity." The emphasis is on unity, and the struggle against all diversity is its chief characteristic. But when we say "Vision of unity" we must not imagine that we have thereby exhausted the conception of the actuality itself. For this purely formal element, this something perceived in unity or as unity, tells us practically nothing as to why this Being in Unity is so palpitating with interest, so filled with value and awe, and at the same time brings so great a liberation and blessedness—says nothing as to why it is the very "unum necessarium." The element of unity is like the pennon of a submerged submarine pointing to something deeper which it indicates but does not reveal. It is the only element which can in any measure be conceptually apprehended and considered, and even then very imperfectly, for what is this unity? Certainly nothing which can be determined by, or compared with, any logical forms of unity that we know.

4. This second form of mystical intuition has, like the first, its "scientific" counterparts. From it there results the "scientific" conception of totality, of the universe, of the cosmic system, which as a system of substances acting and reacting upon one another, is thought of sometimes in terms of vitality as an organism, sometimes in mechanistic-mathematical terms as a mechanism composed of mass and energy. The same applies to the conception of law. Perhaps, as has been maintained, such fundamental conceptions of natural philosophy were once really born "out of the spirit of mysticism," as the disjecta membra, the discarded and soulless members of an originally mystical intuition.

The vision of unity, however, is one which shows stages of ascension. The reader is not to understand by this that these gradations are necessarily separate chronological stages in the history of mystical experience or in the lives of individual mystics, but that there is a gradation which seems to lie in the nature of the vision itself.

In describing these stages we are attempting to trace a "schema" of mystical experience of the second type. It is the peculiarity of all systematic schemes that they do not copy one given form but try to present a sketch of an average type. No single form corresponds entirely to the scheme, but each one suggests it, more or less clearly, more or less precisely, or with a certain amount of distortion. The following schema is to be understood in this sense.

The Lowest Stage

(a) Things and events in so far as they are conceived by this "intuitive" vision, are no longer multiple, separate, divided, but are, in an inexpressible way an All, a Sarvam, a whole, one whole and therefore One. I repeat "in an inexpressible way," for if we add that they now form an "organic whole," "a universal life," or suchlike phrases, these are all rational explanations of the matter, derived from current scientific terminology, which are at most only analogous and not in the least adequate.

Thus Eckhart says:

> In the eternal goodness of the divine nature (as in a miraculous mirror) the essence of all creatures is seen as one.

(b) Further, within this One all otherness as opposition immediately disappears—things are no longer distinguished as this and the other. But, rather, this is that, and that is this; here is there and there, here.[1] This does not mean that all things in the fullness and richness of their individual being disappear, but rather that each with each and all with all is identical—one and the same. The Indian expression for such intuition is: "nanatvam na pasyati," or expressed positively: "samam pasyati," or "dharman samatam gatan pasyati," he sees objects as coalescing in identity.[2]

---

[1] Thus Plotinus says of the locus intelligibilis:

There...they see all, not in process of becoming but in Being. Each Being contains within itself the whole intelligible world and also beholds it complete in each particular Being. Therefore All is everywhere. Each is there All and All is each. (*Ennead,* 5:8)

[2] This is also the chief meaning of the term advitiyam, advaitam, without a second.

In the principal text of the Advaita doctrine, the Chhandogya-upanishad 6.2.1, the word means that the "idam," the "prapancha," i.e. the world apparently

This results in the peculiar logic of mysticism, which discounts
the two fundamental laws of natural logic: the law of Contradiction and of the Excluded Third. As non-Euclidian geometry sets
aside the axiom of parallels so mystical logic disregards these
two axioms; and thence the "coincidentia oppositorum," the
"identity of opposites" and the "dialectic conceptions" arise.
Eckhart says:

> There all is one, and one all in all. There to her (the perceiving
> soul) all is one, and one is in all. It (i.e. the empirical world) car-
> ries contradiction in itself. What is contradiction? Love and suf-
> fering, white and black, these are contradictions, and as such
> these cannot remain in essential Being itself.
>
> Herein lies the soul's purity, that it is purified from a life that
> is divided and that it enters into a life that is unified. All that is
> divided in lower things, will be unified so soon as the (perceptive)
> soul climbs up into a life where there is no contrast. When the
> soul comes into the light of reasonableness (the true insight) it
> knows no contrasts. Say, Lord, when is a man in mere "under-
> standing" (in discursive intellectual understanding). I say to you:
> "When a man sees one thing separated from another." And when
> is a man above mere understanding? That I can tell you: "When
> he sees all in all, then a man stands beyond mere understanding."

(c) Together with (a) and (b) we must take into account what
is called "visio sub specie aeterni": that is, not only the negation
of the usual association of things together in space and time, but
a positive ordering of their existence in and with one another in
a higher but inexpressible way in the eternal "Now."

(d) Closely connected with this as the accompaniment of the

---

extended in name and form, is "one only," without a second—is in itself without multiplicity. That it is "without a second" does not mean here as yet the
identity of Brahman and the inner atman, but the identity of the multiplicity of
the world as the "One only." The same thought often occurs later, cf. Mandukya Kar. 1. 17:

"Mayamatram idam dvaitam, advaitam paramarthata*h.* "

The "idam" here is also the "prapancha" as in the Chhandogya, for as
Sankara expressly states in his commentary: "Idam prapanchakhyam," cf. also
3.19: "Mayaya bhidyate hi etat, na anyatha 'jam kathamchana: "Only by delusion is the (One) divided." In truth it is "samatam gatam" (3.2), and 4.91:

"...sarve dharma*h.*

Vidyate na hi nanatvam tesham kvachana kimchana."

"For there is in them (viz. in all objects) absolutely no multiplicity."

"unification" of things is what we may call their "transfiguration." They become transparent, luminous, visionary. They are
seen—and this relates to their perception sub specie aeterni—"in
ratione ydeali" as Eckhart puts it, that is, not in their "obvious-
ness" but in their eternal idea.[3] "So I see in all the eternal
glory," sings Lynkeus. And Plotinus says: "There is the perfected beauty." Eckhart has expressed it thus:

> The man who has let things pass away in their lower forms
> where they are mortal, receives them again in God (that means
> first in their ideal "unity"), where alone they are real. All that
> is dead here, is life there. And all that is here gross and tangible
> is there (sub specie ydeali) spirit. It is as when a man pours water
> into a clean vessel and lets it stand, and then, if he holds his face
> over it he sees his face at the bottom (resplendent) as it is in itself.

Eckhart here clearly refers to the peculiar transfiguration of the
features seen in water, filled with the light and transparency of
the medium in which they are reflected.[4]

The chief points included in the paragraphs (a)-(d) are em-
braced by the Indian formula: nanatvam na pasyati—"he no
longer sees multiplicity." Such nanatvam we maintain has not
yet in itself any bearing upon the distinction between Brahman
and atman, but denotes the manifoldness of the namarupadi, the
multiplicity of "names and forms," which are at the same time
"kala-desa-nimitta," determined by space and time. Positively
expressed it is: samam pasyati—"he sees all in its identity." The
perception of the samam is, however, the same as perception
freed from space and time, in principio, sub specie aeterni, and
in ratione ydeali.

(e) Together with this there now appears not only the identification of all things with all, but also of the perceiver with the perceived, an identification which is clearly different from that of

---

[3] To see creatures intuitively in their "uncreated" nature.

[4] This symbol of Eckhart's curiously plastic speech, so entirely free from the
ornateness of the schools, shows us much more clearly what he means by his
"sub ratione ydeali" than his whole, scholarly, Platonized system of ideas. At
the same time it is an illustration of the fact mentioned in the previous chapter,
viz. that Eckhart would have expressed his opinions, and perhaps expressed
them better if he had not been a scholar but only a preacher in his poetic German
mother-tongue.

the mystical experience of the first way, the subjective, inward way, and of a different origin. There is here no mention of the soul as an inner reality, and of the soul's unification with the Highest. No consideration is given to the soul of the perceiver, but simply to the perceiver himself. He is what everything is, and everything is what he is. So unified with the All and the One, he then sees all things "in himself," or, more precisely, "as himself"—as not differentiated from himself.

Plotinus, with paradigmatical acuteness summarizes the points (a)-(e) in the *First Ennead*, 8, 1:

εχει παντα και εστι παντα και συνεστιν αυτω συνων και εχει παντα ουκ εχων. Ου γαρ αλλα, ο δε αλλος ουδε χωρις εκαστον των εν αυτω ολον τε γαρ εστιν εκαστον και πανταχη παν και ου συγκεχυται, αλλα αυ χωρις. But he is not spirit in the sense in which we conceive spirit, which gains its content from logical propositions and its understanding by processes of thought and reflection on cause and effect, and which recognizes being by the principle of sufficient reason. Rather, every spirit has all and is all and is with all because he is with it, and possesses all things, without possessing them in the usual sense (as individual objects external to himself. For he does not possess it as something different from himself). That which is possessed is not one thing and he himself another. What there is (of that which is possessed) in him is not each thing separate for itself. For each is the whole, and is wholly all. Yet still it is not mingled but is again itself separate. (Cf. above: "Black does not cease to be black nor white, white. But black is white and white is black. The opposites coincide without ceasing to be what they are in themselves.")

The spirit which here perceives is opposed to the process of "ordinary" thinking—to discursive thought activity. In contrast to the latter it perceives by means of mystical intuition.[5]

---

[5] This spirit is here the divine. But the divine spirit is for the mystic the original type of the mystical spirit itself, the subject of mysticism, and what has place in the divine has place also in man when he perceives aright. This is a fundamental conception of the mystical attitude. This analogous relationship which then passes into a relationship of identity is indicated in Indian writings even as early as the Upanishads by the regular parallels between "iti adhidaivatam. Atha adhyatman": "So with regard to the divine, and now with regard to the soul" (cf. Kena 4, 29). The same distinction of analogy and identity is found also in Eckhart.

Mystical intuition can stop short at this stage, and mystical experience can be indicated and described without going further. There are plenty of examples where such experience has been content to find its expression in the phrases of this first halting place: "To see no other, to perceive in Unity, beyond space and time—to see yourself and all else in one, and all as in yourself," without using the higher affirmations of the later stages. Mystical intuition is indeed present here, though there is no mention of beholding God or Brahman. For it, all is in unity, is indeed in a full mystical unity. When he sees things in such unity, the perceiver himself becomes one with the objects perceived, and sees them now within himself:

> He who has allowed the beauty of that world (seen in ideal unity) to penetrate his soul goes away no longer a mere observer. For the object perceived and the perceiving soul are no longer two things separated from one another, but the perceiving soul has (now) within itself the perceived object.[6] (Plotinus)

The union which here occurs is not yet union with God, but that of the self with the object perceived in the unity of the ideal world.

The Indian expression for the points contained in sections (a)-(e) is "anyad na pasyati"; "he perceives no other." That means both that he sees no variety in the object, and that he no longer sees distinction between subject and object.

The Second Stage

But to go further, we said in the first place that "the many is seen as one," thereby the One is now beheld. This means that the One is no longer a mere interrelation but a peculiar correlate of the many. Unity now becomes "One." "The One" is no longer a predicate of the many but becomes an equation of the One and the many: Many is one, and the One is many. Still further, these pronouncements do not remain of equal value. The One comes to the fore. Oneness is not a result of the many, nor is the relationship such that Oneness and multiplicity are mutual

---

[6] N. B. The "perceiving soul" is here simply the perceiver himself.

results of each other. The One soon receives the emphasis and takes precedence over the many. As Eckhart says: What in many things is one, must of necessity be above things (and that in the following four intermediate stages):

Many is seen as one (and only thus rightly seen).
Many is seen in the One (where the One is still a form of the many).
The One is seen in the many (as supporting and conditioning reality). The One is seen.

The One itself becomes the object of intuition as that which is superior and prior to the many. It is the many, not as the many is one but as the principle in which the many is grounded. In relation to the many it becomes the subject in so far as it unifies, comprehends and bears the many. It is in fact its essence, being, existence. Already at this point the One concentrates attention upon itself, draws the value of the many to itself, silently becoming that which is and remains the real value behind the many. The many is now only the changing modes of the One. It is itself the constant behind these modes, which remains and is identical with itself, the unchangeable foundation as opposed to the changing and fleeting. Thus al Hallâj says:[7]

> Nul ne peut fouler le tapis étendu de la Vérité, taut qu'il
> demeure au seuil de la séparation, tant qu'il ne voit en toutes les
> essences une seule Essence, tant qu'il ne voit ce qui passe comme
> périssant, et celui qui demeure comme subsistant.

It will at once be clear that we have here the beginning of the two elements usually contained in this type of mysticism:

(a) That on the one hand it is necessarily systematized by speculation on the Absolute; the One is the unconditioned, the absolute which conditions all things.

(b) On the other, that it attracts or originates an ontology, or a particular speculation about Being. The One is the only true and complete Being behind the many; the many sinks down into the half-being of changing, becoming, perishing, and of fleeting

---

[7] L. Massignon: *La Passion d'al Hussayn ibn Mansour al Hallâj*, Paris, 1922, Vol. 2, 517.

modes, which compared with the One is anrita, the untrue, and "cannot be defined either as Being or as Not-Being," etc. At the same time it is obvious that the conditioning relation of the One to that which it determines is beyond our rational categories of determination.

In theism the conditioning relation is that of the rational category of cause and effect. But it is not so with the mystical One. It has the power of conditioning but not in the category of causation; it is a mystical and non-rational relation, not to be grasped by rational thought. One can only use an ideogram, and I am accustomed in my lectures to use the expression: "The verb 'to condition,' here means to lie at the basis of a thing as its principle, and to comprise it."

Where mystical intuition is grafted upon Theism (which, as the oldest Upanishads prove, is not always the case) this non-rational One lying at the basis of all things is called God. The name, God, then takes on that opalescence which is so characteristic where belief in God becomes mysticism, or where mysticism includes belief in God. The personal form of address applies without further ado to the mystic One, and mystical and personal attitudes slip into one another.

An example of all these relationships is furnished by the following quotation from al Hallâj, in which the first and the second types of approach are mingled:

> O Conscience de ma conscience, qui te fais si tenue
> Que Tu échappes a l'imagination de toute créature vivante!
> Et qui, en meme temps, et patente et cachée, transfigures
> Toute chose, par devers toute chose. . . .
> O Toi, qui es la Réunion du tout, Tu ne m'es plus "un autre"
> mais moi-même.[8]

---

[8] Massignon, p. 520;

> *O Conscience of my conscience, what is the source of thy existence*
> *That allows thee to elude the conception of all living creation!*
> *And that, at the same time visible and hidden, transfigures*
> *All reality, all conceivable reality...*
> *O thou, who art the all-encompassing unification, art no more to*
>   *me "another"*
>   *but myself.*

Or compare what the Isa says, in verse 6:

> But he who beholds all Beings in himself and himself in all
> Beings...

and in verse 7:

> In whom the self of the perceiver became all Beings—
> What disturbance, what care could be in him who beholds
> Oneness?

In the first place this is simply the "anyad na pasyati," the
intuition of unity, but soon this peculiar Oneness as mere form
rises to the higher stage of vision of "The One" above the many,
till in verse 8 it becomes "He":

> He comprises all things, in a luminous, incorporeal, faultless,
> sinewless, pure, sinless way. He the seer, the sage, the encom-
> passing one, who *is* through himself.

This "He" is "Is," the Lord, of whom the introductory verse
says:

> The Lord is immanent in all that moves in this world.

The Third Stage

Thus, what first began as a mere form of the many appears
now as the *real* above the many. Only a step further is necessary
for it to appear in contrast and opposition to the many. If it is One
it can no longer be many. The many, at first identical with the
One, comes into conflict with it, and disappears. It disappears
either by sinking down into the indivisible One, as with Eckhart,
or by becoming the obscuring veil of the One, the illusion of
maya in Avidya, as with Sankara.

Thereby the meaning of unity and of oneness changes. At first,
Unity, being one, was a fact in the sense of a (mystical) synthesis
of multiplicity, which though not reproducible by any of our rational categories was nevertheless a synthesis. But out of this
synthetic unity, out of this one in the sense of united, grows a
unity as One and Aloneness. That is, in other words, out of the
united comes the One only, out of the All-One the Alone. Imme-

diately, as with Sankara, the relationship of original immanence—the immanence of the unity in and of things and the immanence of things in the One—passes, and is transformed into complete transcendence. The realm of the many is now the wholly evil in contrast to the realm of the One—it is mithya-jnana and bhrama (error).

In Eckhart's teaching the vital immanence of the One which mediates itself is always present and is peculiar to his speculation, but at the same time, above this rises the One in absolute transcendence—the "silent void of the Godhead" into which difference or multiplicity never entered. For him, the second stage remains bound up with the third.

*   *   *

Plotinus' quotation from Parmenides corresponds to our three stages in reverse order of succession:

> Parmenides expressed himself more clearly and distinguished between first, the absolute One, second the manifold One, and third the One and the Many.[9]

*   *   *

The ways of approach described under sections I and II may be called "The Way of Introspection" and "The Way of Unifying Vision." They can result in two distinct types of mysticism which may even be thought of as mutually exclusive and antagonistic. In Eckhart and in Sankara (or more exactly in the mystical tendency which Sankara and his school represent and fulfill) both ways converge, and this on the ground that they had long converged in Indian and German tradition. But Eckhart, especially, does not merely represent a tradition. In him all that is traditional is yet original and new-born. The blending of both types of mysticism, and particularly the vital interpenetration of both, springs rather from his own living experience than from previous representations.

---

[9] Closely akin to this is the saying of Eckhart: "Does the soul know God (Oneness) in the creatures, that is merely evening light (first stage). Does she know the creatures in God (second stage) that is morning light. But does she know God as He who alone is Being (third stage) that is the light of midday."

The necessity for this fusion only the mystic himself can feel and see. Yet we also are in a position to understand at least the motive that prompts it. But we have deferred its investigation to Section C, in order not to disturb the continuity of thought here.

5

Further Consideration of the Stages of the Second Way

1. The first stage of the second way, namely that of the simple "perception of unity" is not in itself necessarily an attitude of the mystical soul, which she must first pass through, before she can press on to a higher stage. It is a "first stage" using that term in the logical sense as of a systematic scheme. Indeed, with a developed mystical tradition this stage will scarcely appear as an isolated phenomenon, and can be distinguished only with difficulty. But sometimes it may occur as a peculiar phenomenon of its own and remain separate. Its formula is then: "To see no other, to behold no distinction, to behold non-duality."

This stage will be immediately recognized as only preparatory as soon as the higher—the positive intuition of the One—appears. But the further development of the intuition may sometimes remain below the horizon, and the soul's action really tarry in the first stage. In any case it is itself a characteristic element in the spiritual attitude of the mystic, and it is interesting to collect sayings in which the experience is exclusively or predominantly determined by this first stage. Such examples are clearly to be found in the extracts from the Vishnupurana 2, 16, which we translate as follows:

1. After a thousand years came Ribhu
   To Nidagha's city, to impart further knowledge to him.
2. He saw him outside the city
   Just as the King was about to enter with a great train of attendants,

3. Standing afar and holding himself apart from the crowd,
   His neck wizened with fasting, returning from the wood
   with fuel and grass.

4. When Ribhu saw him, he went to him and greeted him and
   said:
   O Brahman, why standest thou here alone?

5. Nidagha said: Behold the crowd pressing about the King
   Who is just entering the city. That is why I stand alone.

6. Ribhu said: Which of these then is the King?
   And who are the others?
   Tell me that, for thou seemst informed.

7. Nidagha said: He who rides upon the fiery elephant, towering like a mountain peak,
   That is the King. The others are his attendants.

8. Ribhu said: These two, the King and the elephant, are
   pointed out by you,
   Without being separated by mark of distinction,

9. Give me the mark of distinction between them.
   I would know, which is here the elephant and which the
   King.

10. Nidagha said: The elephant is below, the King is above
    him,
    Who does not know the relationship of borne to bearer?

11. Ribhu said: That I may know, teach me.
    What is that which is indicated by the word below and
    what is "above"?

12. Straight Nidagha sprang upon the Guru, and said to him:
    Hear now, I will tell thee what thou demandest of me:

13. I am above like the King. You are below like the elephant.
    For thy instruction I give thee this example.

14. Ribhu said: If you are in the position of the King, and I in
    that of the elephant,
    So tell me this still; Which of us is you, and which is I?

15. Then swiftly Nidagha falling down before him clasped his
    feet and spake:
    Truly thou art Ribhu, my master.

16. For no other spirit is so endowed with non-duality
    As that of my master. By this I know that thou, my Guru
    art come.

17. Ribhu said: "Yea, to give thee teaching,
    Because of thy former willingness to serve me,
    I, Ribhu by name, am come to thee.

18. And, what I have just taught thee in short—
    Heart of highest truth—that is complete non-duality
    (advaitam)."

19. When he had thus spoken to Nidagha, the Guru Ribhu
departed thence.
But forthwith Nidagha, taught by this symbolic teaching,
turned his mind completely to non-duality.
20. All beings from thenceforth he saw not distinct from himself.
And so he saw Brahman. And thus he achieved the
highest salvation.
21. So bear thyself, O Knower of the Law, to thyself, to
friend and foe
In knowledge of the self which extends through all alike.
22. For as the sky, which is yet one, appears with the distinctions of blue and white,
So also the self, though one appears illusively in differentiation.
23. All, whatsoever is here, that is the One, Acyuta.
From Him, there is no other, nothing different;
He is I, He is also thou, He is all this.
Therefore let go the mirage of multiplicity.
24. Thus taught by him, the King gained intuition of the
highest reality, and let multiplicity go.

The elements and gradations of intuition are unusually clear in
this example—are in fact almost programed. Nidagha does not at
first behold the One itself, whether as the Atman, or the Brahman
or as the eternally-one Acyuta. But the flash of insight begins
with the disappearance of difference, separateness and multiplicity, so that he beholds that which is not separated. This is that
and that is this, and all is one. Hence the naïve questions of
verses 6-11. And where the diversity of a sensual and spatial perception would assert itself with an "I" and "thou," it is forthwith shattered in verse 14, by the revelation that "I" is "thou,"
and "thou" is "I." At once with this perception the difference
between things and the self, which presses upon one through the
senses, disappears for Nidagha, and thereby all diversity in general. He perceives the advaitam in the whole. Verse 20a takes us
so far. Then, quite briefly verse 20b continues: tatha Brahma:
"So then he also perceives the Brahman," which now comes forward as the One itself behind the non-differentiated.

That the glory of the mystical intuition can be fully expressed
at the first stage, without explicitly lifting itself to the consciousness of the Brahman, or without necessarily developing this con-

sciousness, seems to me to be indicated in the vital passage of the Chhandogya 7, 23-25:

24. Yatra na anyat pasyati, na anyat srinoti, na anyad
    vijanati, sa bhuma.

    Where one perceives no other, hears no other, recognises no other, there is fulness.

The anyad here is not first of all an object as distinct from a subject, for it is only the next passage of the Upanishad which enters into the question of the identity of subject with object, and this it does expressly mentioning it as a consequence of the first statement. But it is in the first instance the contemplation of "samam," the identity of things. This identity of all things is here first and foremost the object of contemplation, and to behold it is "fullness," while the perception of the ordinary man as the "alpam" or the "insignificant" is contrasted with the mystic's contemplation of fullness:

    Fullness, however, consists in happiness. In the insignificant (little) there is no happiness. One must therefore seek to know fullness. For fullness is the immortal, but the insignificant (little) is mortal.

This fullness is at the same time the absolute: it "is rooted in its own greatness," while in the region of the little, nothing absolute is to be found, for here "one thing is always rooted in another" (24, 2). The one fullness in which there is no anyad, is:

    Below and above, in West and in East, in South and in North. It is all (in one, without distinction).

The Chhandogya proceeds: "atha ato 'hamkara-adesah' "

    And now following upon this, the instruction with regard to the I: I am below and above, I am in West and in East, in South and in North. I am this whole world.

Thus, the following verse says in 26, 2:

> *The seer sees no death,*
> *Nor sickness nor hardship.*
> *The seer sees only the all,*
> *He penetrates the all everywhere,*

> *He is simple, he is threefold...*
> *Yea, he is twenty-thousandfold.*

He who has attained intuition beholds no longer the little with its suffering. He sees the all, the fullness (which is symbolized in the foregoing verses). He beholds the All in one: "penetrates it," becomes one with it and is then fullness itself.

It is only in 8, 3, 4, of the Chhandogya that the transition to the Brahman stage follows:

> That is the immortal, that is the fearless, that is Brahman.

2. With these statements we may compare certain expressions of Eckhart. If we look closely we shall notice that here also there is at bottom that will-o'-the-wisp, "Perceive no other, no duality, nothing different." True it rises immediately to the fuller development of the second stage, but even in the form of the first it has already its own value.

> So long as the soul still beholds a divided world, all is not well with it. So long as anything separate looks in or peeps out, so long there is not yet unity. Mary Magdalene sought our Lord in the tomb: she sought *one* (dead) and found *two* (living angels). And yet she was still indignant! Then spake the angels, Why are you troubled? As if they would ask: You seek only one dead man, and find two living. (Is that not much better?) Then she might have answered: That is just my plaint and my trouble, that I find two but I am seeking only the One.
>
> The Soul is troubled so long as it perceives created things in their separateness. All that is created, or that is capable of being created, is nought. But that (viz. the thing itself beheld in its ratio ydealis) is apart from all creation, indeed from all possibility of creation. Because it is something united, something without relation to another, which receives nothing from without.

And now compare the following passage and try to see that there is here clearly a transition to a higher stage of mystical perception, into which the first stage glides imperceptibly:

> So long as the soul beholds forms (namarupe, murti), even though she behold an angel, or herself as something formed: so long is there imperfection in her. Yes, indeed, should she even behold God (as separate), in so far as He is with form and number in the Trinity: so long is there imperfection in her. Only when all

that is formed is cast off from the soul, and she sees the Eternal-One alone, then the pure essence of the soul feels the naked, unformed essence of the divine Unity—more, still, a Beyond-Being. O wonder of wonders, what a noble endurance is that where the essence of the soul suffers no suggestion or shadow of difference even in thought or in name. There she entrusts herself alone to the One, free from all multiplicity and difference, in which all limitation and quality is lost and is one. This One makes us blessed.

Just as imperceptibly the higher stage, the intuition of the Eternal-One can slip back again into the lower, the simple perception without difference.

3. For an understanding of the character of the intuition it is instructive to note how it is kindled in Nidagha. The Master does not present him with a doctrine of Atman or Brahman, does not set before him a theory of singleness, does not disconcert him with the logical difficulties of multiplicity. This last is after all a secondary business which makes its appearance only when the first power of intuition itself is already exhausted. His procedure has a curious resemblance to the method of "Koan" in the Dhyana school, of which I have spoken elsewhere.[1] By means of an arresting question, which brings the pupil up short, where hitherto he has been able to answer readily, he is led to the point where intuition suddenly springs into being almost explosively within him. Now he himself has intuition, and there develops within him the perception of non-differentiation, the intuition of unity, the vision of the One, the Brahman, the Vasudeva, which contains all in unity.

4. This stage, where the emphasis falls first upon nonduality itself, or as we say, upon identity of all with all, is frequently illustrated in the Upanishads. And at times they give the impression that there have been philosophic currents of thought in which the mystical intuition of identity of the first stage was so much to the fore that the mystic could perhaps do without the intuition of Atman and Brahman, or at any rate so use it that its content does not reach beyond the first stage. At least that is true of certain sections of the Mandukya-karika, which curiously re-

---

[1] Cf. R. Otto, *Das Geüfhl des Überweltlichen*, München, 1931.

call the speculations of the Mahayana-Buddhist Lankavatara-sutra, and the experience of the Dhyana school (cf. Mand. 4.91).

> All objects are in origin unlimited like space,
> And multiplicity has no place in them in any sense.
>
> Also all are at bottom deeply still, full of serenity,
> And mutually alike and indivisible, a pure eternal *identity*.
> But this purity exists no longer, so soon as it is multifariously
>   divided;
> Sunk in multiplicity, torn asunder they are called poor.
> But he to whom the eternal identity became a certainty—
>
> He knows something great in this world.
> But the world understands him not.
>
> The dark, immeasurably deep, eternal pure identity,[2]—
> Having known the place of Oneness, according to our
>   strength, we reverence it.

Here nothing is said expressly of Brahman and Atman. The direct recognition of "Identity," without taking the way through Brahman, appears to be the complete experience, which at the same time beholds things like and identical with one another, in "serenity," that is, as in their origin quick[3] and blessed—an experience which is itself bliss.

5. Compare herewith passages such as the following, from Eckhart:

> I say, all creatures are one Being.

Or:

> Therefore I give you still another thought, which is yet purer and more spiritual: In the Kingdom of Heaven all is in all, all is one, and all is ours.

Or:

> All that a man has here externally in multiplicity is intrinsically One. Here all blades of grass, wood and stone, all things are one. This is the deepest depth and thereby am I completely captivated.[4]

---

[2] Note the entirely non-rational nature of this identity.

[3] "Quick" is here used in the same sense as in the phrase "the quick and the dead." TRANSLATOR'S NOTE.

[4] This last is a form of the *plastic* Advaita perception, which for those who are visually disposed, takes the place of the more spiritual intuition, which is itself

Or:

> When the soul comes into the light of the supersensual it knows nothing of contrasts.

Or:

> As all angels in their original purity (sub ratione ydeali) are one, even so all grass-spiders in original purity are one. Yes, all things are one.

Or:

> This Knowledge is timeless and spaceless, without Here and Now. In this life (of higher Knowledge) all things are one and all things in common, all things are in all, and are one in the all.

Eckhart recognizes this mystical intuition in other mystics. He relates the following of St. Benedict:

> It is reported of him that he beheld a transfiguration in which he saw the whole world before him as in a sphere all collected together.

The transition to the "higher stage" is described in the words:

> *God* carries all things hidden in himself, not this and that, distinct and separate, but as one in Unity.—And when man finds the One, in whom all is one, he cleaves to unity.

Or:

> . . . a perceptive mind. Herein the soul has God. What does the soul behold, when she beholds God? A *single* power. This single power makes her one with itself.

Or:

> God is neither this nor that, as these manifold things are; God is one. (Evans LXIX, p. 172)

6. A parallel passage to the extract chosen above from the Purana is a song, not of Eckhart but doubtless from Eckhart's school:

---

purely "intellectual perception." In India the parallel is the vision of visva-rupa, which is likewise a fantastically visual disguise of the intuition of unity and of the One. (Cf. Gita, Chapter 11.)

1. My spirit has grown out of all separateness:
   So I stand unformed in my own being.
   I may not bind myself in any otherness.
   I have passed through into freedom and cleave to it.
   I cannot live any longer otherwise.
   My sense-perceptions have passed away,
   My reason can scarcely grasp it:
   My heart would leave me:
   I must live in freedom.
   This you must forgive me.

2. Wouldst thou also behold it
   In its pure being-ness!
   But thou desirest always that which is different,
   And thus art thou betrayed!
   Thou dost not wish to believe me,
   But I swear to thee
   Thou canst become no other
   Than what thou eternally wast.
   Oh, wouldst thou rightly behold it
   What lies hidden there in the Holy Trinity![5]
   I will remove myself from the cares of all things of time,
   And of all things whatsoever.
   Thus I shall live in a free stillness
   And unmoved in all things
   O thou noble, blessed life!

3. He who learns to float high above all things,
   And without ceasing unifies himself. . . .
   Well, then my soul, we must remain unmingled,[6]
   The natural is driven out of the new creation
   And shall not come again into its own aught.
   Therefore I do not find any more createdness in myself.
   Time and eternity have also passed from me
   When I stand entirely in oneness.

The exalted feeling of Eckhartian mysticism is here incomparably expressed: floating high above space and time, above the multiplicity of things, in blessed freedom (mukti), it ascends also beyond the "Holy Trinity" to that which is hidden behind it, to the eternal unity. Here also it is clear that what we said previous-

---

[5] In it lies hidden the "ground," the eternal original unity.
[6] With the creaturely.

ly of the possibility of the mystic remaining largely or absolutely at the first stage, and expressing his full experience by means of this stage, holds good. For of "Brahman," of the Deity, there is scarcely a word. "Is-ness" (Istigkeit) and "Unity" suffice almost by themselves to express what a man here finds and means.

7. This first stage finds expression in Eckhart, (a) particularly in his insistence on beholding all things "above space and time," and on the other hand in perceiving and possessing them "in principio." So to behold things is to behold them from the first stage. Above space and time: both are indeed the principium individuationis, and with them falls, so it was believed, the individuatio itself. If I perceive beyond space and time, I perceive unity, things indistinguishable. For us non-mystics space and time are the conditions *a priori* of the real existence of objects and events. Only in a spatial separation and in a time sequence or proximity are both possible to us. But Eckhart would say: "In space and time the One cannot also be the other; objects fall into distinction. Let me however conceive them without this dispersing prism, then should I see them in their identity.[7] In space the same subject can be only black and white, so far as it is black in front and white behind, or is today black while tomorrow its color changes. Only through spatial distribution and by the change of becoming and becoming different in time—i.e. in the form of opposition, can anything really *be* here. Therefore it is a false and not a true reality. Tear away the fetters of space and time, and objects merge into one another. The true fullness of the unified being enters then into your vision which was dazzled by the veil of space and time. Highest of all you perceive then the One, unity itself, in which all variety has utterly disappeared."

In the same way his so-called conceptual realism is in truth intuition of unity (and is thus perhaps what it had been originally). In space and time I behold Tom, Dick and Socrates. Without space and time I do not behold this man beside that man. Then this is that and that is this.[8] There, in principio, stands man, the

[7] And thereby at the same time "in essence."
[8] That is really the right expression instead of "conceptual realism" or "hypostatizing of species."

one, the whole, all mankind undivided and joined together in him.[9] Next to man in ratione ydeali stand what may be called the other creatures. Yet intuition rises beyond them also. As in the individual man (beheld in unity) the real idea of humanity is contained, so all ideas come together in the unity of the one, complete, undifferentiated Being, which is thereby eternally enriched. Everything has entered into it but nothing is lost.[10]

(b) Beyond the vision "above space and time" and in principio—as forms expressing the first stage of intuition—we must notice further the strange dignity which the name of "the Oneness" can have for Eckhart, in its general sense and apart from the special unio mystica between the soul and God. Oneness is a mysteriously solemn symbol, in itself nearly sufficient to express the fullness of his experience. It can be a complete synonym for the divine, for God and Deity. Already in beholding the One and in "becoming One" the full content of the mystical experience is comprehended. Sometimes the name God or Deity hangs only as a trimming upon the One or upon Unity.

(c) To this conception of Unity belongs that strange mystification which we find occasionally in Eckhart in the simplest act of presentation and cognition. He follows here the doctrine of knowledge of Aristotelian Scholasticism, but the process of knowledge gains with him a sense of which the Scholastic himself never dreamed. Even the simplest cognition is indeed an act of unification and an abstraction. I recognize "per speciem" on the basis of my sense-perceptions, as I relate them to the unity of this one object. And in so far as I can now abstract from the perceptions as such, I advance to that which is no longer sensual, to the abstract concept freed from sense, which is then intellectual, spiritual and a unity evolved from multiplicity. Eckhart

---

[9] And in such a way that we are not left with the pale abstraction of the concept "man," our meager, logical, impoverished "species," but that those elements which here (on the conceptual plane) are separated as Tom's self and Dick's self are blended together in their higher unity.

[10] Tom is not lost. He is only at one with all that is not Tom. Eckhart probably would not have understood the reproach brought against him that he denies personal immortality. He does not think in those terms. But his idea of all variety ceasing to be in the one eternal identity is something entirely different from the denial of immortality.

added no new mystical ingredient to this teaching, but this simple, rational process becomes mystical, in that he discovers a strange and deep significance within it. Conceptual knowledge means now to grasp and to have in one's self the spiritual essence of things. They are now in me. As I lay hold of them in idea, spiritualizing them from sense-perception, unifying them out of multiplicity, I lead them in myself to be one in Unity, and lead them back again to the Oneness from which they have fallen away in their sensual-space-time separation.[11] And in doing that I lead them back again into—God![12] It is worth while noting such indications when discussing the question as to whether Eckhart "really only popularized Scholasticism and St. Thomas Aquinas—with some excusable misunderstandings." The material with which Eckhart is working here is certainly the commonplace material of the Scholastic system. But what he expresses by means of it is begotten of no "school," and even without its aid he and his message would have remained the same.

8. Let us once more set out systematically the symbols which Eckhart uses for the stages of the second way. He has the following very clear gradations:

(a) His effort is to behold beyond space and time and number, with the vision which is outside the corporate body (and tangibility), outside the manifold ("menige"):

> The first thing is that the soul be detached from here and now.

> "Rejoice in God all the time," says St. Paul. He rejoices all the time who rejoices above time and free from time. Three things prevent a man from knowing God. The first is time, the second corporeality, and the third is multiplicity. . . . While there is more and less in thee God cannot dwell nor work in thee. These things must go out for God to come in; except thou have them in a higher, better way: multitude summed up to one in thee.

---

[11] The soul collects together things scattered and dispersed. The resultant of the five senses, when these are recollected gives her a common sense wherein everything sums up to One." (Evans LXXXII, 207)

[12] Guidance into Unity and into God. Cf.: "I alone take all creatures out of their sense into my mind, and make them one in me." (Evans, 143) "Creatures all come into my mind and are rational in me. I alone prepare all creatures to return to God." (Evans, 143)

There develops in him a true hatred of "time":

> ...time, which is what keeps the light from reaching us. There
> is no greater obstacle to God than time. Not only time but tempo-
> ralities, not only temporal things but temporal affections; not only
> temporal affections, but the very taint and aroma of time. (Evans,
> p. 237)

Or:

> Here and now, that, in other words, is time and place. *Now* is
> the minimum of time. Small though it be it must go; everything
> time touches has to go....*Here* means place. The spot I am
> standing on is small, but it must disappear before I can see God.
> (Evans, p. 115)

(b) That means for Eckhart however that in place of the mutual
exclusiveness of things and predicates among themselves, there
arises a mutual inclusiveness:

> Every creature makes a denial: the one denies the other; an
> angel denies being any other creature.

This mutual denial must also go; esse hoc et hoc must disappear,
the hocceitas, i.e. the distinction according to τοδε τι must
vanish.[13]

Thus Eckhart says:

> We shall be like the angels. Perception here means seeing in the
> light that is in time, for anything I think of I think of in the light
> that is in time and temporal. But angels perceive in the light that
> is beyond time and eternal. They know in the eternal now....Yet
> take away this now of time and thou art everywhere and hast the
> whole of time. This thing or that thing is not all things; as long
> as I am this or that, have this or that, I am not all things nor have
> I all things. Purify till thou nor art nor hast not either this or that,
> then thou art omnipresent. (Evans, p. 127)

And again:

> Being neither this nor that thou art all things....Remote from
> time and temporalities. (Evans, p. 127)

---

[13] Hocceitas corresponds exactly to idanta in Sankara. For idanta is not identity
as one might suppose from the similarity of sound, but the quality of being
"id," τοδε τι, the idditas.

Eckhart calls such perception "perceiving distinction without number and without multiplicity."

> But to one who sees distinctions apart from multiplicity and number, to him, I say a hundred is as one. (Evans, p. 81)

(c) Now this is at the same time the "Knowing in ratione ydeali" and "in principio" of which we have already spoken:

> *Unde nimet ez in principio.*

(d) All this then is to see in Essence, in the One, and in unity; it is to see in God, and to see God:

> The Father's eternal One, where every blade of grass, and wood and stone
> (And all Angels, and thou and they and I and all creatures) are one.

It is to be noted that with Eckhart the "Seeing of the One" remains still as the highest stage. Oneness and God are sacred, interchangeable terms, and it is difficult to say which has preference—the fact that God is Oneness, or that Oneness is God:

> The Oneness which is God Himself.
> That is the fulfilment, the full enjoyment of Godhood; that is Oneness. . . . I find two where I sought one alone. (Evans, p. 182)

> Our Lord departed to heaven, beyond all light, beyond all understanding, beyond all human ken. He who is thus translated beyond light of any kind dwells in the Unity. (Evans, p. 182)

> This unity is causeless: it is self-caused. Of bottomless depth the floor, of endless height the roof, of boundless space the rim. (Evans, p. 375)

> All remains the One, which is its own source. Ego, the word, I, belongs to no one but God alone in his unity. Vos (you) means that you are one in the unity. That is to say: ego and vos mean unity. May God grant that we may be this same unity and that unity may remain.

This apparent abstraction, unity, is palpably different from the concrete "Hen" of Plotinus, to which Eckhart himself seems to object in the words:

> It is not One, it is Unity. (Evans, p. 250)

It bears on the one hand the traces of the synthesis of the first stage:

> In this embrace all is dissolved in all; for all encloses all.
> (Evans, p. 285)

But it is on the other hand a much more mystical ideogram of the Ultimate than the "Hen" of Plotinus. It is a looser and more far-reaching notion, escaping definition. This preference for the abstract "Unity" instead of the "Hen" clearly denotes what we have described as the refusal to be circumscribed by conceptual limits:

> But in itself (viz. the all-inclusive unity) it is itself unbounded.

9. We have dealt with the intuition of the "second way" in considerably more detail than with that of the first, because it seems to us that its appearance and its peculiarity in Eckhart as in the Indian mystics has not been realized clearly enough hitherto. But we have done this not because the intuition was the more important element or the one most emphasized by them. Rather one could say that the opposite is the case. It forms the warp of the fabric, but the woof both with Eckhart and with Sankara is the mysticism of the first way. What follows in this book refers more to the latter than to the former. Also the artificial cleavage which we had to make for purposes of our investigation must now disappear. For that which we have separated in the analysis forms in the living experience of both mystics the inmost unity, both elements mutually interpenetrating and permeating one another.

6

Their Common Standpoint against Other Types of Mysticism

I. COMMON OPPOSITION TO THE ILLUMINISTS

Neither the mysticism of Eckhart nor that of Sankara, as we have already said, has anything to do with the mysticism of the so-called "illuminists," with its fantastic visions, occultism, or miracle-hunting. Eckhart never saw "visions" or experienced "occult facts," nor does Sankara appeal to such experiences. Neither of them was ever a "visionary" as were the "illuminists" and the "yogins" of their time. True, their object is completely suprarational and opposed to everything empirical, for both Eckhart's "knowledge" and Sankara's darsanam are utterly different from all knowledge of the senses or of reflection, or anything we can achieve by logical mental processes. Yet, in the deepest sense of "ratio" they have something rational and luminous about them which is in direct antithesis to all occultism and obscurantism.

Again, the illuminist is the "miracle-man" who receives magical insight, special revelations and heavenly visions through supernatural powers. He is an empiricist and a hyperphysical sensualist in so far as he experiences objects of a supersensual but still empirical sphere by means of a sixth sense. One is here trapped in the antithesis between the supernatural and that which is contained within the natural conceived as two levels of existence. And this is a kind of physical antithesis, where powers, conditions and experiences are classified according to the physical and hyperphysical.

The real intuitus mysticus however is beyond this contrast. For it knows one kind of reality only, veiled by sense experience, and not two spheres miraculously intermingling. It is a secret but not a supernatural light. It is depth, ground of the soul, divine, but it is nothing magical; it knows a distinction of natural and supernatural but this is not so much an ontological differentiation as a distinction of sense and value. The power of the higher insight is not supernatural in the sense of a "donum superadditum" but it is just the essential of the soul. It is wonder but not miracle. Thus Eckhart on occasion fights the vulgar supernaturalism and illuminism of his time. He says:

> People try to find out whether it is "grace" or "nature" that saves us and they never reach a solution. How foolish of them! Let God rule within you, leave the work to Him. Do not trouble thyself whether he does it naturally or supernaturally. Both nature and grace are His. What does it concern thee how it suits Him to work in thee or in another? Let Him choose how and in what manner. If someone would like to have a spring brought to his garden, he will say to himself: "So long as I get water I do not care what kind of a pipe it is through which it flows to me."

Mystical intuition is always being confused by the supernaturalists with "mere reason," so that even Eckhart had to protest against the accusation of teaching reliance upon this. But when the idea of the mysticus intuitus is translated into the language of "secular concepts" it becomes not "mere reason" but "pure reason," which is in contrast to sense-perception or to reason conceived merely as the capacity of understanding. Yet to this very emaciated idea of mystical intuition—for that is pure reason—there clings, however faintly, some last remnant of the sacred and sublime, some trace of the original wonder and depth of the soul. The "ratio pura" in opposition to mere sensation or reflection, remains always something creative. As is often said, it is a capacity for principles, a capacity for "ideas," a capacity to pass by "ideas" beyond sense-perception.

At the same time, pure reason according to Kant, is the capacity to produce general and necessary knowledge. It is this which characterizes the mysticism of Eckhart and forms its greatest contrast to all mysticism of the illuminists. The visionary illuminist makes his own little rent in the veil which hides the supersensual world from us, and individual apocalypses, oracles, and intimations are revealed to him in single flashes of light. He recounts the visions and dreams which he alone has received, and his believers accept them on his authority. But Eckhart never tells what *he* seeks, what *he* knows. Not this man nor that man, not the talented, nor the man with special knowledge of God, neither the oracle, nor the ecstatic is for Eckhart the subject of knowledge. It is the soul: the soul in general quite apart from its chance possessor, the soul that penetrates into its own ground and depth and becomes "essential," that does not allow itself to be separated by division into creatures or powers from the knowledge which wells up deeply hidden within, and which must spring from it of necessity when in concentration it meditates upon itself. The samyagdarsanam of Sankara has just as little to do with illuminist-mysticism. Jnana is eternal, is general, is necessary, and is not a personal knowledge of this man or that man. It is there as knowledge in the atman itself, and lies hidden under all avidya, irremovable though it may be obscured, unprovable because self-evident, needing no proof, because itself giving to all proof the ground of possibility. These sentences come near to Eckhart's "knowledge," and to the teaching of Augustine on the eternal truth in the soul, which, itself immediately certain, is the ground of all certainty, and is a possession not of A or B but of "the soul."

II. COMMON OPPOSITION TO THE MYSTICISM OF EMOTIONAL EXPERIMENTALISM

This second point of contrast is connected with the foregoing, but is still distinguishable from it. According to both Eckhart and Sankara, unity with the divine reality is apprehended by knowledge based upon real being, not by extravagant emotion. This knowledge of unity has its emotional side (beatitude, ananda), but unity is neither experienced nor attained by excited states of feeling. Such states are not the criteria of realized unity, nor are they even the confirmation of such realization. Eckhart says, and here he almost anticipates Luther:

> Now you may say: "I feel nothing of it." What does that matter? The less you feel it and the more firmly you believe it, the more praiseworthy is your faith.

Or:

> Satisfaction through feeling might mean that God sends us com-
> fort, ecstasies and delights. But the friends of God are not spoiled
> by these gifts. Those are only a matter of emotion, but reasonable
> satisfaction is a purely spiritual process in which the highest sum-
> mit of the soul remains unmoved by ecstasy, is not drowned in
> delight, but rather towers majestically above these. Man only finds
> himself in a state of spiritual satisfaction when these emotional
> storms of our psychical nature can no longer shake the summit of
> the soul.

Or:

> Verily, whosoever imagines that he has more of God when sunk
> in rapture, in worship, in extravagant emotion and peculiar feel-
> ings of nearness than when he is by the hearth and in the stable,
> does nothing else than if he should take God and wrap a cloak about
> his head and put him under a bench.

Or:

> Those who are out for ''feelings'' or for ''great experiences''
> and only wish to have this pleasant side: that is self-will and nothing
> else.

III. COMMON OPPOSITION TO NATURE MYSTICISM

Whoever affirms the unity and similarity of all types of mysticism
should at least be at a loss to account for one difference, apparent
even to the most superficial observer, i.e. the contrast between
the mysticism of the spirit and nature mysticism. There are, it is
true, certain traits common to both types, and therefore they are
both called mysticism: for example, the impulse toward unity, the
feeling of identification, the disappearance of the sense of otherness
or of the contrast between the particular and the general, the whole
mystical ''logic'' of the ''second way'' as opposed to rational logic.
But, nevertheless, each has an entirely different content. Take,
for instance, the ecstatic verse of the Jelaleddin:

> I am the dust in the sunlight, I am the ball of the sun,
> To the dust I say: Remain. And to the sun, roll on.

> I am the mist of morning. I am the breath of even.
> I am the rustling of the grove, the surging wave of the sea.

I am the mast, the rudder, the steersman and the ship.
I am the coral reef on which it founders.

I am the tree of life and the parrot in its branches,
Silence, thought, tongue and voice.

I am the breath of the flute, the spirit of man,
I am the spark in the stone, the gleam of gold in metal,

The candle and the moth fluttering round it,
The rose and the nightingale drunk with its fragrance.

I am the chain of being, the circle of the spheres.
The scale of creation, the rise and the fall.

I am what is and is not. I am—O Thou who knowest,
Jelaleddin, oh, say it—I am the soul in all.

That is mystical feeling for nature. It corresponds outwardly
to what we have described as stage one of the mystical experience
passing over into stage two of the second way. All the formal elements there described recur again here; and yet, how peculiarly
different are both the mood and the experience here portrayed.
There is not a trace of this mood in Sankara, and Eckhart too knows
nothing of it. This is all the more remarkable in Eckhart since
for him God has in Himself the fullness and the essence (essentia)
of all things. He is, and is the essence of all things from the angel
to the stone: therein would seem to lie the best theoretical basis
for Jelal's mystical feeling for nature. Yet Eckhart's mysticism,
like Sankara's, is a spiritual not a nature mysticism. Nature mysticism, as is clear from Jelal's verses, is the sense of being im-
mersed in the oneness of nature, so that man feels all the
individuality, all the peculiarity of natural things in himself. He
dances with the motes of dust and radiates with the sun; he rises
with the dawn, surges with the wave, is fragrant in the rose, rapt
with the nightingale: he knows and is all being, all strength, all
joy, all desire, all pain in all things, inseparably. The unbridgeable
gulf set between Eckhart's mysticism and this is that here the divine
One is reached and experienced in the essence and joy of nature,
while for Eckhart the very opposite holds good. He views things
and the essence of things from the standpoint of the significance
and value of the divine, in absolute contrast to nature. This is a
spiritual, not a natural nor an aesthetic valuation. The mysticism

of the verses quoted above is romantic,[1] presupposes a highly developed sensitiveness for nature which was present neither in Eckhart nor in Sankara, and is a sublimated naturalism even in its highest and most abstract forms, and therefore easily passes into the fervor of erotic mysticism. But Sankara and Eckhart seek the illimitable as spirit, as knowledge, as consciousness, and Eckhart particularly ascribes to it still higher values, as we shall see later. What we have in Jelal is what William James is accustomed to call "Expansions." Such feelings of expansion are indeed very common in Indian mysticism, e.g. becoming Sarvam, the All-being, and knowing one's self as the All.[2] Certainly, the statement that in intuition the soul expands to the universal would be applicable to Eckhart also. But mere "expansion" itself does not say very much and is only a term for a moment of experience that may include very different elements. What is expanded? What is it that stretches to the infinite? Whereunto does it expand? With what infinite content is it permeated by expansion? That is the question.[3]

This also applies to the definition: "Mysticism is to possess the infinite in the finite," and to the term "mysticism of the infinite." The concept "infinite" if not used in a strictly defined sense is an easy way of leaving the problem as we find it, for "mysticism of infinity" explains nothing, or at most expresses again that moment of expansion. But as to the content of this experience it is silent, and "infinite" can be used as a vessel to hold the most diverse experiences.

---

[1] St. Francis in his Song of Brother Sun shows a closer kinship with the mood of the song of Jelal than with the mystic Eckhart. No wonder, for he is the troubadour of God and permeated with the spirit of the real troubadour.

[2] Prasnopanishad, 9, 5: mahimanam anubhavati.

[3] Compare with this what L. Massignon says in his penetrating criticism of the varieties and contrasts within Sufi mysticism. *La Passion d'al Hussayn ibn Mansour al Hallâj*, Paris, 1922, Vol. 1, p. 116:

"L'ivresse délirante constatée chez al Bistami n'est pas la vraie et durable presence de Dieu dans la mystique (de Hallâj). Dans essence de l'union (en al Hallâj) tous les actes du saint restent coordonnés, volontaires et deliberés par son intelligence,—mais ils sont entièrement sanctifiés et divinisés."

"The delirious intoxication of Bistami is not the true and absolute presence of God in mysticism (of Hallâj). In the essence of the union (as per Hallâj) all the saint's actions are coordinated, voluntary and determined by his mind—however, they are all sanctified and deified."

As religion has manifold varieties—nature religion, spiritual religion, and many other distinct types—so there is a nature mysticism, a spiritual mysticism and many other forms. These differences are revealed in both the East and the West, and are not divided into East *and* West. In Eckhart and Sankara we see clearly how types and combinations of spiritual mysticism, identical or very similar, have sprung to life in the Orient and in the Occident. They reveal indeed a spiritual kinship of the human soul, which transcends race, and climate and environment.

We shall return to these considerations in a separate chapter on the divergences of mysticism.

7

Atman and Soul

I. ATMAN AND BRAHMAN. SOUL AND GODHEAD

The Indian speculation upon which Sankara's system is based had, as we have said above, two starting points and thereby two lines of development along which it advanced.

The one was the discovery of the "thing of Wonder" (yaksha), the Brahman at the foundation of the world, and the other the discovery of the gandharva (the fairy-like being) of the Atman within man's own self. Only later do these two meet and their relationship, indeed their identity, is recognized in mystical intuition. With Sankara they are identical. Brahman is Atman and Atman is Brahman. Even the terms are used as synonyms. Yet if the question were asked: Is Sankara's knowledge Brahma-bodhi or is it "Atma-bodhi?" it would not be easy to give a definite answer. Atma-bodhi is with him obviously accentuated, and it is characteristic that his explanation of the Brahma-sutras, which are intended to teach the Brahma-jijnasa, the study of Brahman, begins with an introduction in which "the Knowledge of the Inner Self" seems to be paramount. This introduction culminates in the sentence:

> The Knowledge of the oneness of the soul (Atma ekatva vidya)—to teach that is the purpose of all the Vedanta texts.

It is only with the first of the Sutras that the term Brahman occurs. It alters the whole emphasis of mysticism as to whether one proceeds from the knowledge of the eternal Brahman and then comes to the astounding perception: Sa Atma: the (Brahman) is the Atman (the self), as Svetaketu does in the Chhandogya-upanishad, or whether, starting with the search after the true nature of the inward Atman, one comes to the knowledge that: aham Brahma asmi (I [this Atman] am Brahman). Sankara belongs to those who take the second line of approach rather than the first.

In this respect he is again like Eckhart, with the difference only that what in Sankara is merely indicated in outline is quite obviously expressed in Eckhart. One might almost say: the center of Eckhart's mysticism is a "Mysticism of the soul": a mystical view of the soul which carries with it a mystical view of God. For him, quite decidedly speculation does not move from above downwards, but ascends from below upwards. (The recognition of this will become important for us later for the fuller understanding of his speculation about God.)

II. MYSTICISM OF THE SOUL

To know and to find one's self: to know one's own soul in its true nature and glory, and through this knowledge to liberate and realize its divine glory; to find the *abyssus,* the depths within the self and discover the self as divine in its inmost depth; in short, "the canticle of the soul as the *homo nobilis*" has been rightly pointed out as the core and pivot of Eckhart's teaching. Absolutely parallel to this is the lofty atman faith of Sankara, and his "inner self." The wisdom of both is first and foremost Atma-bodhi.

With Eckhart the "soul," das Gemüte, the inner citadel, the spark, is more profound, tender and emotional in experience than the inward atman of Sankara. There is nothing of the *Seelenvoll* (fullness of depth) about Sankara's atman. Over and above this the bloom of the gandharva, the gleam of irrationality which the original atman possessed, is much worn away in Sankara's dissertations. It is not surrounded by that play of light and color which Eckhart conjures up about the soul.

Apart from this, however, the inner atman of the one and the soul of the other form very definite parallels.

(a) A common antithesis between the "inward" and the "outward" in general, is characteristic of both masters. For both, deeply hidden "within" is something ultimate, pure, inward, entirely separate from all that is outward. This peculiar possession is absolutely different from all other elements that may be associated with it. It is a "Self"—this expression occurs again and again with the same solemn significance in both mystics—as the spiritual center in a ring of ramparts and courtyards to which it is our task to penetrate. We have to know and liberate this self which is purely spiritual and gives forth its own light. This inward being is for Sankara the atman, for Eckhart the soul.

(b) Similar psychological means are used by both to carry forward this antithesis between inward and outward.

For Sankara, the inward is separated first of all from flesh and body, and the first struggle is against *deha-abhimana,* the false illusion that the body is the self. But further, beneath the *indriyani* (the senses), beneath the *manas* (the organ of thought, which is likewise a sensus communis) and beneath the *buddhi* lies for Sankara the *atman* itself.

With Eckhart, beneath the "faculties," the lower powers of sense-perception, of outward senses, of the sensus communis, the sensuous, impulsive will, the lower understanding; and beneath the "higher" powers, memory, reason and the reasonable will, lies the soul. It is the deepest and the highest, the apex, the summit and the "ground of the soul," the spark, the syntheresis,[1] the third heaven within.[2]

Both atman and soul, however vastly different from all the faculties they may be, however foreign and separate in the psychic life, are yet at the same time the stay and foundation of the faculties, without which they could not function.

(c) Unknown and unknowable, unprovable, self-proved is the atman; unknowable is the soul and the ground of the soul. Deep within the atman there dwells for Sankara (according to the pro-

---

[1] Syntheresis is in Scholastic philosophy a name for that function or department of conscience which serves as a guide for conduct ("scintilla conscientiae" of Jerome). TRANSLATOR'S NOTE.

[2] This innermost something is ineffable like God. Eckhart says: "God is inexpressible and he has no name. At bottom the soul is also inexpressible as He is." The Bhagavad Gita says the same, 2, 39.

visional "middle wisdom") the Lord as guide of the inmost, in mystical union with the atman; for Eckhart there blooms and springs in the ground of the soul, God (so long as He has not "ceased" ["disbecome"]. There God goes in and out; there He has His hidden dwelling place; there He brings forth His eternal word; there He holds converse with the soul.

(d) The soul, like the atman is the "self." Now the self comes into sharp conflict with that which we are accustomed to set up as self, as ego—"I" and "mine" as Eckhart puts it; the Ahankara or "I-sayer" as Sankara says. The Ahankara is the erroneous act by which consciousness relates things to an "I," by which I make the abhimana, falsely imputing a relationship between possessions, relatives, friends, body, senses, will and action and the self, and wrongly calling them "my senses, my body, my possessions." Yet it is that faculty by which I regard myself as individual, separate and different from others. All this does not belong to the true self but to that "ego," which, in true self-knowledge, is brushed aside as alien and false. Thus for Eckhart "I" (ahankara), "me and mine" (mamatva) do not belong to the soul. I must renounce all "me and mine" and enter into complete "poverty" (tyaga) in order to attain the selfhood of the soul.

(e) Both atman and soul must free themselves from the world which surrounds them. They must withdraw from the senses and from sense-impressions, without attachment to the objects of sense; they must free themselves from all outward objects as well as from objects of thought, and thus from all manifoldness, multiplicity, and difference. This both masters maintain.

(f) Thus withdrawn inwards, free from all inclination and attachment, stripped of all sense-impressions and thoughts, freed from an egoistic selfhood, the atman shines forth in its own light as pure consciousness. Yet it is entirely free from the ego, free from differences of subject and object, free from the threefold contrast of knower, known and knowing. For Eckhart, the experience of the soul is the same: entirely withdrawn from all things, all objects, all division into will and thought, the soul knows nothing more of the world or of any object, is modeless and formless, is neither this nor that, neither subject nor object. It has become completely one and is the One.

(g) Here the atman is in truth the Atman, free from the obscurity and restriction of avidya. It is light and spirit through and through, high above all devas (heavenly beings). It is again in truth the ascharyam, the miraculous being which it was by nature, and has attained to highest bliss. For Eckhart the soul stands here in its full glory as the homo nobilis, more wonderful than seraphim and cherubim, exalted above all creatures.

III. THE MYSTICISM OF THE SOUL OVERLAID BY THE MYSTICISM OF GOD

Thus, in both writers, there stands as central to the doctrine of salvation what we can call "a higher faith of the soul, which becomes a mystical conception of the soul." One might be tempted, particularly in the case of Eckhart, to determine the nature of his whole speculative system by this, and perhaps even take his conception of God as an extension of the mystical consciousness of the soul. Does he not himself say—and there are most exact parallels in Sankara's conception of the *Atman*—that with knowledge of the soul God Himself is known, that knowledge of the soul is knowledge of God? Even more: are not his speculations on the modeless, supraconscious, suprapersonal, objectless and subjectless "Godhead" merely repetitions of the mystical state writ large, copies of the soul which has become "one," has sunk into itself, has passed beyond world and things and self-consciousness? Is not "Godhead," or "Brahman" merely a name for the soul which has found its own glory?

(a) This would be a complete misunderstanding, but to dispel that doubt is, nevertheless, very difficult. It is perhaps easier to do so with regard to the Indian teaching, though it is just here that Atman and Brahman seem to be perfect synonyms, and Brahman is supposed to be nothing other than the Atman itself released from multiplicity and limitation. It can be done by comparing the teaching of Sankara with that of the Yoga. In the Yoga, speculation as to the soul is everything. Also in the Yoga, the Atman is to be found, known in its glory and set free. Here the kaivalyam of the Atman is striven for, i.e. its isolation from all additions and connections, which constitutes its aisvaryam (lordship), its complete divineness and onmipotence. This aisvaryam scarcely falls short of that of Brahma-nirvana in the absoluteness and fullness of glory attributed to it. But for the attainment of this kaivalyam and aisvaryam in the Yoga system, the approach through the Brahman is not necessary; one does not need the knowledge of the unity of the Atman with something beyond itself, whereby it first attains its own glory. Atman has this glory eternally within itself which only needs to be set at liberty.

(b) Sankara could really say the same of the inward atman, indeed he does say it often enough. The atman is essentially all that the seeker after salvation needs. Sankara assures us that the atman attains nothing above itself, is united with nothing besides itself. It is in itself the divine glory and has only to be recognized as such. The terms Atman and Brahman seem to be tautological. Nevertheless, there is a deep chasm between Yoga teaching and Atman-Brahman teaching. Those who practice yoga who do not seek the Brahman, and who wish to find the Atman only, stand far below those who know Brahman, and are perilously far from salvation.

It is almost impossible to reproduce the absolute difference in attitude between the two conceptions, apparently separated only by the fact that the one does not use a term, which in the other seems to be merely tautological. Yet this difference of mood is very palpable and is rooted in the deepest essence of the matter. One can express it thus: The Vedantin would indignantly reproach the Yogin with what he himself seems to do continually in his own phraseology: viz. (he would say) the follower of the Yoga is practicing a blasphemous self-deification. The Yogin ascribes to the atman that which belongs only to the Brahman. Theoretically, this charge could not stand, for it is meaningless with the complete identity of atman and Brahman which is maintained. The speculative mystic, if he came across this problem, would know how to wrap it up in dialectic. He could not set it aside. It is obvious here again that one cannot understand mysticism and its terms, if they are taken as they are in themselves instead of in relation to the "soil" out of which they spring. With Sankara this "soil" is the original separation of the Brahman and Atman speculation. To judge by terms and speculative efforts, "Atman is Brahman" is an analytical statement, or rather a verdict of identity. In secret however, it remains a verdict of synthesis. Thereon depends the whole inspiration and attitude of Sankara's speculation in distinction from mere Yoga. Because it is also Brahman, something incalculable has been *added* to the Atman, which is not contained in the kaivalyam of the atman merely stripped of limitations. And exactly the same applies to Eckhart.[3]

IV. THE POINT OF VISION IS FROM BELOW UPWARDS

To the elements named in Section III a fourth must be added equally significant for both masters. We must pay very close attention or this further element will be confused with the earlier ones, while it is indeed something new.

From the terms which they use, the teaching of both masters could be presented as if the whole process described were a matter not of the atman but of the Brahman. It would then run something like this: "Brahman, one only, without a second, is multiplied through avidya. By false representation a world of multiplicity is built up around it. In a multitude of (fictitious) individual souls the one pure Being appears as manifold. The whole significance of the teaching of Brahman is that at various points this net of Avidya is torn and the monstrous error as to true Being is corrected."

But the matter has only to be presented in this way for the reader to feel immediately how little it corresponds to the real purpose of Sankara. His interest is not to correct a dosha, a mistake, that has befallen the Brahman; it is not an objective correction of the nature of Being. His true teaching as he sets it forth with great emphasis and earnestness in the introductory chapter of his principal work, is offered for this purpose: "that none should injure *his own* blessedness, and fall into evil." His teaching is for the purpose of salvation, not for the salvation of the Brahman[4] but for man who has need of saving.

The formula aham Brahma asmi (I am Brahman) expresses this

---

[3] We shall deal with this more fully in the "Transition from A to B."

[4] This it is indeed in Schopenhauer's interpretation of the Vedanta. But to see the Vedanta through this lens is to see it quite falsely. God redeeming Himself, salvation applied to the Brahman, which is nitya-siddham, nitya-buddham, nitya-muktam, would be for Sankara, not only the most repellent blasphemy but pure nonsense. And the same holds true for all religion.

also. In the first case it could only run "Brahma asti, ekam cha asti," i.e. "Brahman is, and is alone; and at one place at least, where formerly an illusion, viz. the ego, obscured his all-oneness the error is remedied." Without question such a formulation might be consistent if it were permissible to draw the logical conclusions of formulas which—in spite of their own assertions—are not theoretical propositions but enigmas. But that would not correspond to the inner significance of a teaching which is not objective metaphysic of the Brahman, but a doctrine of salvation of the atman. This meaning is revealed as the true one in the experience of the man who has attained to saving knowledge. However much in the moment of awakened and achieved fullness of knowledge all ego and all separateness may disappear, as soon as the spirit draws back out of such states it knows these moments of insight in remembrance as salvation which *it* has experienced. The content of this experience is not "there was Brahman" but "there I was Brahman," and that is something that concerns *me* not *Brahman*. In spite of all, the sentence: "Brahma is this atman" is indeed a final synthesis of two subjects.

V. The Mystic Copula

The last sentence is of course not of a logical, but of a mystical nature. The word "is" in the mystical formula of identification has a significance which it does not contain in logic. It is no copula as in the sentence: S is P; it is no sign of equality in a reversible equation. It is not the "is" of a normal assertion of identity. However much the emphatic pronouncements of Sankara and Eckhart strive to attain to the latter, they do not succeed in hiding the fact that their logic is indeed the "wonder" logic of mysticism. One might try to indicate this by forcing the language and making the word "be" into a medium of higher unity of intransitive and transitive. For instance one might say instead of: "I am Brahman," "I am 'existed' by Brahman" or "essenced" by Brahman, or "Brahman exists me."[5]

The reader should compare what is said later in Fichte's words about the mystical copula.

[5] If Sankara builds the forms astitvam and astikata, and Eckhart the corresponding form "Istigkeit," the form to exist somebody (isten) would be permissible in a grammar of mysticism.

8

Creature and Maya

The most surprising doctrine of Sankara is that of Maya. It is a growth which seems only possible on Indian soil, yet there is at least a strong resemblance in Eckhart, in the latter's curious conception of the "creatura" and the nature of the creature.

That the creature, which of itself is nothing, has no essence, being, or value, may come to "being" and "essence" is the meaning of Eckhart's teaching of salvation. It is the same with Sankara, for he uses the same terms: arriving at being; to reach being: to become unified with being: sampatti, sampadyate, apnoti, sad-atma-svarupa-sampatti; to become united with *sat,* sad-atman, sad-atma-brahman, satyasya satyam, the beyond-death, the immortal, yea, immortality itself.

This quantity which is thus to arrive at being, Eckhart calls the creature. Here it is almost forgotten that creature is derived from create and means a creation of God's. All the emphasis lies on the fact that as creature it is what God is not, it is the vain, unreal, non-essential. In this respect it resembles Sankara's world-being, which, set up by Maya and Avidya is the unreal, vain and untrue. The two masters also resemble each other in the fact that this explanation of the creature is built upon a quite realistic, naïvely conceived doctrine of creation. In this conception, creature exists through creatio, through srishti. God is the creator of the creature, and Brahman is "that from which the world has its beginning, its subsistence and its dissolution"; Brahman is jagato mulam, the root of the world. Final-

88

ly, they resemble one another in this, that, as with Eckhart the "creare," so with Sankara the maya, has the opalescence of a curious double meaning. These elements of comparison must be followed up in detail.

Of all Eckhart's ideas none is more elusive and difficult to grasp than that of the creature; but none is more important for the significance of his whole doctrinal system.

1. *Creare,* on the one hand, as "conferre esse," to confer being, is the highest function of God, indeed the whole value and significance of His Being.

(a) In countless instances, when he is talking of creare and creatura, Eckhart is simply speaking the language of the Christian speculation of his age, just as Sankara presupposes the whole realistic doctrine of creation, and presents it over and over again in whole and in part. God is then causa and prima causa of all that is, superior to the world, all-wise, effecting all things. He is in complete transcendence to His creature, preceding it as causa precedes effectus, Himself like every causa, containing all that is to become in effectus, and at the same time containing infinitely more than ever was, or can be, in the world.

(b) God creates through His word out of nothing: no second rival principle, no material, no prima materia confronts Him.

(c) He creates according to the eternal types, the ideas or "rationes" which are eternally in Him. These ideas are[1] the elements of his own rich inexhaustible Being.[2] As He contains them within Him He sees and knows in them and through them His own self in the radiant fullness of His eternal, uncreated and uncreatable Being. This self-knowledge is, vice versa, the setting forth of ideas and the system of ideas and of the eternal mundus ydealis, which Eckhart on occasion also calls a creatio. (See below creatio in principio.)

What can be well-pleasing in things, that should please God? The things must please Him, for He who saw them was God, and

---

[1] Bonitas nec est creata nec facta nec genita. (Goodness is not created nor made nor born) and this applies equally to all ideas or rationes:

Creaturarum rationes non sunt creaturae sed nec creabiles ut sic (the ideas of things created are not creatures nor creatable as such).

[2] Idea in Deo est nihil aliud quam Dei essentia (the idea in God is nothing other than the essence of God). Thus says Thomas Aquinas also.

that which He saw was likewise God: in their eternal types, which He Himself is, God beheld Himself and therein beheld He also all things.

(d) The ideas in their totality are the eternal Word in Him, which He speaks from everlasting to everlasting; they are the eternal thought and the knowledge of His own self through which He is conscious and self-conscious, person and personal.[3]

(e) When He creates the world in space and time, He creates it according to these ideas, and since they are the content and expression of His Being, He creates the world in truth after His own image. Deus est exemplar mundi; the world is therefore a copy, an expression of the eternal God, of His riches, and His glory (Upanishad: "all shines through Him"), though of course infinitely diminished and falling far short of the original type. This empirical world is in space and time, is six thousand years old, and has its beginning not in time but with time, for before the world was, time was not. The creation of this world confined in time is nevertheless for God not a temporal but an eternal act. (This conception is quite self-evident in Scholasticism and in Augustine.)

(f) Following the Platonic precedent, every separate thing is for Eckhart that which it is inasmuch as it "participates" in the corresponding idea: it is album in so far as it participates in the eternal idea of album, in the eternal albedo, the album ipsum. It is bonum in so far as it participates in the eternal bonitas, the bonum ipsum. This participation or having part in the eternal idea, is from the standpoint of the idea, a giving of participation.[4] The idea gives itself to the object, gives it part of itself. The idea is in it or of it. It constitutes the essence of the thing, inquantum est album or bonum, and in so far the idea is the "being" of the thing.[5] Now the ideas are nothing less than the elements of God Himself unfurled. God therefore "is" the nature of the creature, inquantum ea est alba, bona, una, etc.

---

[3] The creation through the "word" has a curious parallel in Indian theology in the idea of the *vag* and the *sakti*. This is the Indian Logos.

[4] Quando dicimus bonum, intelligimus, quod sua bonitas est sibi data, influxa et innata ab ingenita bonitate. (When we call a thing good, we understand that its goodness is given to it, flowing and borne into it by the unborn good.)

[5] Quomodo enim esset quid album distinctum seu divisum ab albedine. (For in what way should what is white be distinct or divided off from whiteness?)

This is true also of the idea of being, of esse ipsum. God is the ipsum esse, Being itself, as He is the Good itself, bonum ipsum. Therefore the creatures inquantum sunt not only inquantum, sunt album, bonum or anything else, but in so far as they exist at all, they *are* because they participate in ipsum esse (Being itself) which is again God Himself.

All that seems to us pantheistic in this teaching is at first nothing more than the attempt to express the Christian conception of creare and creatum esse scientifically by means of the speculative system of the time, but with a more Platonic than an Aristotelian emphasis.[6]

(g) At the same time the meaning of both "creare" and of "world" expands. Without its being noted in the context, world often becomes that original world, the "mundus ipse," the "mundus ydealis," the world of ideas, and the world as idea, apart from its descent into time and its expression as this world here below. The bringing forth of this ideal "world," which is the self-knowledge of God in the richness of His own being, and His eternal beholding of the same, is now also called "creare." Creare is then a parallel term to the "speaking of the eternal word" (begetting the Son). The difference between "creare" and "speak" (or beget) is only this, that the one is generally used when the eternal world is spoken of as a multiplicity of ideas, and the other, when vice versa, the multiplicity of the world of ideas is meant in their unity, as one eternal whole, as one Word, as God's thought of Himself. This "creare" is then also creare in principio: creation in principle, a bringing forth in and as idea. In this sense it is safe to say, that this creatio in principio is as eternal as God Himself. God speaks His word, begets His Son from everlasting to everlasting. It is also safe to say: the "world" is God. For the world in principio, in the fullness of

---

[6] For the Platonic realism of this teaching of participation compare especially:

Bonitas et bonum non sunt nisi una bonitas praecise in omnibus, praeter generare et generari. (Goodness and good are one and the same. Goodness is absolutely and in all things distinguished only as generating goodness and generated goodness.) Eckhart substitutes for the Platonic "methexis" the term "generari" from trinitarian speculation. The idea of the good generates the good in the good individual. And therefore this, in so far as it is bonus (good), is itself something generatus (generated), not something (factus) made, or creatus (created).

ideas, is "God out of God." And the eternity of this "world" is not denied by Scholasticism: it is the logos, "the word."

(h) Eckhart's teaching became "dangerous" only because on the one hand he seldom distinguishes clearly between the "creare in principio" and "creare" in general, and on the other because this failure to distinguish is with him not merely accidental. In consequence of the Platonic realistic conception of participation, something of eternity entered into the idea of the creature—an intimate connection which is indeed the unity of the world and God. By means of a kind of "communicatio idiomatum" there crept into the world something of the divine substantiality and essence, which was more than the fact that it had been created after God as its exemplar.[7]

2. On the other hand, creatura in Eckhart is often a principle directly opposed to God, is indeed in complete contrast to the divine Being itself, as prapancha, the world of things and of multiplicity, is in Sankara's teaching. We can understand this curious fact by considering the common meaning of the word "creature," and the two contrasting valuations attributed to it, which did not originate with the mystic but are apparent also in forms of common religion.

(a) We say "creature" and we mean thereby on the one hand something begotten, caused, called into existence by the Creator. We thus recognize the existence and the real being of the created, and also its value. For if a thing is created it is of God, and therefore it is obviously real, for God creates nothing unreal; and it is good, for God creates nothing evil. Thus the term "creature" expresses a positive reality and value.

But we also say "miserable creature" implying thereby that the thing is miserable just because it is "creature." In this case the creature is not so much considered as a creation, issuing from God, but as a created thing, *merely* a creature and therefore nothing of itself, fragile, unable to stand alone, lacking in value: something pitiable, even contemptible. "Creature" then be-

---

[7] Compare with this what is said below of the madhya vidya in Sankara. Here Isvara creates out of himself, and gives the world thereby a relationship which is intended to be a participation in himself, a tad-atmyam, a weaker counterpart of identity.

comes synonymous with a miserandum or actually with a miserabile. Thus the German says "diese Kreatur" (this creature) when he means an utterly worthless fellow. Here creature expresses a negation of reality and value.

(b) This double meaning has developed from a common religious dual evaluation of world and creature. On the one hand: the "world" and the "creation" is the work of God, is good and a reflection of His glory. On the other: the "world" and all that is "creature," is vain and empty, transient and perishable. It is a fetter and an obstacle, a hindrance and a bedazzlement, "a handful of sand," sorrow, and confusion. The world has to be conquered and overcome; it is opposed to God—is essentially antagonistic to Him. We find the world thus disavowed not only in the mystics but in simple prayers, hymns and sermons of Christian, Jewish and Mohammedan origin. Without resorting to mysticism this negation can make use of expressions which come near to the doctrine of maya: for example, "illusion and deception of the senses," "vanity and hollowness," "vapor and dream."[8] Non-mystics also have said of the creature:

> Formed from the dust, returning to the dust. Like a broken shard and withered grass, like a faded flower and a passing shadow, a vanishing cloud, a dying breath, flying dust and a fleeting dream. (From the Mussaf prayer of the Jews at the New Year.)

(c) Eckhart develops this antithesis and thereby approaches within a hair's breadth of Sankara's maya doctrine:

> All that is created has no truth in itself. All creatures in so far as they are creatures, as they "are in themselves" (quod sunt in et per se) are not even illusion, they are "pure nothing."

> All that is created is nothing.

> Omnes creaturae sunt unum purum nihil. Nulla creatura est, quae aliquid sit. Nulla creatura habet esse. Quidquid non habet esse, hoc est nihil.

---

[8] I have dealt elsewhere with this double meaning as explained in (a) and (b) by differentiating between "createdness" which signifies the nature and value of the creature, and "creaturehood" which indicates the vanity of the creature. Cf. R. Otto: *The Idea of the Holy.*

All creatures are one mere nothing. (Or:) There is no creature
which is anything. (Or:) None of the creatures has being. What
has no being—is nothing.

But this "purum nihil" of Eckhart is a puzzle for his interpreter.
To explain it we should have to invent the very terms which we
find already used in Sankara. It does not mean that the creatures
do not exist at all. They must exist somehow in order that this
judgment of their non-existence may be cast in their faces. They
"are" not, does not mean that they have no empirical existence,
no physical reality. They cannot be non-existent in this empirical
sense, for they could not then be "pure nothing."[9]

They resemble in fact the prapancha of world and multiplicity
in Sankara. According to Sankara, things and the world and its
multiplicity only exist through Avidya. But in what sense then *is*
Avidya itself? And who is it who has Avidya? Individual souls
perhaps? But they are themselves the products of Avidya. Does
Avidya really exist? If so there would be something other than
Brahman, and Brahman would not be "without a second." Does
Avidya not exist? If it does not, how can it then effect the illusion
of the world and set up multiplicity about the one Brahman?
What might be taken in Eckhart as a possible explanation of the
"how" of creation is explicitly formulated by Sankara: Avidya
(and thereby the multiplicity of all Karyam of all "that which is
effected, i.e. created") is sad-asadbhyam anirvachaniyam, viz.
not to be defined either as Being or as Not-Being. Exactly the
same is applicable to Eckhart's creatura.

3. But whence comes this "creature," in the second sense of
the term, for Eckhart? That God created the world, that this
world was six thousand years old, that it was empirically real and
was there through God, Eckhart maintains and believes just as

[9] This being of the creature in its empirical nature and existence, Eckhart
ascribes to the "esse formaliter inhaerens" of the creature. If this were the
"esse" of God, then Eckhart would indeed be a pantheist. He would then set
the natural being of things on a level with the being of God as the pantheists
do. The pantheist deifies the creature. Eckhart does the exact opposite. Where
the creature *ends,* God *begins.* In this sense he says: distinguendum de esse formaliter inhaerente et de esse absoluto quod est Deus. And: Esse est Deus. Hoc
verum est de esse absoluto non de esse formaliter inhaerente. (A distinction must
be made between the empirical being and the absolute being which is God. Being
is God. This is true of absolute being but not of empirical being.)

firmly as every church-goer. But as the orthodox believer already admits the peculiar rejection of the world, of which we have spoken above, yet does not ask whence then is this vanity, this fleetingness, this opposition to God in the creature, so it is with Eckhart's higher speculation. The creatures are simply there with their nothingness, with their lack of real being or value. How they may attain to "Being," how, above all, that creature of most importance, *man,* seeking salvation, can escape this nothingness, can become essential, can attain Being itself, can find himself as Being—that is all that is sought in Eckhart's teaching.

It is exactly the same with Sankara's Avidya. Pressed and plagued by the controversy of the schoolmen one must wrestle with this problem. But Sankara hardly bothers about it. He asks how creatureliness is to be overcome, not how it is to be explained. ("We do not explain the world; we explain it away.") This is, by the by, a new proof of the fact that the interest of his teaching is not a scientific one, which seeks problems in order to solve them, but an interest in salvation, which, starting from a certain given lack of salvation, desires to remedy this need, but not to solve its origin theoretically. And so he quietly ignores the insoluable problem or answers it roughly and incompletely.[10]

4. In his exegesis of John, 1:2, Eckhart attempts to explain his idea of creare. Here he distinguishes between the creata and the facta. The creata, as merely creata—pure nothing—receive Being in so far as they are also facta. Facere is then conferre esse, the true gift of Being by means of which the creature is withdrawn from its mere creatureliness:

> Now listen carefully. I will now say what I have never said: When God *created* (creavit) heaven and earth and all creatures, then God *made* (fecit) nothing. But then spake God: We *make* an image that is like unto us. Merely to create is easy; that one does when and how one will. But what I *make,* that I make myself, with and in myself, and impress my own image upon it. . . . Therefore, when God *made* man, He did more than merely create. He made in the soul a work equal unto Himself, His own efficacious and eternally enduring work.

[10] As Christians we also do not know where the devil comes from.

We might try to develop this thought as follows: Eckhart distinguishes a lower and a higher "creare," viz. a first positing of things—the mere "creare," and a second further making the "facere," through which they receive "Being." This teaching would then resemble the Platonic doctrine of the μη όν, which is not non-being and is also not being. But Eckhart does not draw these conclusions. The doctrine of a μη όν opposed to God, particularly of one which He Himself had produced, would have been forcibly denied by Eckhart. God could not create a μη όν. In Eckhart there remains that curious double valuation of things which is peculiar to all religion: things and men so far as they are creaturely, i.e. as they are of themselves, are valueless and simply nothing. But inasmuch as they were created by God and are of God they have existence, are good and divine. This accounts for Eckhart's favorite "in so far as" ("also verre als").

> In so far as the creature is creature, it carries within itself bitterness, shame, evil and hardship. Whoever forsakes things in as much as they are accidental, possesses them in as much as they are pure Being and eternal.

The simplest expression for the true content of this teaching is:

> All things—in their finite form—have flowed out in time, and have nevertheless—in their infinite form—remained in eternity.

(5) With regard to this double valuation, creare has a resemblance to Maya. Maya has also a double aspect both in its first beginning and in its finest ultimate form in Sankara. Maya is in origin a *magic* force, the power by which the magician obtains his effects. He produces an "existence" through imaginative suggestion which is distinct from being and non-being, which approaches the calling up of a mere illusion, and which yet on the other hand results in extremely real effects.[11]

At a higher level Maya is then *miraculous* power. Brahman is the great mayin, the one rich in maya. According to the original meaning of Maya, this miracle-worker by his power creates the

---

[11] Saubhari, the saint, created for himself through his Maya fifty bodies: an illusion, yet such an one that it could actually marry and have a hundred and fifty children. (See: Vishnu Narayana, p. 19)

world as magic which carries in itself the half-reality of all
magic, but is certainly not mere appearance in the usual sense of
the word. Sankara also on occasion advances this idea with the
utmost naïveté.

But even in the highest form of his speculation Maya retains
a final flavor of this magic. The world which we perceive in multiplicity through Avidya has still its foundation in the Maya of the
great Mayin himself, floats like the magic spell indeterminate between being and non-being. With this hybrid interpretation it
resembles Eckhart's "creature."

6. On the relation between real Being and the being-non-being
of the creature Plotinus expresses himself thus:

> By this non-being, of course, we are not to understand some-
> thing that does not exist, but only something of an utterly differ-
> ent order from Authentic-Being; there is no question here of
> movement or position with regard to Being; the non-being we are
> thinking of is, rather, an image of Being, or perhaps something
> still further removed than even an image. Now this (the required
> faint image of Being) might be the sensible universe with all the
> impressions it engenders, or it might be something of even later
> derivation, accidental to the realm of sense, or again it might be
> the source of the sense world or something of the same order
> entering into it to complete it.[12]

This explanation resembles Eckhart's and Sankara's conception.
Yet there is still a difference. For Plotinus, the creature derives
its non-being from materia. As a Scholastic, Eckhart also touches
upon this idea. But for him, the real distinction is not between
God and materia, but is given in his peculiar expression "in as
much as." Inasmuch as the creature is conceived of God, it is
true being, is unified and one, is eternal and identified with the
Being of God. But inasmuch as it is "of itself," it is vain, empty
and of no account. Sankara expresses precisely the same contrast, for example, in the passage commenting on the Chhandogya-upanishad 6, 3, 2, p. 313.

> Sarvam cha namarupadi vikarajatam sad-atmana eva satyam.
> Svatas tu anritam.

[12] *Ennead* I, 8, 3.

> This whole multiplicity of production (creatures) existing under
> name and form in so far as it is Being itself is true. *Of itself*
> (svatas tu) it is untrue.

This svatas is in Eckhart the creatura per se apart from its existence in Being. For that very reason Eckhart and Sankara are
alike far removed from so-called "idealism"; in a way they are
both staunch realists. This world is emphatically not "my conception." It is, truly conceived (i.e. in unity and as the eternal
one which is Being itself) absolutely true and independent of all
my "conceptions." It is one unified body of reality, and the
satyasya satyam.[13] So too, the inexhaustible fullness of the being
and depth of things[14] is real, for it is Being, Beingness, astitvam
itself, only gathered and blended in the identity of the one complete Being.

Only what the creature (svatas) is of itself—its multiplicity and
division, its dispersal in space and time—is anritam, is untrue,
is to be overcome by the true knowledge of mystical insight.

But how the creature or the vikarajatam which is in truth the
one eternal Being, instead of remaining in this Being comes to
exist per se, or svatas, and thereby falls a prey to vanity, is a riddle that neither the Eastern nor the Western master solves. In this
they are also alike.

[13] "Sad-aspadam sarvam sarvatra"—says Sankara of Gita 13, 14, p. 557. The
all is everywhere a storehouse of sat (Being, reality, truth).
[14] Purnam-dives per se; also in the aspadam, in the stored-up Being, lies fullness
and riches.

9

Religion as Exaltedness of Self

Measured by a simple personal belief in God, mysticism is always bold. It dares to use expressions which overstep the relationship of the simple believer to his God, and from his position must appear astounding, reckless and even blasphemous. There are grades and stages in this boldness, and mysticism shows itself capable of much variety in respect of greater or less temerity. Sankara and Eckhart are at one in this, that they are bold to the highest degree, so daring that their temerity cannot be surpassed. Sankara says in his exegesis of the Chhandogya-upanishad 6, 16, p. 657.

> The Atman, to know whom is salvation, not to know whom is bondage to the world, who is the root of the world, who is the basis of all creation, through whom all exists, through whom all is conceived—the Unborn, the Deathless, the Fearless, the Good, without second,—He is the Real. He is thy Self. And therefore that are thou.

He expresses himself in similar terms again and again. That is his opinion absolutely without qualification. This absolute and immense Brahman with all its awe-inspiring attributes—that art thou thyself, fundamentally. But that is more than *unio-mystica,* than becoming one in a simple close relationship. It is, or should be, complete identity. With what feelings of exultation this certainty was permeated and surrounded, the following verse from Kaivalya, 2, 9 shows:

> *Finer than the fine yet am I greatest.*
> *I am the All in its complete fullness,*
> *I the most ancient, the spirit, the Lord God.*
> *The golden-gleaming am I, of form divine.*
> *Without hand and foot, rich in unthinkable might,*
> *Sight without eyes, hearing without ears,*
> *Free from all form, I know. But me*
> *None knows. For I am Spirit, am Being.*

Eckhart makes the same claim: not only Deo unitum esse (to be united with God) but unum esse cum Deo (to be one with God), to be indeed the One itself, the *unio* as complete and absolute identity. He does not try to soften the astoundingness, even the terror of his assertion. On the contrary he seeks ever bolder and harsher expression. He knows that he is teaching rara et nova, is saying what was never heard before.

There is no question that the two masters here harmonize in presenting a type of religion which goes far beyond what is usually implied by that name. All religion, indeed, seeks the transcendent, and salvation in transcendence; seeks rest and fellowship with something strange, unapproachable, unspeakably lofty. It strives thereby to pass beyond the natural and merely creaturely; to escape limitation and find completion at what appears to the natural eye a giddy and exalted height. But however close the fellowship is thought to be, there remains always the chasm between creator and created. Even in the final consummation of this fellowship the cleft is unbridged and unbridgeable. In the mysticism of Eckhart and Sankara, however, the soul seeks to pass out of the region of the created to the Being and dignity of God Himself. It feels satisfied with its salvation only when it is uncreated with the uncreated, eternal with the eternal, high above deva and angel, blessed with the Blessed, original being with the original Being; when it is this not merely as a part or element of its nature and life, but Being in its fullness and its unity; when it is the One itself.

2. This tendency in Eckhart (particularly in that which we are later to know as his "vivacity"), soars even higher than in Sankara. There is a strange ring of exultation in the expressions

by which he describes the soul as not only one with the eternal ultimate Being, but as creating from eternity with the creator, as the eternal creative power itself:[1]

> God made all things through me, when I had my existence in the unfathomable ground of God. (Evans, pf. 589, 1)

> My innermost man enjoys the creatures, not as gifts but as what is and was ever mine.

True, if we only examine his terminology we can regard even such expressions as quite harmless and not going beyond scholastic philosophy. For Eckhart is here speaking of the soul sub ratione ydeali, i.e. of the idea of man as eternal in God and as one with His own nature, a conception likewise found in Thomas Aquinas. This idea of being in and with God and God Himself is also according to the scholastic doctrine, the creative principle. What is specifically Eckhartian is that this harmless conception sets Eckhart's thought aflame and fires him with a feeling of exaltation of which no Scholastic would have dreamt. According to his conception of the true participation, "I" have part in this idea. Yes, ideally, I *am* this idea. What is true of it, is true of me. So it is verily true that I have existed eternally in God, before the foundation of the world was laid, and that I with Him laid the foundation; that *I* am conceived with the eternal Son from the Father in eternity. Before God was begotten out of the Godhead, before He spoke His Word I was included without distinction in the eternal, silent abyss of the Godhead, and was one and the same with it.

3. This experience is in fact something more than religion or theism could afford to permit. This is "numinous feeling of self" and exalted feeling of self, revealed in sharpest contrast to all religion of "absolute dependence." It seems to be a complete and exclusive antithesis of all theism.

4. Yet a further point of similarity between the two masters lies

[1] Still, there are also many expressions in the Indian mystics which closely resemble the Eckhartian feeling of creativeness: Compare Kaivalya-Upanishad 19:

> *In me arose the whole world,*
> *In me alone exists the All.*
> *In me it passes.—This Brahman*
> *Without second, am I.*

in the fact that both *are* theists, that beneath their mysticism lies a substructure of theism (and in this theism also there are many analogies). This is a fact which must be admitted on the evidence of the original texts, but usually it is not held to be of any importance. In Eckhart it is generally regarded either as simply a matter of accommodation and of adaptation to the traditional conception, or as inconsistency. Sankara on the other hand distinguishes between a higher and a lower knowledge. For the lower knowledge of popular understanding there is the Isvara, the personal, world-creating and world-controlling God. But this lower knowledge is avidya, is Not-knowing, which disappears when the higher wisdom enters. As mystics it is said that both Eckhart and Sankara are esoteric, as theists that they are exoteric.

From such a position the problem of how to explain Sankara's positive theology and his devoted and even passionate zeal for the personal God, fighting and crushing his Buddhist and materialist opponents, remains a riddle, even when one is aided by esotericism. Again, to take Eckhart's real and simple Christian piety, which he acknowledges as warmly as his mystical heights, for mere allegory, compromise or esotericism, is sheer folly.

For Eckhart there is a necessary antinomy arising out of the very experience itself. He who cannot understand this antithesis may at least help himself out with the pitiful (and nowadays so cheap) ''Complexio oppositorum.'' Or he may class Eckhart with Goethe as ''Mensch mit seinem Widerspruch'' (''man with his contradictions''), but should not force him into a scheme of the esoteric and exoteric, which does not fit him in the least, and which he would probably not have understood.

This type of mysticism is accompanied by a certain type of theism which is more than an historical accident. It needs this theism, and that for two reasons: first, for the sake of its own inward tension and aspiration—it is the bow which makes the string tense. Secondly, no mysticism extends like the arc of the rainbow in the blue, without a basis. However high it reaches, it always bears within it some faint scent of the soil from which it rises, and from which it draws the sap of life. In both masters there is a positive relationship between their mysticism and their orthodox religion, and what is still more important, it is this relationship to theism which distinguishes their mysticism and gives it a peculiar note, as we shall show later. First let us deal shortly with their theism.

We need only remark here that the Western sage, although in his higher speculation he is at times even more abstract than the Eastern, in his utterances frequently challenging orthodox religious opinion and intentionally seeking the boldest, the most confounding and almost blasphemous phrases, yet in truth maintains a decidedly more positive relation to personal speculation than Sankara.

10

A Common Theistic Foundation

I. THE THEISTIC FOUNDATION IN SANKARA

When we speak of Indian religion we usually think immediately of monism, pantheism, impersonal mysticism, of the Brahman, which is pure Being, the One without a second, identical with the soul. Often, we do not know that fierce battles have been fought on Indian soil over the question of personal theism, and that a large number of Indian schools have combated and decidedly rejected that form of monism. The most famous pioneers of a personal theism, outside the Sesvara-Yoga schools, are such men as the great Ramanuja and Madhva, whose communities still exist today and are just beginning to show a new zeal. But even with regard to the classical school of Indian mysticism, the school of Sankara, which prefers to be called the school of the absolute Advaita, caution is necessary. For, this school, at least in its substructure, represents pronounced theism of a high type. The impersonal Brahman rests here also on a theistic basis, and this basis is not unimportant for the conception of Brahman itself. It definitely colors the mystical experience of the school. Later we shall attempt an examination of a mystical experience so colored, but here we shall confine ourselves to becoming familiar with this particular form of theism. Apologetically it is at least not unimportant that it exists, and that upon a soil so different from that of our own religious development, a system of thought and experience has arisen which in many respects shows a marked similarity to our own religious ideas. Occasional references to our own conception may therefore also be allowed.

Particularly important for the purposes of our examination, is Sankara's Commentary on the Bhagavad Gita. For the Gita is the great basic text of Indian theistic piety. Garbe has translated the Gita into German and has proved that in its pure form it is one of the original texts of Bhakti piety with its distinctly theistic stamp. Undoubtedly Sankara rather forces the text when he attempts to read into it his own teaching of the suprapersonal Brahman. But we must not overlook or deny the *positive* relationship which he adopts toward Theism itself.[1]

1. In reading Sankara's introduction to his Commentary on the Gita, it would never occur to one that here a Monist is speaking and that the impersonal Brahman, and absorption into him, is being proclaimed as salvation.

Om

Narayana is exalted above the not unfolded [unfolded nature]
(Out of the not unfolded has come the world egg.)

He uses this old traditional verse as a preface to his commentary and then describes how Narayana, that is, Isvara, the Lord, creates this world, and with it the lower demiurges[2] who must fashion it in His name. He then reveals to the ancient wise men the twofold Vedic religion, the lesser religion of sacrifice and other works, which leads only to earthly happiness, and the true religion of knowledge and freedom from passion which leads to salvation. This Lord, possessed of the divine attributes of infinite knowledge, divine majesty, and power, guides nature in its evolution and its course. Though Himself unborn, immortal, eternal, pure and free, he consents to appear in human form as Krishna, in order by revealing the Gita to teach the world anew—that world, which through the passion of desire, has allowed true religion to grow dim. The Gita contains the sum of the Vedic teaching. Its purpose is the highest salvation, which is at first

---

[1] I quote from the Ananda-asrama-samskrita-grantha-avali*h*, 2nd edition Vol. 34.
[2] The highest of whom is Hiranyagarbha.

described simply as the cessation of Samsara and the cause thereof, and which is reached through the constant exercise of Atman knowledge, and the surrender of all sacrifice and other works directed toward earthly happiness.

All this could be affirmed by a purely Theistic Vedantin even if he were not a disciple of Sankara, as for instance Ramanuja or Madhva.

It may be urged that this is an adaptation, a passing allegory, or a compromise with the "lower knowledge" demanded by the text. But that is a very inaccurate statement of the position. Sankara's relationship to the thought-world of the Gita is an inner one. His point of view is no longer simply that of the old Monistic Upanishads. The reason for this, viewed historically, lies in the general development of Indian religion.

2. Long before Sankara, India had developed a distinctly theistic philosophy, partly in striking contrast to the monism of the old Upanishad teaching, partly in close relation to it and even admixed with it. The Gita, the great epics, the Puranas, the Sutras of Badarayana had been its heralds and witnesses. Sankara's philosophy enters into this heritage. He also proclaims and defends Isvara, the Lord, the personal God. The name "Lord" has for him the same full solemnity as Dominus Deus has for the Christian of the West. Brahman is Lord, the Highest Lord, Paramesvara. It is true that, as such, Brahman is the lower Brahman, and for the samyagdarsanam, for complete vision and knowledge, "the Lord" together with the soul and the world is absorbed into the highest Brahman, the Nirguna-Brahman, who is Being only, without qualities and distinctions, one single undifferentiated mass of knowledge without the contrasts of Knower, Known, and Knowing.[3]

But it is not unimportant for this Brahman, nirvisesham and advitiyam, that an Isvara has been submerged and fused into it, for it is unmistakably there. The Brahman conception rises beyond

---

[3] With almost startling agreement, Eckhart says: "But in as much as thereby (through the disappearance of the soul in God) God is no longer there for the Spirit, there is for it no longer any eternal archetype." (The archetype is the eternal idea of the soul. God and the soul disappear together into the eternal One, just as Isvara and Jiva disappear into the Brahman.)

a personal God and yet still bears the fragrance and color of the ground from which it springs.

3. For the apara vidya Sankara is a passionate theist. If he was the greatest teacher of his time, the restorer of the pure Vedantic doctrine, the antagonist and destroyer of sects, false teachers and mistaken philosophers—particularly the Buddhists—he was this in the name of a Brahman whose foremost and fundamental definition reads thus: Brahman is that from which the origin, continuance and dissolution of the world comes. That is, He is a world-creating, world-sustaining and world-dissolving God. That statement is simply the commonly used definition of a strictly theistic conception of God; and in so far as his doctrine of God is theistic, it has far-reaching parallels with Christian teaching. In a short survey we are setting forth here a few of the fundamental characteristics of Sankara's teaching about God, the Christian parallels to which we do not need to mention. They will be evident to every reader.

4. Brahman as Paramesvara,[4] as the Lord, is the One, unique, world-surpassing, free, all-powerful God; He is all-knowing, all-wise, just, good, personal and purely spiritual, not to be known through philosophy, nor by the logical proofs of reason, but through His revelation in the Veda, which He Himself in the beginning of the world breathed forth. Against the attacks of his opponents Sankara, like his colleagues in the West, develops what is for him a proof of God's existence.

As the teachers in the West reason from movement to a mover, who is himself unmoved, so Sankara states (Brahma Sutras 2, 2, 1) that an unspiritual material could not of itself pass from the primary condition of equilibrium into a creative activity, still less into a purposeful activity, i.e. into one which is moving toward a definite effect (a telos, namely a purposively formed world).

> This movement, namely toward a goal, is impossible with a non-spiritual cause. For instance, clay or a wagon, because they are non-spiritual, cannot of themselves move toward a definite end (i.e. their own formation or destination), unless they are directed by potters or by horses.

[4] Among Indian Christians today this is the usual term for God.

Similarly he sees the proof of God in the laws of the universe, e.g. in the regularity of the monsoons:

> The wind fulfills its function, namely to blow, regularly. But such regularity presupposes a guide (who wills and realises this regularity). (Sankara's Commentary on the Taittiriya 3)

He also uses a physico-theological proof similar to those of the West.

> Houses, palaces, beds, chairs, and pleasure gardens are built by judicious artists for the purpose of furthering pleasure or dispelling ennui. It is the same with the whole world. See, for instance how the earth is arranged for the enjoyment of the fruits of manifold works, and how bodily form both outwardly and inwardly possesses a disposition of parts fitting to the different creatures even in detail, and thus forms the basis of enjoyment of the fruits of manifold works. Even intelligent and highly trained artists are not able to comprehend it with their reason—how then should this disposition of the world come from a non-spiritual primary material, since clods of earth, stones, etc. are not capable of achieving this? (Brahma Sutra, 2, 2, 1)

He has something clearly analogous to the so-called cosmological proof, which concludes that the chain of evolution cannot stretch endlessly backward, but leads to a first primary cause, which has no need of an origin (because necessary in and of itself), and which supports the whole chain of creation. Sankara says also in Brahma Sutra 2, 3, 8:

> Brahman exists, for it is the cause of the ether etc. We perceive nothing in the world which has arisen from nothing. If name and form (the multiplicity of things) were products of nothing, they would not be perceived. But they are perceived. Consequently Brahman exists (Sankara's Commentary on the Taittiriya 5).

Or:

> If there were no primary nature as the ultimate root, the result would be a regressus in infinitum (which is impossible).

Sankara also deals with the problem of theodicy. When the Lord creates creatures unequal, the one on a higher, the other on a lower plane of existence, that seems to be unjust, but nevertheless He is acting justly. For He is thereby taking into consideration merit and guilt in an earlier existence. Isvara is also judge of the world, or at least, the guardian of the moral world-order. He ordains reward and punishment according to the work, the Karma, which each achieves. This just Nemesis which inevitably overtakes everyone, whether for good or ill, is not a blind world-order, but is the government of the All-seeing, All-ruling and All-judging.

Brahman-Isvara creates the world without organs, without tools, purely through His decision (sankalpa). For as a purely spiritual Being He has no organs and no need of them. He also creates it without the dualistic rivalry of a world material opposed to Himself. Sankara disposes of this rivalry by the doctrine that Brahman-Isvara brings forth the world out of Himself, that He is both causa efficiens as well as causa materialis. (The tendency of this teaching is expressly to allow of no second beside God as world cause, and thereby to assure the complete conception of creation.)

As in the West, God Himself and His Being are "exemplar mundi" so that the world is the reflection of God, similarly in the East, everything in the world "shines through Him": and mirrors His splendor.

As He Himself is of a purely spiritual nature so the worship of Him should be spiritual. Brahman, and particularly the personal Isvara-Brahman, rejects idolatry and the worship of images (pratika). (See Brahma Sutra 3, 14)

Just as the God of Scholasticism creates according to the eternal archetype of "Ideas," which He, as the eternal Word, eternally possesses, so Brahman creates the world according to the eternal Veda, which has within itself eternally the primary types of all classes of things, and which He recalls in creation.

5. He is the One Highest, above the gods, the devas, who are His creatures, and which as inferior isvaras hold a similar position to Him in the formation and control of the world, that the angelic powers and the directors of the spheres maintain in the heavenly hierarchy of Scholasticism and of Dante.

He is at the same time the Savior-God: He gives forth the Veda. The redeeming knowledge of salvation comes not through effort or reason but through His elective grace (prasada).

The good go to Him after death to attain there the aisvaryam, the divine majesty, which Isvara grants to His own, with the sole exception of the control of the world. Thus the whole Bhakti-marga, the way of salvation, as upasana, that is, personal reverence of worship, prayer, praise, and the private devotion of love and trust in a personal, redeeming God, are also to be found in Sankara.

6. Sankara distinguishes indeed, as we have already said, the apar avidya and the para vidya, a *lower* and a *higher* knowledge. Where he keeps this distinction consciously before him he makes it clearly and strongly enough. Thereby, he differentiates a higher and a lower Brahman, the uncreated and the created. As soon as this distinction enters "the highest Lord," the name which he very often involuntarily uses for the Brahman, is only the "lower Brahman," which disappears in perfect knowledge, and together with soul and world enters into the higher Brahman. But to avoid complete misunderstanding we must keep the following points in mind.

(a) Every reader of Sankara who comes fresh from the interpretations and presentations most usually given of his teaching has the same experience: he is bewildered by a seeming confusion, a constant change and variation of expression, and is conscious of a sense of helplessness in face of his author's assertions. The system of contrasts between higher and lower knowledge often simply will not fit. For pages together, one does not know whether Sankara means the higher or the lower Brahman. At times this thesis is partially or entirely lost sight of, and emerges as a kind of makeshift. But this does not signify hopeless confusion of thought and inconsistency: rather it is the natural result of the intimate fundamental relationship between the two conceptions. The nirguna-Brahman is not the exclusive opposite of the saguna-Brahman, but its superlative and a development of the tendencies which lead to the saguna-Brahman itself.

We can explain this by means of certain conceptions from Western theology: for example the via eminentiae and the via negationis. Both ways are methods of expressing the divine. The via eminentiae is the way of idealization—the setting up of an ideal. Man finds expressions for God by attributing to Him all possible ideals at their very highest, or better still, in their absolute perfection: the absolutely good, wise, righteous, powerful Being, etc. In India they say in the same sense: Brahman is "a collection of all noble qualities." It is saguna-Brahman. The purpose of this expression is exactly the same as with us—to set up the highest absolute ideal, via eminentiae.

The other method of finding expressions for the Godhead is the via negationis. The Godhead is defined by negative predicates, and the purpose of these is exclusion (remotio, vyavritti). This, however, is not meant to indicate impoverishment or emptiness, but the exclusion of all definition as limitation, impoverishment, or creatureliness. So it is negatio as negatio negationis and therefore (as litotes) it is intended as the very highest positive. And so the via negationis emerges not as contrary to the via eminentiae, not even as a merely parallel mode of expression, but really as a continuation of the via eminentiae itself.

The case is very similar with Sankara. When this relationship is understood one is no longer perplexed by his apparent "confusion." The method which he uses is really that of samuchchaya (summing up) with regard to the saguna and the nirguna-Brahman. Only thus is he comprehensible, and from this point the confusion in his writings is solved. Sankara can employ this method quite consistently, for the term "Nothing" which the mystic uses of God is the superlative exaltation of the divine above all "something." In like manner Sankara's nirgunatvam is the superlative of sagunatvam. The former does not deny the latter, but the latter is taken up into the former. Therefore Sankara can justifiably pass from the standpoint of the para vidya to that of the apara vidya and vice versa a hundred times until the distinctions between them are completely obliterated. (Eckhart does exactly the same.) The significance of this process of samuchchaya is obviously to assure to the highest Brahman all the conceivable divine values of theism and include them in the conception of the Brahman.

(b) The following should also be noted. Usually emphasis is laid on the fact that the apara vidya is "only lower knowledge." But the accent can be changed and the fact stressed that the apara vidya is also called and meant to be, vidya, knowledge. It is not a chance notion which could be omitted, or a mere opinion which is as indifferent, as neutral to the samyagdarsanam as any other idea might be; nor does it share the same fate as other opinions, namely to be only bhrama, mithyajnana, error or lie. It is not erroneous but a lower knowledge, yet as such it is still a "knowledge." Apara vidya is in any case related to that which is called vidya; it is a knowing which also aims at the highest Sat, the loftiest truth and reality, even though it be yet imperfect and dim.

This understanding of vidya has consequences even for the highest Brahman. Where a man is not yet Brahman, where there is the contrast of seen and seer, there Brahman must be seen as an Isvara. This necessity lies undoubtedly in the nature of the highest Brahman itself, however much it may be "neti, neti: not so, and not so." In any case where there is a lower knowledge, there Brahman must be looked upon as Isvara. All other perception is false, but this perception does not share the falsity of other vision. As the one homogeneous, white light, seen through a prism, breaks up into seven colors, and as the basis of the existence of the seven colors is not the prism alone, but is chiefly the white light and its own nature, so, in the prism of the Avidya the one "only Being" breaks itself up into Isvara with soul and world. But the reason that it breaks, and must so break, lies unquestionably in "Being" itself. That is also apparent in Sankara's Maya-doctrine. Brahman himself is the great Mayin, the Magician, who "deludes" the man without knowledge; the magician is himself the reason for the world's appearance in its present form to the man who lacks real insight. This deluding is no "action" of the pure Brahman on the consciousness of the ignorant, for Brahman does not act. But such delusion means that the reason for the appearance of the One as the many, when seen through the medium of Avidya, lies in the One itself. Sankara can actually adopt the definition of the Brahman as that from which the world has its origin, duration and solution (which otherwise would be simply misguidance). Therefore all the assertions of the Scriptures about the saguna-Brahman have a very positive interest for him, instead of proving just so many difficulties in his way. It is true of him as of Eckhart, that his teaching leads to a kind of super-theism and not to an anti-theism.

7. This super-theism has its basis in the history of the Brahman-conception. In the very beginning Brahman is that wonderful, numinous, magical entity, which emerges mysteri-

ously from the realm of symbol and feeling of the old sacrificial magic, and in dark irrationality begins to surpass and over-shadow all devas. This Brahman is next invaded and spiritualized by Atman-speculation. Brahman becomes Atman, and thereby spirit, knowledge, light, Jnana. But from the time of the Satapatha-brahmana the theistic conception forces its way in: "Vishnu is the sacrifice." The idea of the God towering above all other gods blends itself with the Brahman-conception, or rather, draws it to itself and makes it serviceable. Thus, in the Gita, the real subject is not Brahman appearing in a lower form as Isvara, but on the contrary, the personal God is the subject, appropriating the dignity of the brahmatvam to himself. Sankara's own basic text, the Sutras of Badarayana, teaches a Brahman which is completely permeated by theism.

8. Therefore, when Sankara employs for his Brahman the terms of honor which, strictly speaking, belong only to a world-creating and world-transcendent God, it is not a question of accommodation but is the very essence of his position. This is particularly true in his exposition of the Gita, though it applies in many other cases. A very favorite expression of his for the highest Brahman is the term, jagato mulam, root and origin of the world. Brahman is sarvajna and sarvasakti, all-knowing and all-powerful: but also as the highest Brahman which can have no sarvani as objects of its knowledge, and needs no saktayas (powers)—as pure, motionless Being, it does not act. Sankara purposely uses the solemn names of the personal God for the highest Brahman itself: the personal name "Narayana" or "Vasudeva," as well as the greatest titles of honor, Bhagavat and Paramesvara, highest Lord. With the utmost simplicity he applies the terms of highest Lord and eternal Brahman quite indiscriminately:

> I (the constituted highest Lord) of an eternal, pure, awakened, and ransomed nature, the Atman of all beings, free from guna, which brings the seed of the samsara-evil to maturity—I am not known of the world. (Gita 7, 13a)

Indeed, in the passages where unity with the Brahman is described with particular solemnity, these personal designations are freely used:

> I (namely, the soul) myself am Bhagavan Vasudeva. I am not
> distinguished from Him. (Gita, 7, 18)

> He attains to me, Vasudeva, to the inner Atman. (Gita, 7, 19)

It is obvious that at the same time these titles definitely color the
conception of Brahman with the true dignity and value of a God.[5]

Or take the great passage of the Gita, 10, 14-16:

> For, the gods and the spirits themselves, O Bhagavan, may not
> perceive you clearly. Only thou, oh highest Spirit, knowest
> thyself, through thyself.

Sankara felt impelled to relate this passage to the Brahman who
is beyond all power of conception and to its svayam-prakasata
(its "self-evidence"). But he does it in this way:

> Because thou art the origin of all gods (and thereby removed
> from them all) therefore knowest thou only thyself, the Lord
> boundlessly rich in knowledge, glory, strength and power,
> thyself through thyself.

Strictly speaking these expressions should only apply to the apara
vidya, the lower wisdom, and were Sankara challenged by his
opponents, he would doubtless retreat to this position. But the
true position is easily seen: the para vidya exists by virtue of its
own lower stage, and bears the color and fragrance of its native
soil even in the finest sublimations. This is particularly clear
where Sankara includes in the eternal Brahman not only the attributes of power and wisdom, but also those of salvation and
grace. He even calls the eternal Brahman, Sivam—"benevo-
lent." In commenting on the Gita, 18, 54, he says:

[5] S. on Mund., I, 17: "What is the glory of Brahman? By its command the earth
is maintained and the heaven endures; by its command the sun and the moon
run their course as flaming fire; by its command the rivers and the seas do not
overflow their boundaries. Its command is obeyed alike by all which moves and
all which does not move; the seasons, the solstice, the years do not overstep its
command; by its command all Karma and actors under Karma and the fruits they
bring forth, do not continue beyond their allotted time. . . . That is its glory."
All that is here praised as of worth and dignity is simply Brahman's glory. In
relation to it all distinction of higher and lower knowledge disappears from the
horizon.

Whoever comes thus by stages to the Brahman and has attained to the grace of highest Atman, is free from care.

Saving grace can only really be attributed to Isvara, the Brahman as personal God. Here, however, it is an act of the highest Atman itself. It is no wonder therefore that Sankara declares the passage 11, 55,[6] which is an indubitable witness to the personal love of God, to be the whole aim and purpose of the Gita. According to him, this passage is intended to proclaim unity with the highest Brahman:

54. "Through Bhakti, directed to nothing else," that is, through faithful love which is directed toward nothing save Bhagavat Himself and which does not turn for a moment from Him and which with all its faculties perceives only Vasudeva and nothing more. He can be known through Scripture, but not only through Scripture, for He can be seen in essence and in truth.

The meaning and purpose which is the core of the whole book of the Gita and which leads to the highest salvation is declared as follows:

55. Who, what he does, does for me only, is inclined towards me only, and true to me. Free from envy, free from dependence on the world, he goes to me, O Pandava.

Sankara adds:

A servant carries out the work of his Lord, but he does not say of his lord that he is the highest goal to which he hopes to attain one day after his death. But he who has surrendered to me, who does my work, he attains to me as his highest goal. He who cleaves to me, in all things with his whole soul and with utmost zeal, he has surrendered to me. He comes to me; that is: I alone am his highest goal.

9. Sankara distinguishes between the higher and the lower Brahman. According to the usual presentation, the lower Brahman is the Brahma-Hiranyagarbha, a demiurge within the world of appearance, himself succumbing to the changes of the world, who arises as Karya-Brahman at every world-beginning

---

[6] It is called the charama-sloka, the most important passage of the Gita.

and is dissolved away at every world-ending. Placed on an equality with Isvara himself, Isvara then would in like manner succumb to this fate. There are some passages in the Commentary on the Sutras which have a tendency in this direction. But in the main lines of Sankara's presentation the relationship is quite different. There Hiranyagarbha has the same position of the subordinate and created demiurge, which he also has in Ramanuja. He is clearly distinguished from the "highest Lord," as a created being, as a lower demiurge, as a single Jiva placed high in the hierarchy, an individual soul, which again is a different one in every creation. But high above him stands Isvara Himself, as the eternal God, who is not drawn into, but directs the play of worlds that rise and perish and is Himself absolutely transcendent, existing from all eternity. This is clearly evident in Sankara's Commentary to V. S. 4, 4, 19:

> There is one form of the highest God which is eternally redeemed, taking back into itself the created.

According to the quotation from the scripture, this form cannot be the modeless Brahman, but it is the world-creating and world-dissolving Isvara, as in Ramanuja. Thus, in the foregoing passages which speak of the "eternally perfect" God, He is yet at the same time the One who is given dominion over the world. Hiranyagarbha is not by any means this eternally perfect God. Compare also such passages as V. S. 1, 4, 1:

> God who once *created* the Brahma (Hiranyagarbha), and delivered the Vedas to him.

See also 1, 3, 30. Here again it is the highest God not as the impersonal Brahman, but as the real world-creator. With his consent the world-drama is played out. From world to world Brahma and the other gods are created anew, analogous to the preceding world-creation. They themselves are part of the rise and decay, but not directors and lords of this process. But not so the "Lord" Himself. He remembers what existed in His former creation and in accordance with what has preceded it He fashions the new. He is eternal; the One existing through Himself: V. S. 1, 3, 29. Ramanuja's whole theory of the relationship of this eternal creator to His world is presented in V. S. 1, 2, 22. So it is obvious to Sankara (V. S. 2, 2, 19) that the reigning God is constant and enduring. His consciousness of world and objects remains unchanged and undiminished even when the worlds have passed away. V. S. 1, 1, 5:

> How much more must an unceasing knowledge relating to the origin, duration, and decline of the world be ascribed to the pure, eternal God.

That is not, of course, the "higher Brahman," for that has no object. Still less is it the lesser Brahma-Hiranyagarbha, for that arises and perishes. But it is the personal, eternal creator-God, who eternally produces and outlasts all the drama of the worlds. The clearest passages are those in which Sankara speaks of the difference between the individual soul and the highest God: V. S. 1, 1, 2. He recognizes this as the world of lower knowledge. Here the highest God is naturally not the impersonal Brahman, that knows no differentiation. Still less is it the lower Hiranyagarbha: such an assumption would be simply blasphemous. It is Isvara, the personal God, who is different from the individual soul, but is, at the same time, her inward guide. This inner guide is described in terms which otherwise apply to the pure Brahman itself, but which, as we have said, are also evident and customary in any purified form of theism. The "distinction" between the higher and the lower Brahman does not help toward an understanding of this relationship, so long as we allow the lower Brahman to be obscured by the figure of the Hiranyagarbha. The true relationship appears particularly clearly in Sankara's comment on 11, 37 of the Gita:

> . . . thou, the primal Creator (adikartri) thou who art worthier of honor than the Brahman.

The text of the Gita contains obviously a frank polemic against the monistic conception of the Brahman: it attempts to exalt the original Creator above the Brahman itself. Sankara naturally cannot accept this. He declares that the Brahman named here is the Brahma-Hiranyagarbha. But, at the same time, he sets the first creator, the saguna-paramesvara or the creator-God, high above the Brahma-Hiranyagarbha, the lesser demiurge.[7]

---

[7] The passage on the Aitareya 5, 3, in Sankara's Commentary is also very definite on this point. Here the one Brahman without upadhis, beyond all word and

In Sankara, G. 5, 29, the acknowledgment of Isvara is solemnly consummated, and to Him is attributed salvation itself, the final liberation from Samsara:

> He who has known me, Narayana, the receiver of all sacrifice and all penance, both as their instigator and their end, Lord of all the world, who benefits all beings without reward, who dwells in the heart and controls all works and their fruits, who witnesses all thoughts—he attains santi (rest), the cessation of all samsara.

10. The same acknowledgment is clearly seen in the conception of Maya, which at first sight seems to be directly opposed to it. According to Sankara the world exists through Maya; a phrase which is usually translated as—"the world only exists through illusion (appearance)." Now the last expression applies to the para vidya, but Maya is here not illusion itself but that which produces the illusion. And that which produces illusion is not itself illusion; it is, and remains also for Sankara, the Maya of Brahman. Brahman is the Mayavin, the one rich in Maya, the one exerting Maya. However difficult or even impossible it is to determine the relationship of Maya to Brahman, it is nevertheless indubitable that somehow or other in Brahman lies the reason for the existence of Maya, and for its result in a world of purpose, aim, order and wisdom.

11. Finally, when Sankara distinguishes the higher from the lower knowledge, he does not sufficiently clarify his point of view. He should at least distinguish still another vidya, a madhya vidya, an intermediate knowledge. For Brahman, even as Isvara, has pronounced mystical tendencies which continually underlie, mingle and often combine indistinguishably with the elements of the higher knowledge.

In any case, where it is not a question of artificially constructing a strictly rationalistic deism, there are characteristics in God

---

thought, becomes Isvara, through combining with the upadhi of pure wisdom. He is All-knowing, the Lord of all atmans, the Principle of the mula-prakriti, and at the same time, the inner guide of all things and all souls. From him there proceeds the Brahma-Hiranyagarbha, who as demiurge, fashions the created world. Finally, from this last develops a still lesser demiurge, Virat, who indeed only arises within "the world-egg," and has his realm here. In other passages Virat and Brahma mingle or are equalized, which simplifies the universe but does not touch the relationship of Hiranyagarbha to Isvara.

Himself which are more or less mystical and upon which is founded a mystical relationship to world and soul. This is true of the Isvara of the Gita and of Badarayana; it is true in large measure also of the Isvara of Sankara. God under this aspect pours Himself into and unfolds Himself in his creation; He is and remains its transcendent Lord, but as its causa materialis, He is at the same time immanent in it. He is especially present in certain exceptional phenomena of nature and can there be contemplated. With his jiva-atman, i.e. with the sum of the individual souls which were included in Him before the world was, He enters into His creation, and is thus both immanent and transcendent. As Antaryamin, or inner guide, He dwells within man; not in identity with the soul, but in mystical union with it. As such He is the soul of the soul. Sankara, referring to the Upanishads, so emphasizes this "Madhya vidya" that often enough it gains the significance of the vidya itself.

Eckhart presents very clear parallels to the relationships described above. The firm theistic foundation of his mystical speculation (which possibly soars even higher than that of Sankara) is without question sincerely and truly accepted by him. It is the simple, Christian belief in God, and at the same time, the Scholastic, theistic, speculation of his age. High above it towers his mysticism. But even more palpably than in Sankara, it is permeated and transfused by the life-sap of the ground from which it springs. Central for him also—unbounded by any limits either above or below—is a simpler form of mysticism. It is the mysticism not yet of identity, but of indwelling, of immanence, of a secret mutual relationship and interpenetration of God and soul. These are transitional stages to the more deeply mystical experiences of perfect unity, but are likewise their rivals, and often enough their equally important counterparts.

12. To this Isvara and faith in Him there belongs in the Gita an ethic of great beauty and severity. Religion and morality are here intimately related. Through the ethic which he demands the character of Isvara is also essentially determined. Let us consider this briefly.

(a) The whole of the Gita develops around an ethical question. Arjuna is in strife against his honored kinsmen and his feudal lords, against his teachers and masters in the art and discipline of chivalry. His heart sinks, and doubt assails him: Is it right to fight? Were it not better to give up the labor of strife altogether? This question broadens into the general one: Is work right, or is the surrender of all work (nyasa and tyaga) the true way?— Krishna, the incarnation of Isvara, now instructs Arjuna. He teaches him the high ethic of knighthood which permeates the whole Mahabharata, finding its embodiment in the devout Yudhishthira, where it is made known in his great conversation with his likewise doubting wife.[8] Strife, righteous strife, is knightly duty, which, surrendering self-interest, is waged for the defense of the true, for the maintenance of the order willed by Isvara, and for the protection of the oppressed. Strife belongs to the svadhama, the particular duty of knighthood. To fulfill his particular duty according to the rank in which the individual stands, is the highest task of every man.

(b) From this conception of svadharma there develops an ethic of rank and profession which has the most remarkable similarity to that adopted by Luther. According to Luther the three classes ordained by God are: the teaching class, the class of defenders, and the working class. The various professions are distributed within these ranks. Following this conception it is a man's Christian duty not to stray beyond the borders of his own profession, nor to intrude into the sphere of another, but to serve within the ranks of his own calling. In the same way, Isvara has ordained the four castes in India: the Brahmana's, the Kshatriyas, the Vaisyas, the Sudras—the teaching, defending, trading and serving classes. It is possible for each caste to attain to Isvara and his salvation. But each caste has also its svadharma, its particular duty, which it has to fulfill. Herein man is to follow the example of Isvara Himself; for He also "does his work," namely, the task of controlling the world.

(c) Within time limits of his own asrama (rank) each individual is to do his necessary work. This term "necessary work" is almost identical with our term, "duty," and comes near to the Kantian conception. Such duty is not to be performed by "clinging to work" nor for the sake of the fruits of labor: that would

---

[8] Cf. R. Otto, *Vishnu-Narayana,* p. 24, "Battles of Faith."

bind man to samsara. But it is to be done without self-interest, without expectation of reward, simply because it is "necessary":

> *He who wishes to milk virtue,*
> *Who leads duty to market,*
> *Who does his work without*
> *The strength of faith in his heart,*
> *Knows neither duty nor virtue,*
> *And thereby loses his reward.*[9]

The upright man is he who does his duty in the manner described previously; it is he who exercises the right tyaga and nyasa, the true renunciation and sacrifice, but not he, who inactive, withdraws himself and preaches withdrawal from the world. The way of work and the performance of duty is the path to salvation, and the kingly sages of ancient time, like Janaka, trod this road.[10]

(d) Krishna thus develops for Arjuna as his svadharma the knightly ideal, opposed to unmanliness and inert skepticism; the ideal of courage and valor which is ashamed to disgrace itself in the eyes of honest men and before posterity. It is not the Christian ideal of a burning love into which faith pours itself; or of a faith which itself becomes a "driving urge to seek expression in deeds and works"; least of all is it the ideal which Luther sets up—to be a fellow worker with God in His own work. It is a calm submission to the "necessary" task, the aristocratic ideal of the soul unmoved, standing above the play of impulse, resting assured within itself, doing the task which falls to its lot but without "clinging" to it. It has a stoic quality: the power to face alike, inwardly unmoved, joy or sorrow, misfortune or fortune, friend or foe. It is composure in quietness of soul, inner independence, self-assurance and ascendancy. This composure does indeed mean a superiority to the world and the things of the world. It comes as with Eckhart from a repose in God. And that

---

[9] See R. Otto; *Vishnu-Narayana*, p. 29.

[10] This passage later caused the preachers of salvation by grace in India some embarrassment since salvation should come from grace and not from our works. But this is unjust. For the point of the passage is directed not against grace, but against the path of renunciation of svadharma, against the idle monk and the wandering ascetic. The doctrine of grace has indeed deep roots in the Gita.

is the meaning also in the Gita. Bhakti is here permeated with prapatti, which is literally a drawing near. To surrender one's works without self-interest to Isvara, to do them because He Himself is working and because He wills that we should work; to do them in His service, indifferent to their fruits and indifferent to the course of the world, especially to its evil, while the heart remains serene in God—that is bhakti and prapatti.

(e) This utter composure which can here at times be called faith (sraddha) is the true ideal, the emotional background and also the source of this ethic of the Gita. Its assurance and strength and its character of world-surpassing tranquillity of sense-control, of inward quiet and immovability, come from repose in God. The Gita expresses this inner relationship in the incomparably devout words:

> *Man is made by his belief,*
> *As he believes, so he is.*

His God is reflected in his faith, and his God determines his faith. Both make the man and his character—make the idolater and the devil-worshiper, make the servant of Isvara strong, free, just and of a noble virtue.

(f) This ethic unites itself with the Yoga, not to gain magic power, but released from the play of passion, to attain independence. It is easily understandable that a refined form of Yoga, dependent upon an inner ascendancy, integrity and steadfastness, must have had a particular attraction for the knightly rank.[11] Its purpose is to direct the soul to Isvara Himself, in an iron effort of will and concentration, and to hold Him fast (dharana) in faith and knowledge.

(g) Strict discipline of the will and dedication to God, not mortification; svadharma, not self-chosen piety, inner renunciation of the reward of works with a full practice of works ("in activity rest, and in rest, activity"),[12] and upon this basis the building of a richly varied structure of altruism and noble living—that is the

---

[11] It is not by chance that the Knighthood of Japan, the Samurai, train themselves in the Yoga school of the Zen sect. Cf. my introduction to Schuej Ohasama: *Zen, Living Buddhism in Japan,* Gotha, 1925.

[12] Eckhart could say precisely the same.

ethic of Isvara. It is not glowing with the pathos of the Christian experience of God which is vital in Eckhart, but it is analogous to the Christian ethic, just as Isvara is analogous to the ethic of the West.

This ethic of the Gita, with Isvara as background and as goal, Sankara completely accepts as preliminary to his system. He not only recognizes it—he comments upon it finely, penetratingly and in detail.

13. Thus, we realize close resemblances between Sankara and Meister Eckhart. In both men mysticism rises above a personal theism. The interpenetration of the theist and the mystic is much more marked in Eckhart than in Sankara. Yet the greatest mystic of India is himself a witness that theism is not an accident of Western development, but somehow arises out of the deep necessity of mankind in general. In the language of religion he also attests to that statement of Paul's in Acts 14:17:

> He left not himself without witness.

II. THEISTIC GROUNDWORK IN ECKHART

In his *Collations* and in his *Book of Divine Consolation* as well as here and there in his sermons, Eckhart preaches a very simple and genuine faith in God, both before he comes to his mystical speculation and as part of it. This he does out of a rich and deep experience and knowledge, with inward fervor and tenderness, with warmth and power, and with a personal note which is interesting in itself quite apart from his mysticism. The mystic has always been too narrowly sought in Eckhart. But it is well worth while to get to know him in his simple piety, and to understand his originality in this realm also. He would remain a great phenomenon in history had he never been a mystic or a schoolman— a rare example of a profound and resolute Christian soul, standing out from his age and environment as an originator and a reformer. It would be valuable to trace the quiet working out of his simple religion in contrast to the religion of experts and scholars, to sacramental magic and ecclesiasticism, to the religion of works and monastic discipline, or to fantastic legendry and the mediation of priests. It would be profitable also to follow the undercurrent of evangelistic preaching which arose from his "simple" religion, and passing into his school prepared the way for the Lutheran reformation. We shall try to trace some of the features of this evangelistic undercurrent in Eckhart's works, seen most clearly and simply in his *Collations*. Lehmann rightly places them in the forefront of Eckhart's writings; they are indeed the best and necessary introduction to his thought. At the same time we shall gain a clear conception of how even his mystical ideas have their germ and prototype in simple and common religious faith.

1. The key to Eckhart's whole position is given in the section of his writings which Lehmann finely calls, "Of Possessing God."

To will to possess God: that is indeed the secret significance of his teaching. To will this in all humility, with all the powers of the soul, in rigorous obedience, with deep feeling and concentrated will so that God Himself becomes the soul's deepest comfort and its blessedness, is his demand.

> Of that shouldst thou be inwardly assured, that He alone is the treasure which can satisfy and fill thee.

But God is still more than that: He is the ground and the power of a renewed, sanctified life flowing in an unbroken steam from the depths of the soul. Eckhart here conceives an ideal of human life which is purely spiritual, standing aloof from all "natural" ideals; one that is neither "aesthetic" nor "classic" and not in the first instance even "moral," but purely religious. For to have God in most intimate communion is for Eckhart the very meaning of the life of man. From this ideal there grows as its antithesis Eckhart's idea of sin as first and foremost a purely religious abnormality. Sin is not conceived by him in the first instance in a moral sense. It is in essence neither libido nor cupiditas but selfhood, that is, the self-centeredness of the ego, "I," "me," "mine," etc. This is not egoism in the ethical sense of self-seeking at the expense of other men, but it is the self-sufficiency of the creature set over against God. It is superbia in the purely religious sense, the lack of adjustment and subordination to the divine, by which man first gains his true being and his ideal raison d'etre.[13] It is only when based on selfhood as separation from God that life becomes self-seeking and egotistical as regards other people, and that lust, libido and fleshly desires enter in. The roots of all these evils are cut off where that selfhood as opposed to God disappears. For these experiences, however, there is no need of mysticism, and Eckhart can speak of these things in such a way that they appeal to the very simplest:

That the human soul may be fully turned toward God.

Or:

Set all thy effort upon this, that God may become great to thee, and that all thy endeavor and all thy effort be set upon Him in all thy doings and dealings.

In other words, this means "clinging to God," and that is the simple and unpretentious root of all Eckhart's lofty speculation of unity with God, as illustrated in such passages as the following:

He has simply and solely God. Whoever has simply and solely God in mind in all things, such a man carries God in all his works and in all places within him, and God alone does all his works. He seeks nothing but God, nothing appears good to him but God. He becomes one with God in every thought. Just as no multiplicity can dissipate God, so nothing can dissipate this man or make him multiple.

Or:

Though I should live here in the flesh until the judgment day, learning the pangs of hell, it would be a small matter by reason of my Lord Jesus Christ, since I have received from him the certainty of never being parted from him. While I am here he is in me: after this life I am in him. All things are possible to me united as I am with him to whom all things are possible. (Evans, p. 353)

[13] It is obvious that this conception of ideal and opposition to the ideal accords with that of Luther. He likewise sets up as the ideal not a "morality" but communion with God in the spiritual acts of fearing, trusting, loving. Sin is the antithesis of this. For him also, sin is the superbia which seeks an independent life in works instead of living by grace. Compare, R. Otto: *Religious Essays,* the chapter on "Sin and Original Guilt." Oxford Press, 1931.

These things are self-evident to the simplest Christian belief.

2. Such "clinging to God" is first and foremost a demand upon man. He is to cling, he is to direct all his attention, all his will power toward the one good in deepest concentration, from "the bottom of his heart." Thus already in Eckhart the simple preacher, there develop warnings against dissipation into the manifold—the multiplicity of senses, thoughts and objects. So the demand arises to become "simple" (simplex) to come to "unity" in work and being. In the first instance this is nothing more than a thorough collectedness, and the simple knowledge that only he who is completely concentrated can come to have and to hold God. He only who is concentrated in "real earnest" will perceive what God is and what God is to him; he alone experiences God as the sum and substance of his own salvation, as his blessedness. Further still: only in such a man is found the divine power for conversion, repentance and penance, the power of a liberated and fortified will.

3. Eckhart knows full well the blessedness of possessing God, he knows His consoling power (witness *The Book of Divine Consolation),* the joy in God which is beyond all delight, which is participation in the blessedness with which God Himself is blessed. Yet higher still for Eckhart is that other experience: the possession of God as the power of renewed and liberated will. Not ecstasy in God, not visio beatifica, is for him the highest, nor ecstatic ebullitions and emotions, but obedience to God in deed and life. It is primarily for this reason that he wages war against emotionalism and the inducement of rapturous states.

An unqualified surrender of self is involved in this obedience. It means the absolute subjection of will and personal desire to the eternal will of God. Yet it is more than mere resignation to God's will. It means making the individual will a vessel and medium of the divine will. This alone is the meaning of a Christian life to Eckhart, that our will becomes none other than the very will of God, who wills and works, lives and creates through our will, so that there is but one will, which is likewise essential justice.

4. The divine demand is thereby enhanced, for not only the will as such, nor activity as an outward fact, but "to be essential" is the important thing.

> Men should not think so much of what they ought to do, as of what they ought to be. Think not to lay the foundation of thy holiness upon doing, but rather upon being. For works do not sanctify us, but we should sanctify the works. Whoever is not great in his essential being will achieve nothing by works, whatever he may do.

Thus even in the sphere of simple faith it is a new "Being" (Esse), which itself is the foundation of a new will, that, unitary and potential, precedes all volition, and in which alone there is real value. This is more than a mere "attitude of mind," more than Kant's "good will." It is the goodness of the ground of being itself, out of which the good will and all disposition flows as a stream from its source. This is itself the "inward work," which is no longer really work but rather the hidden ground of the possibility of all work and all activity. So there arises the wonderful teaching of the Master concerning the "inward work," which is often the theme of his sermons, and is dealt with most concisely in his tractate, *The Book of Godly Comfort.*[14]

5. Eckhart says:

> Therefore there is an inward work which neither time nor place can limit nor comprehend. In this, is what God is and what is divine and like unto God, whom neither time nor place can limit. It is everywhere and at all times equally present.

The vital point here is a fundamental good, which does not consist of single acts of our empirical and self-active will or emotional life, but which precedes all these as the hidden "intelligible" ground of our being itself. This is primarily not a fundamental "moral" disposition, but something much deeper. It is an intimate relation of our deepest self to God:

> This work shines and beams day and night. This work praises and sings unto God. It sings a new song.

It "loves God" and thereby it is distinguished from all outward works, and indeed from all "works" whatsoever.

---

[14] Evans trans., p. 419.

The work that is outward does not love God, for time and place limit it, it is narrow; man can prevent and force it; it becomes tired and old with time and exercise.

But the inward work

is to love God, to will God, and the good, so that by it all that a man may ever will or do has now been done with one undivided (entire) will in all good works, and in that he is like unto God. David writes of this when he says that all that he would have done and worked is now completed.

With one undivided will: that is, in essential unity of our will before any dissipation into individual acts of empirical volition occurs. In this state everything that may be of value and appear in time as a good deed, is already completed, and in principle determined and anticipated.

He explains this "inward work" by the illustration of the stone, which without falling, i.e. without realizing its weight in an act of falling, is yet heavy, though at rest all the time. The stone's activity in time arises out of its being, which it possesses essentially quite apart from time.

The stone performs its work without ceasing day and night.

Such inner work, which is being, has real value, independent of all appearance in outward works. This value is neither increased nor changed by the "accident" of external works.

Therefore I say, and I have said before, that the outward work, neither its length nor its breadth, neither its quantity nor its magnitude increases the goodness of the inward work. That has its goodness in itself.

6. These expressions, deeply significant and entirely independent of "mysticism," close with the words:

Whoever has the inward work all the time within himself, takes and draws all the magnitude, breadth and length of the inward work only from God, and from the heart of God.

All demands therefore finally turn into a gift of grace. (We shall have more to say of this later.) But this is not sacramental grace. It is the experience of the great just, and holy, and at the same time, merciful, forgiving, and loving God. It is the experience of the absolutely true and simple God of the Christian gospel, Who meets man's trusting faith, confidence and love when he opens his heart and surrenders himself in repentance, humility, and dedication.

This simple teaching of Eckhart is quite in line with later evangelical preaching. True, there is a significant distinction between Eckhart and Luther. For even in his simple piety and not only in his mysticism, Eckhart falls considerably short of the deep experience of the Reformer. The depth of Luther's sense of sin and guilt, the whole orientation of Christianity to the terrores conscientiae and the forgiveness of sin, the consolation of the stricken conscience, grace as the favor Dei per Christum, and thence the sharp and final denial of all propria merita, opera, vires, are not yet to be found in Eckhart with the same acuteness. For their development was needed the ever-increasing growth of the sense of sin, whose awakening is shown in the struggles and convulsions of penance in the second period of the Middle Ages. But faith as whole-hearted trust,[15] a sense of the consoling God, and moments of pure repentance and penitence were central to Eckhart's own preaching. All insistence on merita and opera and even upon opera superogationis are quite foreign to his thought. Eckhart has already proclaimed in all its purity that recognition which expresses the deepest meaning of the Lutheran faith, namely that the foundation of all Christian life and all right being is the certitudo salutis, complete assurance, and that to be a Christian means to live in this assurance. To have a God, says Luther, means to trust and believe in Him with the whole heart. And Eckhart also says:

> All that man dares to expect confidently from God, that man will actually find in Him and a thousand times more. Just as one cannot love God too much, so one cannot trust Him too much.— However much thou lovest Him, be sure that He loves thee incomparably more and is incomparably more faithful. For He is faithfulness itself. This certainty (of faith) is far stronger, fuller, truer than that (which comes from alleged supernatural illumination). It cannot lie.

[15] R. Otto, *The Idea of the Holy,* Appendix VI, p. 209.

And:

> This he does purely because of his simple goodness and mercy.
> For God needs nothing for all that He does but His own goodness.
> Our works serve in no way to induce God to give to us or to do
> anything.

This intimate and confident relation of the soul to God is clearly
very similar to what he calls in his "mystical" phraseology,
"united with God" or "being in God."

7. The foundation upon which Eckhart's mysticism rises, and
which is itself a simple basis of faith, is most clearly shown in
such words as the following:

> God never gives, nor did he ever give a gift, merely that man
> might have it and be content with it. No, all gifts which He ever
> gave in heaven or on earth, He gave with one sole purpose—to
> make one single gift: Himself. With all His gifts He desires only
> to prepare us for the one gift, which is Himself.

That is not yet "mysticism." It is what the Psalmist expresses
by the words: "Whom have I in heaven, but thee? and there is
none upon earth that I desire beside thee" (Psalm 73:25). Or, if
it is mysticism, then faith itself has the seed of mysticism within
it, and this is only the development, or maybe the exaggeration
of certain non-rational elements that are contained in faith. In any
case, what these words express is the core of religion; that salvation is to be found not in what God gives but in the possession
of God Himself. Where this core reveals itself in its non-rationality (for that which is indicated in the words "to have God Himself" is already non-rational, it escapes every attempt at
formulation)—there, so it seems, the intuitus mysticus appears
with a certain inevitability, breaking forth out of the depths of the
soul, with its vision of unity, its peculiar dialectic, its bold and
daring ideographs.

8. Even more important is the following. It is true that mysticism results from a special aspect of the Deity, and that it conceives this Godhead and sees it otherwise than in the relations
between I and thou, of distinction and antithesis. But even this
aspect is not solely and primarily peculiar to mysticism. It belongs to a certain extent even to the simple ground of faith itself.
Within it there are already two clearly distinguishable aspects of

God. They stand in a polar antithesis to one another, though often permeating and completing each other: the one is the aspect of transcendence, the other of immanence.

It is supposed to be peculiar to mysticism to conceive God not as transcendent but as immanent, and this was said to be the most prominent trait in Eckhart's teaching. But two things should be noted: first, that what is meant here is true of Eckhart not only in his mystical experiences but even when he preaches devotion and speaks as a simple Christian. Secondly, that the antithesis between transcendence and immanence is not only too colorless and cold, but is inadequate to give the true and living content of this antinomy. The antithesis is rather this: that the divine, which on the one hand is conceived in symbols taken from the social sphere, as Lord, King, Father, Judge—a person in relation to persons—is on the other hand denoted in dynamic symbols as the power of life, as light and life, as spirit ebbing and flowing, as truth, knowledge, essential justice and holiness, a glowing fire that penetrates and pervades. It is characterized as the principle of a renewed, supernatural Life, mediating and giving itself, breaking forth in the living man as his nova vita, as the content of his life and being. What is here insisted upon is not so much as "immanent" God, as an "experienced" God, known as an inward principle of the power of new being and life. Eckhart knows this δευτερος θεος besides the personal God, and in his capacity as a simple Christian preacher, proclaims it.

9. What he thus proclaims is indeed the most ancient treasure of Christianity.

(a) It lies concealed already in the strange ambiguity of the old evangelical idea of the "kingdom of God." On the one hand this is an absolutely future state, upon whose coming the Church of the new dispensation waits in expectation. On the other hand it is said in the Gospel itself: "The Kingdom of God is among you." The future Kingdom throws its mysterious shadow before it and secretly lives and works here and now as the hidden power overcoming Satan and the world in the germinating faith of the early Church, in renewal and transformation, in "peace and joy in the Holy Ghost."

(b) This indwelling Kingdom of God is identical with, and only becomes more explicit in, the later idea of the outpouring of the

Spirit, and a life in the Spirit. That Spirit is none other than the Godhead itself as the foundation and power of life. The figures of fire, of life, light, truth and knowledge, of the water of life, of the spikenard outpoured, of the divine seed and the indwelling χαρις only serve to strengthen this conception of divine self-communication.

(c) Indeed, what we have called the double aspect of the Godhead is really the ancient, fundamental meaning of the biblical teaching of hypostasis developed in trinitarian speculation. The other hypostases of the Godhead are "Word and Spirit." They are the divine essence itself in so far as it is found indwelling in the world and in the human spirit. They form the two viewpoints of what we have called the second aspect of the Deity. But they are certainly not two other "persons" besides the one original person of God, and they do not concern us as that miracle of logic, the three egos in the one God. They do however concern us as the insoluble mystery of a Divine Being, which is on the one hand by its very nature *beyond* all creation, but which under a second form of being is indwelling as word-spirit, and so becomes itself the foundation of life for the renewed creature. Without *this* mystery Christianity were no Christianity. But with it, "simple" Christianity itself claims real possession of God, and a real self-communication of God. It knows Godhead, not conceived of here in any relationship of I to Thee, but as a permeating principle of light and life, not to be addressed, but to be experienced.

The mystical teachings of the master are therefore rooted in his simple and first-hand Christian experience. In these teachings he concentrates with special fondness upon the divine hypostases, and it is clearly the aim of this hypostatical speculation in Eckhart to revivify the rigid formulas of the traditional Trinitarian doctrine by giving it the interpretation we have used above. This is particularly true of his teaching of the birth of the eternal Word in the depths of the soul. At the same time it is obviously only a developed form of what, in Christian teaching, has always been meant by the communication of the Spirit. It is no false exegesis when Eckhart often enough describes it as the "inward kingdom of God," for, as we saw above, the synoptic idea of the Kingdom, already present in early Christian teaching, is the germ of the fully developed idea of "life in the spirit." Eckhart's evident failure lies in the fact that he does not sufficiently recognize the condition necessary for all communication of the Holy Ghost, namely, the God-given "objective Word." But it is just those elements which are supposedly "mystic" in his teaching, such as the true participation in the Divine through the indwelling of the Holy Spirit, which are really purely and simply Christian. Whoever denies this real participation in the Divine denies the divinity of the Spirit, which Christians should be receiving as their own life principle.

10. Thus even the very boldest teaching of Eckhart, the teaching that man must get rid of God, must put off God, must "know nothing of God," belongs in its fundamentals at least, to the sphere of his first, simple piety. One might be tempted to regard such expressions as used merely for the sake of emphasis, since they can be interpreted in a way which is deep and true but not specifically mystical. That would be wrong, of course, for it is palpable that Eckhart wishes by their aid to suggest secrets, which are astounding even to him. But still the simple, religious foundations are easily recognized. It would be possible to say, in the sense of Eckhart: He has not God who merely believes in Him, or is merely convinced of His existence, and who regards Him in thought and feeling as an "objectum." He only has God for whom God is no longer objectum but injectum, who lives God, or rather "is lived by God," borne up and impelled by the Spirit and the power of God. But the more this is realized the more God as merely an object "disbecomes" from the sphere of his conceptions and thoughts. God becomes the inward power and the health of his spiritual life, so that the "living waters" flow from him, the living fruits spring forth in righteousness and holiness, love is radiated, and the spirit itself goes forth passing to others and working the same effects in them. He has got rid of the conceived and apprehended God, because God has now become his inward power, by which he lives, but upon which he reflects less, the more completely and powerfully he lives in the Divine.

Eckhart says:

> To him who asked of life a thousand years "Why livest thou?" life might answer: "I live that I may live." That is because life

lives out of its own depths, and wells up out of itself. Therefore it lives without wherefore, living only in itself. In exactly the same way, if one asked a true man who acted from the depths of his own nature: "Why dost thou work thy works?" he could give no other answer than: "I work that I may work."

His work flows freely, "knowing" no goal and setting none before it, because it no longer needs knowledge.

In the same way, whoever "knows" nothing more about God, because he is willing and living in God, is most near to God:

When the soul beholds God purely, it takes all its being and its life, and whatever it is from the depth of God: yet it knows no knowing, no loving, or anything else whatsoever. It rests utterly and completely within the being of God, and knows nothing, but only to be with God. So soon as it becomes conscious that it sees and loves and knows God, that is in itself a departure.[16]

It is necessary to understand this fundamental position in order to realize how widely different is Eckhart's mysticism from that of Plotinus or Dionysius. The parallel expressions used by both must not deceive us as to their entirely different meanings. Both say that for the true knower the contrast between subject and object disappears, as the knower becomes the known. But this happens for Plotinus in the rapture of ecstasy, where normal states of consciousness cease altogether, and abnormal ones intervene. The ecstatic condition of Plotinus is entirely foreign to Eckhart; for him, God disappears as object when man becomes living and active in God. He then becomes as unconscious of the principle and power of his life as life itself, which springs, and blossoms and puts forth its life's work "without a wherefore" (sunder

---

[16] The simplicity with which Eckhart can say these things is exemplified in the passage from the "Talks of Instruction": "This true possession of God lies in the heart, not in an even, continuous thinking about God. Man should not have merely a God intellectually conceived. For when thought passes then God (intellectually conceived) also passes. Rather, man must have an essential God, who is high above the thoughts of men (because He is inwardly possessed and lived). This God does not pass away unless man turns from Him of his own free will. Whoever has God thus in his being conceives Him divinely. For him God shines in all things. In him God has His eyes open at all times. In him there is a quiet turning from outward things and a penetrating into the beloved, ever-present God."

warumbe), in a free outpouring with no question of wherefore and without any reflection upon the Why. This does not happen in ecstatic states of the soul, but in essential being and working;[17] it is not known under exceptional emotional conditions, induced by mystical exercises, but in the vigorous life of every day. It cannot be attained in the contemplation of Mary but in the active zeal of Martha; it is life and action, not the sublime ecstasy of Eros:

> Only think! God is then born in us when all our powers of soul, which hitherto have been bound and imprisoned. become liberated and set free (for spontaneous action).

Plotinus and Eckhart agree in this that they are both mystics; for that very reason they are so fundamentally different.

The two aspects of God in the Christian faith of which we have spoken stand in a direct polarity to one another, and the same is already true of God in Eckhart's simple teaching. The matter we discussed in sections 8 to 10 is still only one side of the question for him, which does not exclude but complements the other. God as the object of humble love and trust in nowise disappears from his sight behind the Godhead as indwelling power. It would be superfluous to attempt to prove this in detail; one would have to copy out half his writings to do so. The man who speaks in such a fashion of the consoling God as does Eckhart in his *Book of Divine Consolation,* and for whom mystical communion immediately turns into relationships of the most personal love, devotion and fellowship, is fundamentally a theist despite the highest flights of speculation, and is that neither by concession nor exoterically.

11. Even more than Eckhart's mystical teaching, it is the sublime flight not only of his daring thought but of his very mood and emotional attitude itself which seem strange to us from the standpoint of ordinary Christianity: the note of high and noble self-consciousness, which is so powerfully stressed in his praise of the homo nobilis. But is it Eckhart's fault that these things are strange to us? Or is it the fault of our one-sided judgment, if we

---

[17] We have in doing (action) just what we have in intuition. The one rests on the other and completes it.

do not see that in Christian consciousness itself the basis is laid for Eckhart's conception of the homo nobilis? It is said, and not by Eckhart: "What shall it profit a man if he gain the whole world and lose his own soul!" Why is that true? Because the soul, and a hurt to the soul, is more than the whole world. (Is this not also a supreme feeling of self?)

The Christian consciousness of self has a double orientation: toward God and toward the rest of creation. Toward God it is humility. But toward the creation it is pride and the sense of an exalted position, if the teaching that man, and man alone, is created in the image of God, is Christian. This sublime self-consciousness is expressed in the Scriptures themselves as that of standing with God and akin to God opposed to the whole creation:

> For we are His offspring.

That is more than a consciousness of similarity. It is already a sense of relationship. Thus it is entirely in keeping with Eckhart's Christian background when he says proudly:

> What would the whole world profit a man if he were not more than it!

*   *   *

The masters of the East and the West agree in the demand that "God should disbecome." But they agree also in this, that each in his time and place is a faithful theist, that their mysticism towers above a theistic basis, and that however high their mystical speculation soars, they never deny the ground upon which they stand.

Transtition from Part A to Part B

Differentiation of Mystical Experience in General, Developed by Means of Indian Examples[1]

In Part B I intend to show the difference between the mysticisms of Eckhart and of Sankara and thereby to prove by a classical example that mysticisim allows of diversity. This transitional section will serve as an introduction to that task, for quite apart from the particular comparison between Eckhart and Sankara it discusses the possibility of diversity in mystical experience in general, and illustrates this by examples drawn solely from the sphere of Indian religion.

1. Sankara is the classic representative of Indian Vedanta mysticism, which is itself regarded by many as the classic form of mysticism. Our concern with him is in line with our efforts to determine the nature of the mystical experience itself. In this attempt I am guided by a theory which I hope to substantiate by the example selected here, and I have purposely chosen this example because it seems at first sight to run directly counter to my theory. It is still very generally held that mysticism, however diverse the sources from which it springs, is fundamentally one and the same, and as such is beyond time and space, independent of circumstances and conditions. But this seems to me to contra-

---

[1] The following section appeared as a whole in the *Jahrbuch für Religionspsychologie*, 1926. It is printed here in its original form. This involves some repetition, which however in view of the difficulty of the subject, it is hoped will be not without value.

dict the facts. Rather, I hold that, in spite of all the similarity of terms, which can be surprising enough, there is a diversity in mystical experience which is not less than that of religious feeling in general. It is true that somehow or other the word "mysticism" must have one identical meaning, otherwise there could be no conception of mysticism, and the use of the expression as a general term would be impossible. For, logically, we can only use the same term for several objects when they are in some determinable aspect always "the same." This is true, for example, of the term "religion." We call Buddhism, Hinduism, Islam, and Christianity religions, and thereby convey the sense that they are to be ranged under the one classification, "religion." But that does not exclude, it rather includes, the possibility of "religion" differing in each of these examples, and that within one and the same genus very diverse spiritual forms may be found.

2. In defining the nature of mysticism it is common to affirm that mystical experience is experience of the immanence of the divine, and of unification and unity in essence with it, in contrast to the experience of the divine as transcendent. But we have at once a criticism to make. From its inception this definition is burdened with the error of *equivocatio in terminis*. The expression "the divine" used in both cases hides the fact that the object of relationship is of a different nature in these two contrasting experiences. The word is not used in the same sense in the two instances. It is clear that Godhead as an immanent principle is different from and means something other than the transcendent God. Not only is the relationship different in the two contrasted cases, but the essential form of the divine itself is different when the Absolute, or, better still, the religious object of the relationship is conceived as an immanent or as a transcendent God. The difference cannot therefore be determined by a formula which, according to definition, is concerned only with the relationship of the worshiper to the object of his worship, but does not at the same time emphasize the inherent difference in character of that object; and make this distinction of primary importance. The point of departure and the essential distinction is not that the mystic has another and a new relationship to God, but that he has a different God. This difference of object results in a difference

of relationship, but it is the difference of the object itself which is the determining factor.

It is characteristic of certain types of mysticism to seek the *Deus sine modis* (the God without modes) and to cherish Him in the soul. "God" is then experienced in an act of union. But man is a mystic as soon as he has this conception of God, even when the element of union recedes or remains unemphasized, which can easily happen in mysticism. It is the wholly non-rational character of this conception of God with its divergence from the intimate, personal, modified God of simple theism, which makes the mystic. Mysticism is not first of all an act of union, but predominantly the life lived in the "knowledge" of this "wholly other" God.[2] God himself is mystical, for a relationship of union is only possible with an object which is itself mystical in the first instance.

Mysticism enters into the religious experience in the measure that religious feeling surpasses its rational content, that is, as I have said elsewhere, to the extent to which its hidden, non-rational, numinous elements predominate and determine the emotional life.

3. This definition of the concept of mysticism is supported by the etymology of the words "mystical" and "mystic." Etymologically, "mystic" has nothing at all to do with a "union." Our modern use of the word is derived from the Scholastic tradition. "Mystica" was originally an adjective qualifying the substantive "theologia." The essence of the mystica theologia in distinction from the usual theologia lay in the fact that it claimed to teach a deeper "mystery," and to impart secrets and reveal depths which were otherwise unknown. In this the Scholastic usage was following a still older trail. For long before men spoke

---

[2] In Rudolf Otto's *Das Heilige*, 20th edition, will be found the Hymn of Gregory of Nyssa. This hymn is mystical not on account of the unio mystica which is not mentioned at all, but because he lives in the wonder of the "Modeless One" who is called "O Thou entirely beyond all being." The basic meaning of mystes is not "the unified" but epoptes, drashtar, "the man of the divya-chakshus" (qui videt oculis Dei) the "seer" in whom the intuitus mysticus has dawned and who perceives the "Wholly Other," be it atman or Brahman, or unity or sunyata, or soul or modeless Godhead or One indivisible, and who lives in this vision.

of mystical theology they spoke of a mystical *sense,* and of a
mystical interpretation of the Scriptures. Such an interpretation
was mystical not because it was concerned with a "unio
mystica" but because it unfolded a threefold or sevenfold hidden
meaning of the scriptural text, and revealed mysteries which only
the eye of the enlightened could perceive.

4. Mysticism appears where God is seen in a deeper sense as
a mystical Being (e.g. as "Deity without modes"). But with our
definition it is possible to understand what is otherwise quite incomprehensible, that mysticism can also exist where there is no
conception of God at all, or where for the final experience itself
His existence is a matter of indifference. This is particularly the
case in an example of mysticism which comes to mind directly
the subject is raised, for who can speak of mysticism without
thinking immediately of the Yoga of India? In fact, for many people Yoga and mysticism are practically inseparable. This is
wrong, though Yoga is indeed deeply mystical in both experience
and method. It is not, however, God-mysticism, but soul-
mysticism.

We distinguish a sa-isvara-yoga and an an-isvara-yoga, i.e. a
yoga with God and a yoga without God. That the latter cannot
be a unio mystica with God is clear; but in the former also God
and union with Him is not the goal. There is here no effort after
such a union, but after the "isolation of the Atman" for which
God is merely an aid. Even when achieved it is not a relationship
with God. The goal of salvation is to free the Atman by the
method of Yoga from all false ties and limitations which impede
the pure being of Atman itself. The process is indeed a mystical
practice, for the ascharyam of the Atman—the miraculous being
of the Atman—must be sought and found in its unique spiritual
essence, which in relation to all other beings is the "wholly
Other." Yoga has arisen from magical conceptions and practices, and it always remains a refined form of magic. Its ultimate
goal, the "Kaivalyam" is magical—a miraculous state; it is connected not only with the acquisition of magical powers, the sid-
dhis and the riddhis, but it consists in attaining aisvaryam—a
supernatural, miraculous "glory" with an abundance of power
and knowledge.[3]

[3] For the relationship of the "Magical" to the Numinous compare what I have
said in *The Idea of the Holy,* p. 69.

The same is true of original Buddhism. It has been seriously maintained that Buddhism is not religion at all because it denies God. This it certainly does, but it is nevertheless religion, for it lives in the numinous. The salvation sought in Nirvana, like that sought in Yoga, is magical and numinous. It is the utterly supra-rational, of which only silence can speak. It is a blessedness which fascinates. It is only to be achieved by way of negation—the inexpressible wonder. Here, as in all mysticism, negation does not mean nullity. The null is entirely rational, comprehensible, definable; it is not ineffable, it could not bring the soul to silent astonishment. Of all *fabilia* it is the most *fabile*. Buddhism's very denial of atman only increases its mystical nature, for in so far as this final limitation is passed, the mystical, paradoxical character of Nirvana is revealed. Nirvana is an absolute, supranatural, mystic state to the same extent as is the unio mystica between the soul and the eternal God, and by virtue of that state both are forms of mysticism though with a very different content.[4]

5. Yoga is not a mysticism of union, but purely a mysticism of the soul, a development of the numinous sense of "soul." Soul, and belief in the soul, in its peculiar and incomparable being, and in its nobility because it is destined for salvation are part of religious faith generally. Every higher faith includes in some way a belief in the soul. Such faith becomes a mysticism of the soul to the extent that the "wholly other" of the soul is experienced—the miraculous character and the supreme mystery of the atman. That is, in other words, inasmuch as the numinous nature of the soul, latent in every "faith of the soul," is aroused and becomes the dominant factor. As God-mysticism appears where the Deus sine modis, God in His complete non-rationality, is predominant, so soul-mysticism arises when its hidden character becomes vital and active.

6. Mysticism can become merely a mysticism of the soul as in Yoga and Buddhist teaching, though as we have said even these two forms are widely different in content. But soul-mysticism can also be combined with God-mysticism, and then another and

---

[4] Buddhism has this in common with Yoga—it is not a mysticism of union. At the same time it is obviously distinguished from Atma-Yoga by an essential difference, difficult to grasp, but yet so radical that the two are irreconcilably opposed.

entirely different type of mystical experience evolves. Both Eckhart and Sankara represent this type. In Sankara, as we have
seen, Atman-mysticism is the foundation and skeleton of his
scheme. That statement applies with even greater force to Eckhart, for it is hard to say which is more mystical in his teaching:
the ''modeless Godhead'' or the ''homo nobilis'' the supreme
wonder of the soul, which he glorifies and strives to illuminate
in ever fresh aspects. He writes of the miraculous depths of the
soul and submersion in those deeps, of its marvelous structure,
its ground and summit. He speaks of the soul as the ''wholly
other,'' which lying deep below all powers, is eternal beyond
space and time. Even God (conceived as a personal God with
modes of being) has never looked into those depths and cannot
comprehend them. This is mystical wonder, and the striving to
attain and to live in that experience is in itself completely
mystical. Certainly Eckhart is a mystic not alone by virtue of his
God mysticism; he holds that title already by reason of his doctrine of the soul.

On the other hand, Sankara, judged by his introduction to his
Commentary to the Brahma-sutras, must also be placed first
among the ''mystics of the soul,'' since the quest for the Atman
and for the right knowledge of Atman is here so predominantly
in the foreground. In that very important introductory chapter of
his great work the Brahman is not mentioned at all. Yet Sankara
stands in sharpest contrast to the pure atman-mysticism of the
Yoga. This distinction makes it particularly clear that Sankara is
not ''the mystic'' as usually understood, that his attitude is not
that of mysticism in general, but that he represents a mysticism
of a very special type which stands in the same sharp antithesis
to other types of mystical experience. There can be no doubt that
Sankara, the mystic, had he been compelled to choose between
the mystical attitude of the Yoga and the personal theism of his
great rival Ramanuja, would have rejected the former and chosen
the latter. Surely, the contrast in mood and the difference in
experience is tremendous between the proud ''Brahmasmi'' (''I
am the Brahman'') on the one hand, and the Bhakta's humble,
trustful submission to the God of personal theism on the other,
and is a difference which permits of no compromise. Yet both,
when compared with the ideal state of the Yoga, hold a position

equally distant from it, and in sharp contradistinction to that experience, because for both the ideal of the mere Yoga-Kaivalyam would appear as complete Godlessness.

This contrast between a Yogin and a Sankara is very difficult to define. Very often, even by Indologists, it is overlooked. Or the contention is sometimes made that although the Yogin does not recognize a Brahman, his mystical experience is at bottom the same as that of a Sankara. I have heard the same argument put forward regarding Buddha's Nirvana. But the belief in the "oneness of all mysticism" here deceives the eye of the observer. Sankara as well as Buddha would have abhorred such a claim. It is true that the difference is very hard to make clear in words, for the very verbal expressions of the two opponents seem to disavow it, so alike are they. Both appear to be striving after the same thing, or at least after something extraordinarily similar. For what is the Kaivalyam of the Yoga? It is the Atman in its supreme glory, and this does not appear to differ in the slightest degree from the experience of the Atman (soul) when it knows itself as Brahman. The atman in its absoluteness, opposed to and set free from all that is not atman, brought to its pure being as clear self-knowledge, freed from all sense of the "I," unfettered from the world, blessed in itself—that is what the Yogin seeks. But the brahma-bhava, the state of complete oneness with the Brahman, is described in precisely the same way. For Sankara likewise "Brahman" appears to be the atman (soul) come to itself, in the glory which belongs to its own eternal nature, which has only been obscured by avidya. Brahman and Atman appear to be simply interchangeable terms for the same thing. Where Atman has been found there Brahman is reached. It is not easy to see what the Atman would gain by being given now the name of Brahman also. True, the Yogin maintains the plurality of the atman, but as regards the quality and content of the atman it makes no difference. In both cases the final state is governed by those feelings of infinite liberation and exaltation of which it is customary to speak in any religious-psychological discussion of mysticism. In both we are dealing with liberation from the bonds of self-consciousness, in both the Atman is pure Jnana without the distinctions of Knower, Known and Knowing; in both it is complete consciousness. Nor is there any doubt that the degree of blessedness of those who have reached the Kaivalyam of the Yoga is not less nor less important than of those who have achieved Brahma-nirvana. The distinction here is in no way one of mere quantity.

The later Bhaktas condemned the Yogins with their Kaivalyam, and denied them the final capacity for redemption, which they allowed to every denizen of hell, so conscious were they of the wrong path upon which the mere Yogin is set. Sankara's attitude toward the Yogin can hardly have been more charitable than that of the Bhakta.

Brahman mysticism is qualitatively different from Atman mysticism, however much the terminology of the two may seem to agree. Their respective contents are separated by a great gulf which can be distinguished by any painstaking observer. The difference between them however, is itself as non-rational as the difference in character of the two mysticisms; it is not to be reproduced in intellectual conceptions and is only comprehensible in mystical experience itself. I must again remind my readers how insufficient to any treatment of mysticism are the usual terms—"feeling of exaltation, liberation, and expansion, or infinity." All these terms would apply also to pure Yoga and describe it tolerably well. But the sense of Brahman is obviously something different from all this.

7. This fact is important in another connection.

(a) The mystic is often reproached for differing from "real" religion, and for his lack of humility, the fundamental religious feeling. His ideal, it is said, is like that of the old serpent "to be as gods" or, still worse, to be God Himself. And in truth mysticism is characterized by peculiar numinous and lofty feelings, which do indeed prove that religion is not exhaustively defined as "the sense of absolute dependence." But this definition is indeed obviously too narrow, for there is a sense of exaltation in every religion. It is true even of simple Christian piety that to define it as the feeling of "complete dependence" is to present only one factor in Christian experience, which gives a false impression if not immediately supplemented by the admission that this complete dependence upon God results at once in the strongest sense of freedom and victory over "the world, sin, evil and death." "Our faith is the victory which overcomes the world." A sense of exaltation is the complement of Christian humility, without which the latter is cant. "The Christian is a free lord over all things." That sense of genuine lordship which Luther describes in his *Freedom of the Christian Man* is a very real experience of exaltation, and it is doubtful if any mystic has felt the antinomy of that experience more profoundly than Luther. There are here the beginnings of mysticism also, in so far as such feelings of exaltation, proper to all true religion and having strong numinous characteristics, rise further and further into the sphere of the non-rational and the inexpressible.

(b) Secondly, it is certainly true that from the standpoint of Sankara's mukta (the redeemed) there can be no more talk of humility. But that does not exhaust the question, for we must again note his relationship to Yoga. Seen from the standpoint of Brahma-nirvana, the Yogin's striving after Kaivalyam is revealed in its true character as without Brahman, and must be reproached by a Sankara as sheer blasphemy. Sankara cannot accuse the Yogin of lack of "humility" for he is certainly not any "humbler" than they, but he can say that the Yogin is absolutely "secular," and sacrilegious in his arrogance in so far as he seeks salvation, and supposedly attains it, apart from the one, eternal, Brahman and his blessedness. This element in Sankara's teaching is sometimes the cause of a seeming lapse when he comes to the doctrine of grace. Sankara cannot admit a "grace" of Brahman. Brahman as the higher or supreme Atman, which is identical with every atman (soul) cannot strictly speaking be gracious. But the fact that a man can achieve the highest state not in mere isolation like the Yogin, but only in and through the attainment of Brahman, has indeed an analogy to the bhakta's "salvation by grace," so that for Sankara there is here a possibility of accepting the doctrine of the Gita. He adopts this teaching not only in the sense of the personal God who helps man along the path of knowledge by His illumination, but occasionally in the sense of the supreme Atman Himself "bestowing grace." Thus in Gita 18, 54 he says:

> He who has become Brahman, who has attained to the grace of the supreme Atman (adhyatman) is free from sorrow.

The relationship here is analogous to that mentioned on page 94. Just as Brahman must of necessity be seen as Isvara and Creator-God when a world of contrasts appears in multiplicity, so salvation in Brahman, seen in the refraction of "lower knowledge," must appear as a revelation of grace. A doctrine of grace as the reverse side of this mysticism is not merely a concession—the relationship can also be expressed thus: "It lies on the one hand in the character of the Brahman itself, that, when a world appears in the magical mist of Avidya,[5] it must appear as a world of order, of wisdom and justice. But it also lies in the nature of the Brahman, that when a world appears, there are found in it souls which attain to salvation and overcome Avidya." To that extent, to speak of a "grace of the adhyatman" is not a mere slip of the tongue.

In any case, it is true that in Brahman alone lies salvation. To seek salvation without Brahman is sacrilege. It would be an overweening attempt at "self-redemption"—a conception foreign alike to Sankara and to Eckhart.

(8) The peculiarity of Sankara's mystical experience would be thrown into still stronger relief if it were contrasted with non-Indian forms of mysticism, as for instance, with the Taoist and Zen schools of China. The Tao teaching and the experience of a Laotze is indeed mystical and here also it is not difficult to find similar, or like-sounding formulas, to those with which we have been dealing. Considered only in relation to these similarities, it is easy to let Indian and Chinese forms of mysticism disappear "into the one night in which all cats are gray." Yet Tao is fundamentally different from Brahman. Since it concerns the absolutely non-rational, it is again only possible tentatively to indicate these differences and to understand them by feeling rather than through the intellect. But the sensitive observer must easily perceive that Tao has a much greater affinity on the one hand to the bhuta-tathata and alayavijnana and on the other to the mysterious sunyata of Mahayana than to Sankara's Brahman. These out of an inner affinity mingled with Tao and interpenetrated one another, and at the same time, in consequence of their peculiar character and content, they produced a mysticism of nature and an incomparable art, such as the masters of the Chinese and Japanese Zen schools have created. It was the outcome of their experience of the mystical and paradoxical "Void": while from

[5] "In the double, magic, fog of space and time," as our Jacobi says.

Brahman no such form of art could ever have developed. The same mistake has been made here as that we noted and disapproved above: Mahayana Buddhism has been understood as a "gradual relapse" to the general Indian level—as a disguised or complete return to the Vedanta. The comfortable theory of Syncretism was speedily adopted. Undoubtedly, there have been reciprocal influences and counter-influences and attractions between Vedanta and Buddhism, but the similarities are due less to mutual plagiarism than to that curious law of the convergence of types of which I have spoken in my book *Vishnu-Narayana* and in *Religious Essays*. Here also this convergence of types does not lead to an identity of content. Within Vedanta and Mahayana, in spite of mutual convergence, there lives an entirely different spirit, which needs to be perceived in its essence and cannot be exhausted by generalities. The alaya-vijnana is in its profounder depths different from jnana, which is Brahman. To indicate the difference roughly in words, the latter is the static, massive, and quietly immobile; it is quite distinct from the highest principle of Mahayana-mysticism, which is dynamic and vital, with its stimulating influence upon mood, fantasy and creative imagination, and its experience of the wonder of the world and of nature in their beauty. On account of this dynamic character the idea of a static "Atman" which is indispensable in Vedanta must be passionately rejected here, and the "Anatmata" *must* become the shibboleth of this experience. The antinomies and paradoxes and the inner driving dialectic of the Anatmata teaching must be carried almost to the verge of sense, as a protest against the firmly fixed, four-square character of the Atman conception, and the massive substantiality of the Brahman idea. Without any doubt, a genuine disciple of Vasubandhu could not find in the Vedanta anything "fundamentally similar," but he would asphyxiate in the Vedanta atmosphere and having freed himself from it would feel like a bird released from the snare. What would be sheer madness on the basis of Sankara's teaching, namely, that "Nirvana and Samsara are one and the same," becomes necessary and vital to the mood of the Mahayana. At the same time it is understandable that between this Mahayana and the piety of the Bhakti there must be a much stronger mutual attraction than between Advaita and Bhakti. The Buddha-hridaya, the eternal Buddha heart of the Mahayana, is emotionally the reverse of the Bhuta-tathata; and this because it is the eternal Buddha heart is a much more immediate source of the Bhakti than the Brahman. Therefore it was not a mere historical chance but an inner necessity which caused the Dhyana school of the Mahayana in China to build up the Bhakti cult of Amida and Kwanyin as the second mainstay of its practice.[6]

9. Sankara's mysticism has a particular emphasis through its relation to Theism; not to theism in general, for that does not exist any more than does mysticism in general; but to Indian theism.

Even with this limitation, our statement will meet with opposition. True, the traditional claim which Troeltsch still repeated in his early writings, viz. that the mysticism of India rises upon a foundation of "naturalistic Polydemonism and Polytheism," will hardly be repeated today, when at last the great religious systems of India are better known to us. That a lofty and advanced theism and not a "heathenish polytheism" is the basis upon which the mystic speculation of India rises is a fact so evident to those circles in which Gita is a holy book, that there is no need to spend time upon it here. But another objection will be raised, and at first sight appearances support it. It may be said: Belief in a personal savior-God, who is to be found and reverenced through the loving faith of the Bhakti, is for Sankara only "lower knowledge" (apara vidya). This God disappears so soon as samyagdarsanam (perfect knowledge) is attained—the knowledge which pronounces the "great word": *"tat tvam asi,"* "That art thou" (namely, Thou art the eternal impersonal Brahman, which is pure knowledge, beyond the distinction of Knower, Known and Knowing). The mystical experience of this Brahman entirely excludes the personal God and the personal relationship necessary for the functions of trustful love; indeed it stands in complete contrast to such a conception of God. The

[6]It becomes clear thereby, that the Bhakti itself is not the same in the Mahayana system as in the Hindu system. Amida, in spite of all similarity, is not simply the Isvara of the Indian Bhakti schools. He has his origin in an entirely different emotional background, must be viewed against this background, and is, with all his superficial similarity, very different from the Isvara of India. The misunderstanding would be still greater were Amida interpreted in the sense of Christian Theism, or were we to see in him a second Christ.

whole varied world together with its Lord disappears in the illusion of Avidya (Not-Knowing), and is itself merely Avidya. Thereby, the vision of "him who knows" is lifted above personal theism as above every other explanation of the world. An unbridgeable gulf separates him from others. Mysticism is here pure in itself, unspotted and untouched by foreign elements, in a cool stillness beyond the emotional stimulus of theistic or "believing" piety, in an ice-cold clarity of pure Being and Knowledge. This mysticism is consistent and is of the type to be found wherever there is "consistency" in experience.

10. Against this contention we maintain, first: The mysticism of Sankara is certainly "cool" and unimpassioned, still and unmoved by any agitation. But (a) that is already a proof that it is a mysticism of *peculiar* character. As a "cool" mysticism it is distinguished from a mysticism of "hot" feeling, of a strongly emotional nature. Persian mysticism, Sufi mysticism is heated and impassioned. The mysticism of an al Hallâj is fervent, that of a Jelaleddin is intoxicating. The mysticism of Plotinus is saturated to the very depths of its non-rational experience of unity with erotic delight; that of Meister Eckhart is steeped in "gemüt"; that of St. John of the Cross is lyrical throughout.[7]

These mystics all differ from one another and from the experience of Sankara. On the other hand, the "icy-coldness" of his mysticism must be restricted. Certainly Sankara's experience and the condition of the man who has attained to Brahma-nirvana is distinguished above other forms of mysticism by its restrained and profound peace and immobility,[8] and by its static character. But the condition aimed at is not by any means a state of no feeling. Brahman is ananda, deep joy.[9] Again Brahman is not "joy in general." There is no such thing. Joys differ very much among themselves. Joy in Brahman is not the same as other joys, or even as other mystic joys; it is a joy which also differentiates this form of mysticism.

10. (b) Secondly, Sankara's mysticism is distinguished by the

[7] For St. John of the Cross and the special character of his mysticism cf. Jean Baruzi, *Saint Jean de la Croix,* Paris, 1930, 2nd. ed. Cf. p. 703ff.
[8] In this respect very clearly distinguished, for example, from that of the Mahayana.
[9] Indeed it is a completely non-rational joy. It is not rationally clear from the words "Being" and "Knowing" what joy there is in Brahman.

fact, that it is not indifferent to theisim, out of which it emerges, but however far it rises above it, it maintains a fixed relationship to Indian theism, and particularly to that of the Gita, and this relationship gives it a special character. Some observations may be made here to supplement what we have said before on this question. They will, at the same time, make clear a certain feature of the emotional side of Sankara's mysticism.

The great opponent of Sankara and his doctrine of the impersonal Brahman, and especially of his doctrine of Maya, is the strict theist Ramanuja. He fights passionately against Sankara for the personal conception of Brahman.[10] Vishnu, Narayana, Vasudeva, the personal Isvara, i.e. the Creator, Guide and Destroyer of the World is for Ramanuja the eternal Brahman, who exists as the immortal God above all world events, all evolution and devolution. Far below him stands the Deva Brahma, a Demiurge of His creation, who in the name and at the bidding of God formed the lower world. But Isvara, is himself the cause of the world, and is so much the absolute cause, that he is both its causa instrumentalis and its causa materialis. Before the creation of the world Isvara (the Lord) had name and form in unity within Himself as the cause.[11] Out of this, by His will, wisdom and creative power, He forms the differing multiplicity of names and types; He fashions this real evolved world in an unending series and repeats its creation and dissolution, but is Himself eternally living, and as God is ever the same above all worlds and all time. By His grace He saves the elect out of the world to His communion and His blessed service in "Vaikuntha," the place above the world where with Him they are eternally blessed. Knowledge of this God is *"the* knowledge," which cannot be surpassed by "higher knowledge," but is this higher knowledge" itself.

If we compare this doctrine with Sankara's system, we find that his teaching is not simply that of the impersonal Brahman, but is a curious twofold structure on two levels. The relation between these two levels is expressed in his terms—the lower and

---

[10] Cf. R. Otto, *Siddhanta des Ramanuja* (2nd. ed. Tübingen, 1923).
[11] Just as the Deus of the West contains the ideas eternally within Himself, which are one with Him and His nature.

the higher knowledge. But this distinction does not imply simply a rejection of the lower knowledge; it is rather a necessary relation between the two. True, the lower knowledge compared with the higher is the one which is to be surpassed, and is surpassed, but it is nevertheless lower *knowledge,* in its own sphere *vidya,* and to be clearly distinguished from error in the ordinary sense of the word. This means that the higher knowledge stands in an entirely different relationship to the lower, than say, to merely personal opinions, or to the doctrinal systems of "false teachers." The higher knowledge is not indifferent to the lower knowledge, but presupposes it in its own place. Materialists, Vaiseshika's, Sankhya's and such like are simply and entirely erroneous and possess no "Vidya." But whoever believes in God has a Vidya, a "knowledge" even though a lower knowledge, which exists in a weaker and more indistinct form, but is not deception or mere error. Sankara himself, on the lower level, is a thoroughgoing theist, and that with ardor and holy zeal. His theology is here almost identical with that of the later Ramanuja outlined above, and his opposition to those who deny God and to those rival systems which opposs theism, is as great as that of his successor (Ramanuja). Therefore, he takes it for granted that the man who is redeemed of God does not turn back, but on the path of gradual redemption finds at last Brahma-nirvana. This explains as we have noted before, the curious elasticity of the borderline of: en entirely disappearing, between higher and lower knowledge—a phenomenon which cannot be dismissed as merely "Indian synthetic thinking." It depends, as we said, upon the nature of the Brahman itself, that when it is refracted by the prism of Avidya, it must necessarily appear as Isvara and as the souls confronting Him.

11. The same relationship is reflected in Sankara's conception of Maya. Maya and Avidya overlap sometimes, yet there is a significant distinction between them. The man who perceives the eternal One as Multiplicity has Avidya, but Brahman has Maya. Brahman is the great Mayin, which implies that the universe, this great Fata Morgana, is not merely subjective imagination. An objective factor is required for its existence. The world of multiplicity has a ground of reality—firstly because Brahman himself is its real ground upon which multiplicity is erroneously imag-

ined. But secondly, the fact that it exists as such a world as a
highly purposeful, wise and meaningful combination is somehow
or other dependent upon Brahman himself. Brahman, as Sankara
passionately assures us, is therefore rightly to be called the material and the effective cause of the world. He is the material cause
inasmuch as he is the existing substratum upon which the
multiplicity of all things is built up. He is the effective cause inasmuch as when this world of appearance and of multiplicity is
there, it is through his Maya that it appears as such. As soon as
this connection is clear, we escape from the apparent confusion
of higher and lower Vidya, which seems so hopeless in the first
Adhyaya's of Sankara's Sutras. For this reason it is by no means
compromise or inconsistency when like Badarayana, Sankara
adopts as the very definition of Brahman the words: "That from
which the world has its beginning, its subsistence and its dissolution." Just as little is it inconsistent when he turns fiercely
against the materialists or the naturalists and uses the cosmological and physico-theological proofs of God. But all this would
be absolutely meaningless if his Brahman were indifferent to
Isvara, if his mysticism were without the special note of which
we have spoken. For then the evolution and subsistence, the
sense or nonsense of the world would be matters of complete indifference to him. Indeed, the greater the nonsense the better it
would be. But when this relationship between higher and lower
knowledge is properly understood, the first great sections of his
book become clear and consistent. He can now rightly claim for
the Brahman all the value which the theist claims when he
describes his God as the sole ground of the world, as almighty,
all-wise, all-knowing, all-righteous. And because of this,
Sankara on occasion can rightly take a neutral attitude between
the higher and the lower knowledge.

12. Sankara believed himself to be maintaining the teaching
and the mysticism of the ancient Upanishad wisdom. Here a significant change had already taken place with regard to Brahman.
The ancient Brahman, the completely unrationalized indefinable
magic world power, the somewhat uncanny Yaksha[12] was experienced as the Being of Atman, as spirit. Also Atman is

[12] See Kena Upanishad 3, 15. This Brahman was certainly not yet Atman.

Ascharyam, is something miraculous, but is much clearer and more nearly approaching the rational. Atman is "self-evident, Consciousness and Knowledge"; is in fact spirit, and though we must guard against robbing these attributes of their mystical character which they always retain, and against using them in the sense of empirical psychology, yet there is no doubt that they are far removed from the original sphere of ancient magic and cosmological myth and legend. But the penetration of the Brahman by this atman alone does not explain the whole content of Sankara's conception of Brahman. It is clear that for him, a third element has entered into and been submerged in the Brahman not without imparting to it again its special hue—and that is the conception of Isvara. It is revealed in the fact that Sankara likes to use for Brahman the term which would fit neither the old conception of Brahman nor of Atman, namely, Paramesvara, "Highest Lord," the name under which God is generally known and worshiped in India. The ancient Brahman thereby has become "Deity"; true a *mystical* deity, but a deity which is not in mere contrast to whatever else is called God, but is at the same time a mystical superlative of God. This is substantiated by the solemn creedal phrases, which Sankara chooses in certain especially impressive passages, and which have an almost liturgical ring about them. It is not the keen dialectician speaking here, but a man in whom the full emotion of mystical Brahman experience has broken forth:

> His Being is by nature eternal, pure, wise and free, all-knowing and endowed with omnipotence. (V. S. 1, 1, 1)
>
> They teach Him as the eternal omniscient, omnipresent, complete, eternally pure, wise free Being, as Knowledge and Joy, as Brahman. (V. S. 1, 1, 4)
>
> The absolutely real Being, exalted, eternal, all-penetrating as the ether, free from all change, all-sufficient, indivisible, self-luminous. (V. S. 1, 15, 4)
>
> The one identical, all-highest, eternal spirit. (V. S. 1, 1, 4)
>
> The eternal pure God. (V. S. 1, 1, 5)
>
> The eternal, perfect, highest God. (V. S. 1, 1, 20)

13. These descriptions of his "indescribable Brahman," which Sankara uses when he gives rein to his religious emotion and is carried beyond his Scholasticism, show what he really means and

give to the apparently cold, abstract "Pure Being" an inner content of feeling. The Brahman here is not far removed from those definitions which theistic speculation also uses in its attempt to free "God" as far as possible from anthropomorphic elements. A comparison makes this clearer. Sankara's Brahman—and in fact just his "Higher Brahman"—bears a striking resemblance to the theistic speculation of our Western Scholastics. Not only Eckhart but Thomas Aquinas before him describes God as Esse, Esse purum et simplex. To him also God is Esse and Esse is His Essentia. He does not come into a genus with other beings, He has no genus at all. He is His own genus. In Him there is no distinction between being in general and particular being. In Him there is no "distinction" whatever. He is simpliciter simplex, is strictly as nirvisesha as the Brahman, and also nirguna, for He is Pure Being without distinction of attributes (Guna's). All diversity and multiplicity exist in Him only "nomine" and "a parte intellectus nostri." As with Brahman, the "Intelligere" of God is identical with his "Esse." Likewise in God the contrast between the knowing subject and the known object is lost. For God knows Himself not through representations of Himself, but without mediation, through His own Being (atman). The motives of such pronouncements are not "an impersonal conception of God fundamental to scholasticism," but the attempt, essential to theology, to think of God in terms of the Absolute, in distinction from dependent and conditioned being. For that which, like God, is to be the ground of an ordered multiplicity, must itself be One. That which is to be the ground of multiplicity in general cannot itself be multiple. That which is to make all conditioning possible cannot itself be subject to conditions.[13]

14. Sankara has often described the true relationship between the higher and the lower Brahman as he sees it. The two Brahmans, the higher and the lower, are not really so distinct that the second is entirely different from the first, as is the case, say,

[13] It is obvious in both cases that this speculation about the Absolute reduces to a rational system that which I have called the numinous "Wholly Other." Sankara uses two distinct terms for this: The Brihattvam, the majesty of the Brahman, and the Atigambhiratvam, the measureless depth of the Brahman (cf. V. S. 2, 1, 31).

with the lower demiurge, who is continually evolving and de-
volving with the world of appearances. But they differ in this,
that one and the same Being is at one time conceived as the object
of the samyagdarsanam, at another as the object of upasana, i.e.
the object of personal devotion. This devotion is not directed to
any other object than the samyagdarsanam, but the apprehension
of it is a "lower" perception. And in countless passages, the
conception of the "Highest Lord," is so fluid that it is impossible to say whether the higher or the lower Brahman is indicated.
This ambiguity is quite intentional, it means that none of the dignity of the world-creating and world-governing God must be lost
to the eternal Brahman. The latter is to be very greatly exalted,
but in such a way, that all value that pertains to the lower shall
be taken up into the higher.

15. Of the Gita, 10, 10, Sankara says:

> Through such exercise of knowledge (in the form of the
> samyagdarsanam) do they reach me, the Highest Lord, being
> Atman.

Is it not obvious that this expression is richer and fuller in content
than when, as often, he speaks of attaining Brahman as the sat
or sad-Atman? The bliss of this feeling is permeated with the
sense of being one with a "Lord and Creator of All."

What takes place in the soul of a man who becomes this Isvara-
Brahman, only he can tell who has experienced it. Or rather, he
would not be able to "tell" but he would know it without words,
and he would also know wherein lay the distinction between
Brahma-nirvana, where the Brahman has absorbed Isvara, and
the state where that absorption has not yet taken place. In distinction from the ancient dim and abstruse Brahman arising out of
the magical world of the old sacrificial cult, such a Brahma-
nirvana must bear within itself, first, luminous clarity, complete
awareness, pure spirituality. It contains these elements in so far
as it is not only Brahman, but is, and has long been, Atman. Over
and above this, however, he who has come to this experience by
the way of Sankara, will know and bear something further within
himself which will be palpable in his attitude toward his sur-
roundings. This something is realised in very fact, when one
meets the true types of those who use the word of greeting—

"Brahmasmi": it is an impressive *dignity* and a rare *nobility*. It is not only complete repose and balance in gesture and speech, feature and expression, but a fine and lofty poise which, one might almost describe as a lordship. Such a mystic is not only filled with light but is also "lordly." This cannot be explained alone by Brahman and Atman, by pure Being, and consciousness, by chaitanya and jnana. But it is explicable when the Brahman here experienced has taken up into itself a Paramesvara, a "highest Lord."

16. We said that between Brahman and Paramesvara there was a shifting and interpenetrating relationship, and that the contrast between the higher and the lower Brahman was not clearly definable, while the relation through jnana and through upasana more clearly and precisely expresses Sankara's meaning. The discussion of this latter relationship now helps us to distinguish the character of Sankara's mysticism more definitely from a further type of mysticism which closely enough resembles it in terminology and which is yet again of a new aspect. This new type is also a form of "Advaita" but an advaita which widely differs from Sankara's in mood and experience. It is that advaita which for example, lies at the root of Vishnu-purana and the Bhakti-sutras of Sandilya, and has an essentially different relationship of Bhakti to Jnana than that of Sankara and his disciples. We will try to make these differences clear.

17. With a Sankara two conditions are plainly discernible, that of Samadhi and that of ordinary consciousness. In Samadhi the Jivanmukta realises his moksha. Here he is really Brahman. The world of distinctions actually disappears in the moment of Samadhi from his gaze; Brahman is then in his experience One and All and he is himself Brahman. When he returns out of Samadhi again into ordinary consciousness the knowledge remains with him that Brahman alone is, and that he is himself Brahman, but it is then *only* knowledge and not knowledge in experience. The false appearance of multiplicity presses in upon him once more. In spite of his better knowledge that all is but the One, he again beholds the manifold. It is with him as with a Timira patient, who sees two moons though he knows that there is only one. The false vision "persists in consequence of his Kar-

ma which must work itself out.'' Nevertheless such bedazzlement of vision does not disturb him in his assurance that, in spite of appearances, Brahman alone *is,* without a second, and that the appearance is *only* appearance, even when he cannot for the time being get beyond it. In this state when he thinks of Brahman, the latter is undoubtedly an object of his reverence. Yet his condition is not at the moment that of the Bhakta. He will not return to Upasana, to a worship of a personal Isvara, he will not think of getting into touch with God through prayer, sacrifice, ritual or other karmani. ''We are above it,'' said a Sankara to me, with conviction. Works, prayer and Upasana are done with, and thereby so soon as knowledge has been attained, all *personal* relationship to a transcendent object. For a real Sankara, bhakti or states of emotion are not a step on the ladder to Samadhi. The union with Brahman or, more accurately, the state of being Brahman, does not lie for the Sankara in the continuance of a devotion emotionally aroused.

But that is exactly what happens in the second type of Advaita mentioned. Here the example of Prahlada, which is found in Vishnu-purana, is instructive. Prahlada, cast into the depths of the ocean by his unbelieving father on account of his belief in Vishnu, remains firmly true to his faith, directs his thought unperturbed to Vishnu in prayer, and brings Him daily his offerings of praise. This elevation of his spirit to the Lord, this upasana, passes *gradually* into mystical experience:

Reverence, worship, honor be to Him For ever and for ever, to Vishnu the Lord. From Him and to Him is all that lives.	Upasana Bhakti
He is all, comprehends all that moves. His being comprehends all space and time.	Transition.
I also am He, and all is mine. I am all, All is in me, I am eternal, unending, through and through As the abode of the spirit most high I am called Brahman, World's Highest Spirit, Who holds beginning and end and all things.[14]	Samyag- darsanam.

[14] Cf. R. Otto: *Vishnu-Narayana*, 2nd. ed., S. 50.

Thus he feels himself Achyuta, loses himself and knows himself as Brahman:

> Eternal am I, changeless,
> Am myself the highest Self.

In this instance we see that the mystical experience arises from a determined act of Bhakti (State 1). In State 2, the personal, beloved, trusted Lord of ordinary theistic religion expands into the mystical All-Being, which is the One. After He has been "seen" in such form, the state of union results; the object seen consumes the seer. He is Me[15] and so I am He. Object and subject glide into one another, and he who experiences is himself this Lord of all being. In the reverse order, this mystical experience afterwards slips back into simple Bhakti worship, and Vishnu then appears again personally in heavenly form as the gracious and merciful One in converse with Prahlada. But without doubt, this personal intercourse is here not something lower or of less value, which could be sacrificed or must pass away, but is equal in value to the mystical experience. One might say: The characteristic of this God is that he can be interchangeably present with the soul, either as blessed all-absorbing All *or* as personal lover and friend of the soul. We have here what we must call a "mysticism of poise."

18. At the same time, we may take warning from the example of Prahlada against trying not to solve but to explain away deep problems of religious experience by "syncretism" or by "inconsistent mysticism," or other easy catch phrases. The religious experience of Sankara is not more "consistent" than that of Prahlada. From Prahlada's point of view it would seem "one-sided" and also poorer in experience. Prahlada's religion is thoroughly consistent. It is by its nature "polar," but that is not inconsistent. Such a nature is rather consistent in itself when it acts in a twofold way. A magnet from which I break off one pole immediately establishes its field of attraction or repulsion at the broken end. That is its consistency.

19. Finally—within Bhakti mysticism itself, there are again differentiations, which can lead to sharp emotional antitheses.

[15] In the sense of "mystical copula."

This is obvious, if we compare, say, the type of Prahlada (who stands nearer to the quiet, collected Ramanuja) with that of the Bengalese Chaitanya. In this type Bhakti becomes "Prema," a fevered, glowing Krishna-eroticism, colored throughout by love passion; and intoxication enters into the experience. In the heat of love's emotion, which breaks through the limitations of the individual in ecstasy, and seeks union with the beloved, the state of unity is striven after. With Prahlada it is clearly different. On the contrary, for him Bhakti is the stilling of the soul before God, a trustful, believing devotion, which has more of Eckhart's "composure in God," than the glowing excitement of the Prema. Neither fiery Eros nor sentimental Caritas, but complete Faith as Fiducia,[16] a trustful, concentrated, believing contemplation leads here to the loss of self, and to becoming one with Him. Not only amor, but fiducia also has within it the possibility of passing into mysticism.

20. Christian analogies might be found for all, or almost all, the above-mentioned forms of Indian Mysticism. Together with the latter, they would prove that mysticism admits of wide variations and they would also serve to show how, in spite of "convergence of types" between East and West, the inner spirit yet differs, and that the very different ground upon which mysticism rose in Europe also colors the highest mystical experience in a way which is Christian and not Indian. To show this differentiation between the mysticism of Eckhart and Sankara will be the task of Part B.

---

[16] Cf. R. Otto: *The Idea of the Holy,* p. 209.

The Differences—
Eckhart versus Sankara

Introduction

1. We have compared the mysticism of Meister Eckhart with the great mysticism of India, and have tried to distinguish features of surprising formal similarity or equality between them, and we have seen that in such similarities there are revealed likenesses in the human soul, which transcend the barriers of nation, time, race and culture. But as I have said elsewhere, the task of comparative religion is not completed by the demonstration of similarities, its finer work then begins. This is to show within the framework of formal agreement the peculiar spirit, the genius et numen loci, which, in spite of structural resemblances, colors very differently the inward experiences of mysticism in the two regions of East and West. This difference is important not only in a comparison relating to mysticism, but in comparing higher forms of religion in general. Beyond the borders of mystical experience also we are surprised by convergences of types,[1] which appear to produce the very same phenomenon in very different circumstances, and present the most amazing analogies to the Christian doctrine of grace. But here too, if one knows how to penetrate to the inmost heart, the spirit and therefore the essence of experience is not the same. Christ is not at bottom, the same as Krishna. Just as little is mysticism "the same" in the East and in the West; Christian mysticism is not Indian mysti-

---

[1] Cf. R. Otto: *India's Religion of Grace and Christianity*, Oxford Press, 1930

cism, but maintains its distinctive character, clearly explicable by the ground from which it rises.

2. Brahman, high above the personal God; the personal God submerged and disappearing in the suprapersonal Brahman; the identity of the soul and Brahman; salvation as identity with Brahman; Brahman determined as the unqualified, pure Being and Spirit, without attributes, without distinctions within itself; the world lacking real being, floating in the indefiniteness of Maya and Avidya—all these have, point for point, their parallels in Eckhart, extending even to a surprising identity of phrase. For Eckhart too speaks of the suprapersonal "Godhead," into which no distinction has ever penetrated, high above the God of person and persons; of "God disappearing" in the suprapersonal deity; of the soul and God merged in this divinity as a single indivisible One; of salvation in this Oneness; of the world and things floating in the indefiniteness of the "creaturely," which is not being but entirely lacks being, and which in itself is "nothing" and "is" not. Can expressions be more alike? Is the likeness merely in expression? Is there any distinction in salvation itself, when on both sides it is described as a losing of self, and a submergence into the absolute, unqualified, one divinity? Are not both mysticism, the consistent mysticism in which all distinctions disappear, and which is one and the same wherever it may arise in humanity? Is it not the same mysticism which, with its abstract and empty goal of Pure Being, of Super-Being, of Nothingness, its theologia negativa, weakens, dilutes, suffocates and clouds concrete religious experience?

3. What follows is divided into two sections. (a) The two mysticisms as different in themselves in the two masters; (b) the two mysticisms as different regarding certain contents for which they provide comprehensive forms.

A foreword prefaces the whole.

Foreword

The reproach is often made against Eckhart and against mysticism in general, that the full, vital, individual life of religion, of personal faith, love, confidence and fear and a richly colored emotional life and conscience, is finally submerged in pale abstractions, in the void and empty formulas of systematized nonentities: to become one with the One, with Being, with that which is robbed of all ideas and all positive content; a game with abstractions like finite and infinite—dissolution into the rare atmosphere of ghostly metaphysical forms; the "nought," which even if it is perhaps not completely a zero made absolute, yet stands very near to it, and is at least entirely indefinite and therefore without purport.

As we have seen above, such reproaches are misunderstandings of the experiential content of Indian mysticism. But applied to Eckhart they are simply monstrous. To say that this "Gothic" personality, absolutely permeated and glowing with the urge of a tremendous new life-impulse, lived in abstractions is absurd. His master, Thomas Aquinas, is much more abstract, in spite of his correct theism. In comparison with Eckhart, he is looking backward, summing up the results of a preceding period, but not opening up a new era; seriously striving to quadrate the circle, and to amalgamate his Christian heritage of tradition and authority with the rationalism of the Aristotelian system. It is true that Eckhart works with the instruments of his own and of earlier

Scholasticism. Judging the current of his thought by the details of his separate formulas, instead of integrating these with their profounder meaning, it would be easy to prove him a thorough Scholastic. But that is not to be able to see the stream for the single drops of water. With the intellectual material which he snatches from the Schools, he builds a thought-system which might be called fantastic rather than abstract, and does in fact bear in itself those elements, which Worringer has recently disclosed in his *Problems of the Gothic*. Worringer calls these elements "magical." Strange and bewildering they are, leading to a new and unknown emotional world, awakening new and unaccustomed powers of the soul. They are non-rational, and their non-rationality is increased by contrast with the austerity of the construction. An example of this is found in Eckhart's "modeless Godhead," the "wheel revolving out of itself," the "stream flowing into itself," "God flourishing and growing in the ground of the soul," Himself an abyss of wonder, bristling with paradox and contradiction, which yet resolve and are fused together in the unity of one great fundamental intuition, that burns and stirs in the soul of Eckhart like the word of Jehovah in the bowels of Jeremiah.

His mysticism is quiveringly *alive* and of powerful vitality, and therefore far removed from "Abstraction." It is therefore also very far from Sankara and Indian mysticism, and the reason for that difference lies in the foundation from which it rises.

In spite of great formal equalities, the inner core of Eckhart is as different from that of Sankara as the soil of Palestine and of Christian Gothic Germany in the thirteenth century is different from that of India. These distinctions we will now try to understand.

1

Vitality. Dynamic Mysticism

1. Sankara's Brahman is sat, chit and chaitanyam; is Being and Spirit through and through, utterly opposed to all "deafness" (jada) and all matter. No one can deny the lofty spirituality of this conception of God. But the difference between this and Eckhart's conception is at once palpable, if the question is asked: Is this Brahman a *living* God? "I am the living God"—that is more than a God who lives. I have dealt with this "living" Christian idea of God elsewhere and must refer the reader to that.[1] It can be re-discovered in all its strength in Eckhart, not in his theistic sub-structure but in his mystical conceptions. This God becomes a mystical God because He is a stream of glowing vitality. The eternal "repose" of the Godhead, which Eckhart maintains, has a different meaning from that of the resting Sat in India. It is both the principle and the conclusion of a mighty inward *movement,* of an eternal process of ever-flowing life. "A wheel rolling out of itself," "a stream flowing into itself": these are metaphors which would be quite impossible for the One of Sankara. The Deity of Eckhart is causa sui, but this not in the merely exclusive sense, that every foreign causa is shut out, but in the most posi-tive sense of a ceaseless self-production of Himself. In fact:

> ...*der sich selbst erschuf*
> *Von Ewigkeit in immer schaffendem Beruf.*[2]

[1] Cf. R. Otto: *Religious Essays.*
[2] *Goethe,* ...who created himself from eternity in an ever-creating vocation.

When Eckhart insists that we must also leave God and climb beyond God, that God disappears and enters into the modeless Godhead, it might seem as if this going forth of God and of the world with God out of the depth of the Godhead, were only an unhappy anomaly, a fate to be redeemed or a great cosmic mistake to be corrected. This is indeed the case with Sankara, for whom the coming forth of God and the world from the primeval oneness of Brahman is the great "mistake" of Avidya. But it is not so with Eckhart. God is the wheel rolling out of itself, which, rolling on, not rolling back, reaches its first position again. That it rolls from inward, outward and inward again is of deep significance. God is, in Himself, tremendous life movement. Out of undifferentiated unity He enters into the multiplicity of personal life and persons, in whom the world and therewith the multiplicity of the world is contained. Out of this He returns, back into the eternal original unity. "The river flows into itself." But it is not an error to be corrected in Him, that He is eternally going out from and entering "into" Himself; it is a fact that has meaning and value—as the expression of life manifesting its potentiality and fullness. The issuing forth becomes itself the goal again of that process enriched by the course of its circuit.

> Indeed, God Himself does not rest there where He is merely the first beginning of being. Rather: He rests there where He is the end and the goal of all being. Not that being comes to nought there; rather it becomes perfected there to its highest perfection.

Let us examine this more closely. We say:

2. This God is in Himself a living *process,* not a static Being. We may here use the word "process" but only for want of a better, for it has nothing of the nature of any ordinary process. A process is a natural event, but this is no event; it is activity, mighty self-positing, a procreation not under the compulsion of laws or blind impulse but in the creative power and freedom of sublime wonder. The terms used by Eckhart to describe it are borrowed from tradition, from the speculation as to Persons in the doctrine of the Trinity, from the current distinctions between persona, substantia and natura, between deitas and deus, which were all familiar. But what an amazing divine drama he fashions from these things! This dross of Scholasticism glows fantastic,

Gothic, marvelous, when his wand touches it. Did ever a schoolman, in spite of identity of terms build from these formulas such
a divina comedia? All these expressions about God are abstruse
with the abstruseness of Scholasticism, when considered as
dogma and particularly if any attempt is made to string them together into a coherent system. But they are extraordinarily powerful taken not as pronouncements of a schoolman but as oracles
hurled into an audience of amazed hearers. And even today, they
awaken premonition and find an echo within the heart, where
there is little or no understanding of Scholastic terms, but where
there is a personal sensitiveness to the intuition of the Master.
The transcendent which is sensed here is dynamic and vital! Even
in his Latin writings, which are much quieter than his sermons
and tractates, Eckhart can say of this divine Being:

> Sum qui sum. Hic notandum est, quod repetitio (quod bis ait
> sum) indicat ipsius esse[3] in se ipsum et super se ipsum conver-
> sionem et in se ipso mansionem et fixationem (The flow and still-
> ness). Adhuc etiam quandam bullitionem sive perfusionem sui in
> se, fervens et in se ipso se ipsum liquescens et bulliens (a god
> boiling within with life!) lux in luce se totum se toto penetrans.
> Propter hoc John 1. dicitur: in ipso erat *vita*. Vita enim quandam
> dicit exscaturationem, qua res in se ipsa intumescens se profundit
> primo in se toto quodlibet sui in quolibet sui, antequam se effun-
> dit et ebullit extra.[4]

Or:

> That must be a vigorous life in which dead things revive, in
> which even death itself is changed to life. To God naught dies:
> all things are living in Him. (Evans 207, cf. also the whole sec-
> tion LXXXII. pp. 205-207)

---

[3] Esse is here used in the genitive case.
[4] "I am that I am." Here it must be noted that the repetition (he says twice "I
am") indicates a turning of Being itself in itself and above itself and yet a remaining and being fixed in itself. Yet it indicates also such a boiling up and
pouring out of itself in itself, scalding and melting and bubbling itself within itself, light penetrating light, itself whole penetrating the whole self. On this account John 1 says: "In Him there was life." For life is as it were a gushing up,
a thing welling up in itself, pouring any part of itself into any other part, before
it runs forth and bubbles over without.

Or:

> It is like a horse turned loose in a lush meadow giving vent to
> his horse nature by galloping full-tilt about the field: he enjoys it
> and it is his nature. And just in the same way God's joy and satis-
> faction in His likes finds vent in his pouring out his entire nature
> and His being into this likeness. (Evans 240)

3. Being is God, says Eckhart. And God gives being. That
sounds an abstraction, but it is obvious that for Eckhart this Being comes within the framework of the ancient biblical conceptions, chajjim, ζωη (Zoe), vita, vivificatio, Life and Life-giving,
and that it receives its special vitality from these conceptions. All
that is characteristic of Eckhart's "Being" is also characteristic
of the biblical ζωη (Zoe); the double meaning, the sense of salvation, the participatio realis, the mystical aspect. Life in the usual
sense of the term is the common predicate of the living creature;
it is the creature's created possession. But the creature does not
have *"the Life."* What the creature has and is in itself, as Eckhart would say, is not the true Life; it is rather basar, flesh,—
death and impotence. Only the "living" God has "the Life,"
and He is that Life Himself. This Life is salvation, Light and
Truth, ruach or pneuma, and He imparts it through His own
spirit. To have part in life and spirit is somehow to share in the
divine. That is the incontrovertible meaning of all the scripture
teaching about the spirit, and of the confession: credo in spiritum
sanctum, dominum, vivificantem. When Eckhart goes back beyond Aquinas' half doctrine of participation to the old Platonic
meaning, and teaches a real participation in Being, he is only following the example of Peter Lombard and of Paul, according to
whom the newly bestowed life of the spirit is the very spirit and
life of God Himself. In biblical terms—the imparting of "being"
is nothing less than the imparting of divine life.

4. This Being is in truth the eternal "vivere," hence its glowing vitality, its stir and movement:

> In him will God rejoice, yea He will rejoice through and
> through: for then there is nothing in His depth which is not stirred
> by joy.

Or:

> In this power God glows and burns without ceasing with all His
> riches, all His sweetness, all His joy.

Hence also especially its character as action and activity:

> He loves for its own sake. That is, He loves for the sake of loving, and creates for the sake of creating. Therefore He loves and creates without ceasing. Work is His nature, His being, His life, His happiness.

This is also revealed in the man who has become "Life," "Being," God." Such an one becomes "essential," and for Eckhart that is more than mere reality. It means, what it does not and cannot mean for Sankara, because he does not know the "living one," that a man becomes actually real as one who *acts and works*.

The goal for Sankara is the stilling of all karmani, all works, all activity of will: it is quietism, tyaga, a surrender of the will and of doing, an abandonment of good as of evil works, for both bind man to the world of wandering. The real Being does not work. It would be possible to find even in Eckhart the most astonishingly parallel passages and to make him also into a quietist, and we ourselves have done it above. It would then also be possible to find counter-passages, which show him to be the most zealous actualist. He could be drawn in this way into the most hopeless contradictions, but there would be no realization of the profound unity of his fundamental intuition. In some ways, this intuition reminds one of the paradoxical Mahayana doctrine: "Nirvana is samsara." Eckhart's position is neither mystical quietism nor secular activity, but an identity of the deepest unity and the most vivid multiplicity, and therefore of the most profound quiet and the most vital motion. It is therefore both a complete inward composure and a most powerful actualization and exercise of the will. These terms are well advised: they describe a chain of three links hanging together in a strictly logical order.

Both masters seek and behold unity and the Eternal One in contrast to multiplicity, but with this difference: the relationship of the One to the many is for Sankara one of strict exclusion, but for Eckhart one of the most live polarity. Sankara—in his para vidya—is a strict monist, but not like Eckhart, a philosopher of identity, as regards the One and the many.

(a) First, Eckhart establishes a polar identity between rest and motion within the Godhead itself: the eternally resting Godhead is also the wheel rolling out of itself; it is stillness and flux at the same time. The modeless, void Godhead, one and the same, in whom there was never differentiation, is also Father, Son and Holy Spirit. "One and the same," which, as the eternally resting unity without any wherefore is still and without activity, also gives Being and life, acting unceasingly:

> For this divine ground is a unified stillness, immovable in itself. Yet from this immobility all things are moved and all receive life, which lives above the senses, drawn into itself.

The one aspect is as necessary for Eckhart as the other. This diastole of the original One in the multiplicity of its elements, and the systole of its manifoldness back into the eternal resting unity, is the eternal life-process of the Godhead.

> When he begat all creatures, He was begetting me; I flowed out with all creatures while remaining within Him. It is like the word which I am now saying: it springs up within me as an idea, then I pause in the idea, and thirdly I speak it out, and all of you receive it; but nevertheless, it is in me all the while. So am I abiding in Him (although I went out from Him). (Evans 221)

The going forth is itself a remaining within:

> The more God is in all things, the more He is outside them. The more He is within, the more without.

But further still, outgoing is incoming:

> In principio signifies, in the beginning of all things. It also means the end of all things, since the first beginning is because of the last end. I trow that God Himself is not at rest as being the first beginning: He is at rest where He is the goal and abode of all being.

This is no mere lila, no playing of the Godhead, as in India, but the divine revolving within itself, in which it displays the richness of its own inner life. The resting unity is the raison d'etre of the moving multiplicity, and it is by reason of the oneness of these two that the Godhead is dives per se.

(b) Secondly, the same is true of the relation between God and the world. The creation and the gift of Being to the creature is likewise no mere disturbance of the eternal unity, no mere fateful mistake. Rather, creation and creature are as necessary for God, as God for the creature. Only in the being of the creature does God himself come to His own goal and purpose. That is to say, only as the eternal and ceaselessly creating God, is He God. For only thus is He a "living" God. This is the Christian God, who is not like the God of the ancient world sufficient unto Himself, blessed in Himself.

(c) Eckhart's conception of God is thoroughly voluntarist. His Esse is will as an eternally active and dynamic principle in contrast to a rigid and static Being. This is reflected in the image of the divine, in the soul and its attitude toward the world. In fact, Eckhart is here first and foremost, the teacher of a magnificent quietism. The soul is to leave all objects, resolve itself from all attachment, lose all that is creaturely, enter into unity out of multiplicity, into stillness out of all busyness, into gatheredness out of all unrest, and is to stand again in the first silence and void of the eternal Godhead. It is to be without differentiation, in the eternal Sabbath of its unmoved, united, gathered God-nature, which it had before all time, as it was "in principio," in ratione ydeali. It is to be as it was even before this, when it was yet enclosed within the still and void Godhead without difference or distinction. But at the moment when the soul passes from all works into complete devotion and composure, it achieves the real "inward work": the one, whole, true, undivided and indivisible. Where this work is performed in the ground and the stillness of the soul, above space and time, it breaks forth in temporal works, without ceasing, "without wherefore," without compulsion, without seeking for reward, without secondary purpose, in the free-outpouring of a new and truly liberated will; and it is as incapable of resting as is the creating God. Thus Eckhart becomes the panegyrist of the strong and active will, and the powerful act—of a voluntarism which alone truly deserves this name. To speak in a paradox: his quietism *is* active creativity. That is why this mystic upsets all ordinary mystical practice: not the quiet, contemplative Mary but the active Martha is his ideal. For Martha with her never-wearied doing and acting proves that she has already found what Mary still desires and seeks: the deep unmoved repose at the center, in unshakable unity and security. It is this inward calm which lying below the play of "forces," gives them power and is the ground for ceaseless living activity.

Here also unity is itself the manifold, repose the eternal mobility, the systole the diastole, the Sabbath the day of labor, the outgoing is the incoming, the departure the return, and the most inward, most mysterious gatheredness of soul is the mighty tension of the will in concentrated force. That is what the following extract means.

> Not as if a man should escape from or be unfaithful to his inward being, but rather he should work in it and from it, so that his inner self breaks forth in activity and the activity is drawn into his inwardness.

And on the other hand:

> Thou shalt have a flaming spirit bathed in a void and silent.

Or:

> Let us use a simile: the door has a hinge on which it moves. I liken the door to the outward and the hinge to the inward man. When the door opens and shuts it moves to and fro, but the hinge remains unmoved in its place and is not affected by the movement.

The distance between Eckhart's conception and that of the Indian can be measured by the following words:

> What thou willest powerfully and with thy whole will, that thou hast already, and neither God nor creature can rob thee of it, if thy will is whole and thou willest for God's sake and standest in His presence. Therefore: let it not be "I would"—because that is still in the future—but "I will that it be so here and now." Verily with my will I can do all things.

5. No wonder therefore, that "life" is a favorite expression and a thing beloved of Meister Eckhart, and that he takes from it his comparisons and metaphors. It is from this love of life that he derives his expression "the budding and blossoming" of God in the ground of the soul. It is from life that he gets his "without wherefore," when he wants to visualize what a purpose is in itself, or what the free flow of mood, will and spontaneous activity is in contrast to reflection, consideration, and the reckoning of reward or of success. It is from this source that he finds what is the "work of unity" in distinction from single "bona opera" ac-

cording to outward rules and formal regulations and in multiplicity and externalization.

6. This extremely vital and spiritual conception of God, soul and creature, defies the impeding gown of the schoolman, and, continually rending it, exposes itself in the wonderful poetry of his thought and language. His speech glows and sparkles in living colours. He is still the poet even when he is forging Scholastic terms. But at the same time, he who says "life" expresses something suprarational, and particularly so when he uses the word in the biblical sense. In the conception of the "living" God, as we have shown elsewhere, the suprarational elements of the idea of God are included and symbolized. These elements are especially revealed in the language and style of Eckhart, which may appear to us sometimes ecstatic or eccentric. But he knows that he has that to say, which must bewilder and baffle the uninitiated. He does it assiduously seeking the very boldest expressions. He tells his listeners what they "have never yet heard."

> Now mark, now will I speak what I never have spoken.
> Apprehend me, I beseech you by the eternal truth and by the ever valid truth, and by my soul. For now I say a thing I never said before. (Evans 142)

He attempts ever yet more daring paradoxes, and loves to do so where the subject could be stated simply in current phrases or in ordinary terms without danger of misunderstanding, or accusation of heresy and blasphemy. While Sankara and his school try rather to rationalize the paradoxes of mystical language and even on occasion reduce them to the trivial, thereby transforming the original mystery-filled figures of the Upanishads into abstractions, Eckhart on the contrary excites his listeners by unheard of expressions, and makes the conventional terminology of scholasticism pulsate again with the old mystical meaning. He causes ideas derived from mysticism, but long tamed and reduced to respectable mediocre conceptions, to flame anew with their ancient color and depth.

7. These peculiar traits of Eckhart which we have gathered together are nowhere better exemplified than in his sermon on "the Soul's Rage" (Evans 389), which Büttner calls a "capriccio." In fact the preacher, through the urge and uprush of his emo-

tions, here falls too much into the style of the artist or the poet. His pulsating vitality breaks forth all too strongly. Boldness almost becomes presumption, and paradox, rashness.

But the fact that this could happen lies in the inspiration of his inward experience. How remote this inspiration is from Sankara's, how deeply different one mysticism is from the other, can be easily seen in this treatise. It would have been absolutely impossible both in spirit and in form for the Indian master.

This poem, a flight of most daring ecstasy, arises from the demand for holiness. (Later that will be significant for the understanding of the inmost experience of his mysticism.) It is the will of God that thou shouldst be holy, says St. Paul. Now holiness is to know God and the self aright, then to love all things only in God, and finally to offer the self to God, as a good and fitting tool with which the great craftsman may do his work. For:

> As many as are led by the spirit of God, they are the sons of God.

But that is not sufficient for the soul, for this means that it still falls short of the highest. The soul desires not to be holy, but to be Holiness, that is, to be God! In this longing the soul becomes a raging soul:

> The soul becomes furious. Her face is lit with passion, red with rage for the arrears withheld from her in God, because she is not all that God is by nature, because she has not all that God has by nature. (Evans 389)

A friend wishes to possess his friend as his own and all that he possesses, say the masters, and thus the soul

> proclaims her rage so boundless, she cannot be appeased by Him.

She complains of the injustice done her by the creator and reproaches Him: were she the creator and He the soul, she would willingly give up all her glory and for His sake become the creature, that He might become God. She rages still and would in very wrath give up her own being, since it is only a gift of God and not God's own self:

> For she had rather be nothing than have or take anything that only *belongs* to Him.

She desires that God should not even *remember* her, because upon that rests her true salvation:

> For then, as she well knows, she has not first disappeared from His consciousness. And that is her blessedness.

Thus the soul wishes she might be God Himself and that there might be neither herself nor any creature. But, it occurs to her that then God would not *love!* Were the creature to disappear love would be torn from His heart. So finally in her greatest rage she wishes to be not "God" but simply pure "being" in which God and the self together disappear.

And thus stripped of her separate being, when God Himself is her being, she conceives God with God. Then she hears without sound and sees without light. Her heart becomes bottomless, her soul senseless,[5] her mind formless, and her nature essenceless.[6] Transcending her own rational powers she comes to the "dark" power of the Father where all rational distinctions (and predicates) end.

> Without sound, for it is an inward immediate perception in pure feeling: without light, for it is an apprehension, beyond determination and opposites, of the "nothing" (not this, not that); without ground for every attempt to love sinks endlessly away before the overwhelming miracle; without form, for the spirit then is informed by that form which has neither form nor figure, by God himself. It is without essence, for her separate essence so completely disappears, that there is nothing left but one single "is." This "is" is the Oneness which is Being itself—her own and that of all things.

Then says the soul, there is no longer a God for me. And I am no longer soul to anyone. True, the bride in the Song of Songs says: "He is mine and I am his." She should rather have said: He is no longer there for me nor I for him. For God is only there for Himself since He alone is in all. Therefore, in another passage, the bride cries: "Depart from me, beloved." That means: everything which can be represented to me is not God. So I flee from God for God's sake.

---

[5] Stripped of the senses.
[6] Without a Quidditas specialis.

Thus the soul becomes the unchanging—more unchanging than that nothingness itself from which she was once created, through union with the eternal unchanging God (Godhead) Who as such was never concerned with any work. (All work concerns God only in the multiplicity of the three persons, not God in His Oneness.)

With a magnificent finale swelling like a Bach Amen, the tractate ends:

> The soul from knowing becomes not-knowing, from willing will-less, from enlightenment dark. Knew she still ought of herself, she would feel it as an imperfection! The inconceivable Being itself she bears in herself beyond all knowledge—and this through grace as the Father through His own nature. She steals out of herself and so enters into the pure Being, and there concerns herself with all things as little as when she went out from God. The "I" is reduced there to utter nought and nothing is left there but God. Yes, even God she outshines here as the sun outshines the moon, and with God's own all-penetrativeness she streams into the eternal Godhead, where in an eternal stream God is flowing into God.

Truly, this soul that seeks God with rage is neither Indian nor Plotinian. It is Gothic.

2

Exalted Feeling and Humility as Two Poles of Experience

1. It is true that such a capriccio would be impossible on the basis of Sankara's mysticism. Yet there is a trait in the character of Eckhart which—distinguishing him from the Christianity of the ordinary or "simple" Christian faith—is common both to him and to Sankara. Not in the creature, not in gifts can the mystic find rest. Nothing satisfies his longing for salvation save "God Himself." "Not only united with Him but absolutely One"; that is the meaning of the capriccio and of the mystical rapture of Eckhart. Therein his experience agrees with that of Sankara. To have or rather to be the one, undivided, eternal, imperishable Brahman, which is wholly Being, wholly Spirit, utter Joy, that alone, and that entirely—this is also the thirst and pride of the Indian seeker after salvation. There can be no doubt that this is also its meaning for Eckhart and that it differs fundamentally and essentially from the simpler Christian conception of salvation, to which it must always seem an extravagance, a Titanic pride, and a transgression of the impossible limitations of the creature—a "Faustian urge," as we call it today. It is indeed closely related to the impulse which expresses itself in the Gothic cathedral, with its vaulted roofs and towers, and its restless upward striving into greater and greater heights. We have already indicated that Eckhart's experience is akin to this urge which finds its expression in Gothic architecture when we described him as the first great Gothic figure.

181

2. But whether this is in truth a "Faustian urge," Titanic pride, an attempt to reach the superman, we dare not say. We should need the soul and the very experience of Eckhart himself to be able to express an opinion. Eckhart would probably have denied such an urge and would certainly have remonstrated against the accusation of Titanic pride, for—this is the curious fact—no man was ever more humble than he! "See to it that God becomes great to you," he said. Humility is to him the cardinal virtue, the beginning and end of all virtue; and this is not a concession to a lower standpoint; but humility as an ideal and as an unmediated attitude of soul is most intimately connected with his mystical experience itself, and is indeed prompted by it. The humility which he has as a simple Christian does not disappear in the sphere of his mystical experience, but is increased and gains an emphasis and a dignity which of itself has something mystical about it. His type of mysticism demands humility.

This distinguishes him from Sankara. Eckhart's mysticism is to a large extent, although not exclusively, the mysticism of numinous majesty, as I have termed it elsewhere;[1] it grows out of the experience of the overwhelming and annihilating divine Majesty, and ends with the absolute nought and nullity of the creature. But above all, there is the same paradoxical relationship between humility on the one side, and being God Himself on the other, as there is between multiplicity and unity, voluntarism and quietism, life in the multiplicity of works and rest in the One. For Sankara these opposites are exclusive. For Eckhart the one demands the other. And it is the same with rapture and humility.

These relations we have described as polar, but even that is not quite adequate. We have to proceed to the paradox: *Because* one, *therefore* many, because eternal rest in God, therefore movement, because complete non-action, therefore most vigorous will. Thus also: because one with God, and God with God before time was, *therefore* nothing, dust, humility.

This relationship is apparent in the following passage:

> Ours to contain all things in the same way as the eternal wisdom has eternally contained them. Ours to know all and deify our-

[1] R. Otto: *The Idea of the Holy,* p. 23.

selves with all. Ours to be God by grace as God is God by nature; but ours also to resign all that to God and to be as poor as when we were not. (Evans, 381-2)

Here, Eckhart sets the eternal modeless Godhead itself before us as an example:

> Godhead *gave all things up* to God: it is as poor, as naked, and as empty as though it were not; it has not, wills not, wants not, works not, gets not. ... It is God who has the treasure and the bride in Him, the Godhead is as void as though it were not.

These are certainly not relationships conceived by the power of logic; even Eckhart has to express them paradoxically. But undoubtedly, to his vision they were no paradoxes, but the most obvious necessities. Later we shall come across these relations again when he at last reveals his final and deepest meaning: namely, in his doctrine of grace.

3

The Gothic Man

1. We have said that Eckhart's teaching increases rather than decreases the Christian attitude of humility toward God. But it is equally certain that there are also religious elements and emotions in his mysticism analogous to Sankara, wherein he shatters any such definition of religion as Schleiermacher's, which would simply identify religion with feelings of absolute dependence. It contains powerful numinous feelings of self, emotions of the "homo nobilis." And in this connection it is particularly true, as we have remarked before, that Eckhart is capable of bringing back into the old and worn-out formulas of the schools their original vitality, so that they glow once more with their primitive mystical coloring. The expressions as such which Eckhart uses, even in relation to his "homo nobilis," can all be found in contemporary writings, and proved to be orthodox Scholasticism. His "homo nobilis" is the "homo sub ratione ydeali," the idea of man; and the fact that these and all ideas are eternal and eternally in God, one with the eternal Word, and thus one with God Himself, and that through them the world is and was created—is to be found in Thomas Aquinas also. So it would seem quite innocuous even without a covering phrase to say that man, viz. the "real man," as the idea with other ideas in the eternal Word, was a principle of creation. But this is exactly what is peculiar to Eckhart, that a phrase which had become fossilized in an attenuated Platonic doctrine, suddenly flames up with its old mystic fire. The doctrine of participation according to which the individual

object is a participator in the idea, is revitalized, and a mere metaphysical relic becomes for him the immediate impulse to fresh and powerful thought and experience, which no Thomas Aquinas could have conceived. We might express it thus: "Man, even I, stood with God before time was, before the world was; I was contained in the eternal Godhead before it was God. With man, even with me, God created and God is eternally creating. In me He first became God. And if I were not, then He would be as little God as I am I." Here we have the vitality that, later tamed and castrated, once pulsed even behind the old ideas and formulas of the schools, and then the melody rings out thus:

> Therefore I pray God that He make me quit of God. For "modeless Being" is exalted above God and all that has distinctions. In it (in modeless Being) I was myself, I willed myself, and knew myself as Him, who made this man. Therefore I am the cause of my own self according to my eternal and to my temporal nature. And hence was I born, and can never die because of the manner of my birth, which is eternal. Through my (eternal) birth I have been eternally, am now, and shall remain for ever. That which I am in time will die and become nothing, for that is ephemeral and must therefore pass away with time. But in my (eternal) birth all things were born. I was the cause of my own self and of all things. If I had not so willed neither I nor all things had been. Were I not, neither would God be...

2. That is indeed numinous rapture. At the same time it is subtly different from that of Sankara. This difference moreover is connected with what we have already described as the Gothic element in Eckhart's conception of God in contrast to Sankara's static Indian conception of Brahman. This distinction between the Gods occurs again in the emotions with which they are sought, striven after, experienced. For Sankara when the soul (atman) has "come home" to the eternal Being (Atman) it is there, it has arrived (apta), it is at rest and fully content (santa). But Eckhart is, in truth, never "there," never in a final static rest:

> When the soul crosses over, then she sinks down and down in the abyss of the Godhead nor ever finds a footing. (Evans 355)

Just as the slender columns and responds of the Gothic building rise and climb and do not finish in the repose of a semicircle, but by an urge after the infinite, thrust up in the incompleteness of the pointed arch, so Eckhart demands "the climbing spirit." And this spirit is of groundless depths and aspires to a goal most limitless:

> For though she sink all sinking in the oneness of divinity she never touches bottom. For it is of the very essence of the soul that she is powerless to plumb the depths of her creator. And here one cannot speak about the soul any more, for she has lost her name yonder in the oneness of divine essence. There she is no more called soul: she is called immeasurable being. (Evans 282)

He further describes this spirit striving upwards:

> Even so the mind, unsatisfied with this infernal light, will press through the firmament and press through the heavens to find the breath that spins them. Yet this does not satisfy it. It must press farther into the vortex, into the primal region where the breath has its source. Such a mind knows no time nor number: number does not exist apart from the malady of time. Other root, the mind has none save in eternity. It must surpass all number and break through all multiplicity. Then it will be itself broken through by God, but just as God breaks through me, so I again break through Him. God leads this spirit into the Wilderness and into the oneness of its own self, where He is a sheer one and welling up in Himself. This mind has no longer a Why. . . . This mind is in unity and freedom. (Evans 180)

Even to stand in the wilderness of "welling" unity and freedom is not to stand at the end of experience. The soul must go "always further" (semper ultra):

> (Already) in her first breaking through (into eternity) she lays hold of God, no longer as being good nor yet as truth: she delves deeper and goes on searching and grasps Him in His unification (simplification), and in His solitude (simplicitas); she finds Him in His desert and in His actual ground. But being still unsatisfied, she "goes further" in quest of what it is that is in His Godhead, of the special property of His peculiar nature. (Evans 209)

> You see then that as you "go further" to the source, wonder after wonder is wrought with the soul. (Evans 217)

The surpassing good, always above that which is already grasped, must remain eternally in its final depth beyond her reach—the alluring abyss in which, lost to herself, she eternally sinks. Further and ever further, semper ultra, climbs the way. The ''oneness'' to which the spirit strives is never closed as a boundary, it is continually opening afresh above her. It is like a vault with an ever-rising roof:

> What is the last end? It is the mystery of the darkness of the eternal Godhead which is unknown and never shall be known. Therein God abides to Himself unknown. (Evans 224)

Such words are by no means a complaint over the unachievable goal, but indicate the tempting ''immer fürbatz,'' the ''semper plus ultra'' for the climbing spirit of a Gothic soul, striving after an ''end,'' which is yet never an end.

4

The Ethical Content. Salvation as Objective Value

1. In spite of what we said in our last chapter, Eckhart's mysticism is not to be cut off from the natural foundation of his Christian religion. Indeed it bears the special hue of his Christianity and is permeated by it. That was evident in the "vitality" of his mysticism, and is still more obvious in another element, which further distinguishes him decisively from his Indian rival.

Both masters, we may say, are teachers of salvation; both seek a salvation that is transcendental. But salvation has two distinguishable factors within it, and according as to which of them is emphasized the emotional content of salvation is determined. The same holds true of the mystical emotional content. Whatever its content may be, in each case salvation is a peculiar value which is sought and striven after for its own sake. But a thing can be valuable in a double sense; on the one hand subjectively, that is, as it has value for me, in relation to me, something which causes me pleasure, joy, rapture; or, on the other, it may be valuable in an entirely different, in an objective sense. That is, it has value in itself, quite apart from whether any man is rejoiced or pained by it. A good deed for example, has its "value" whether or not anyone rejoices over it. It has an "objective" value. This is true also of the "salvation of the soul" in religion. Salvation has its subjective value, a ground for rejoicing, but he who seeks the salvation of his soul, in the Christian sense, is not in the first instance searching after something to make him happy, but to

188

make him "holy," that is, for something which is of utmost importance quite apart from his happiness or unhappiness. It should be salvation from objective lack of value, from sin, guilt, damnation, into "the righteousness acceptable unto God," into holiness and purity, the ideal of his own Being at its very highest. It is important to realize that all religious salvation includes both elements, that of a subjective and that of an objective value, but at the same time to understand how absolutely different the search after salvation will be, according as to which of these two polar extremes is emphasized and given the prior place—the subjective over the objective, or the objective over the subjective. That is, in other words, whether I ask first of all, "How can I win perpetual happiness?" or, "How can I become righteous in the eyes of God?" There is here at once a palpable difference between Eckhart's mysticism and that of Sankara, and of Indian mysticism generally. Sankara is so deeply interested in the subjective pole of salvation, that the other is scarcely noticed by him. The whole construction of his doctrine of salvation, and of the Indian teaching of salvation, is based upon the subjective element, and in speculative systems as well as in popular preaching the matter is thus subjectively presented. It is superfluous to amass examples here. A single example must satisfy us for countless others—a very early one, which also determines the direction of all further pronouncements on this subject in India.

2. In the fourteenth section of the sixteenth chapter of the Chhandogya-Upanishad, there is told most forcefully the story of a man, lost in the misery of the world, yet longing to return "home" to eternal salvation. Sankara in his commentary on the text and his interpretation of it gives a further exposition as follows:

> It is, my beloved, as with the man from the Gandhara-land. A robber fell upon a man from Gandhara, dragged him away from his own people, and left him with bandaged eyes and fettered hands alone in a desolate wood, devoid of human life. There, ignorant of the points of the compass, he calls East and West, North and South: "A robber has bound my eyes, snatched me away from the Gandharenes and left me here alone." As he calls a sympathetic passer-by comes along, releases his bonds and says to him: "In this direction toward the North the Gandharenes live. Follow this route."

So he asks his way from village to village. And enabled by the instructions of those he questions to choose the right way to the next village, he comes home at last to the people of Gandhara, because he is sensible, whilst an unintelligent person, or one who desires to go to another village than the right one, misses the way.

Now, it is with the soul, like the individual who is described in this parable of the man from the Gandharenes, amongst whom he desires to dwell, whose eyes are bandaged by robbers, and so rendered incapable of distinguishing anything, who is confused as to the points of the compass, dragged away into a wood full of tigers, highwaymen and other evils, plagued by hunger and thirst, and who, standing there with a great longing for freedom from his bonds, tortured by suffering, calls for help; then freed by a sympathetic human being and returning to his own people obtains a joyful salvation.

Thus it is also with man (in Samsara) caught away from Being itself, from the World Atman, by the robbers "Merit, Demerit," and so on and ensnared in this body composed of the earthly elements of fire, water and food, which is infected with the sources of evil—with wind, gall, phlegm, blood, fat, flesh, bones, marrow, seed, worms, excrement and which is subject to such pairs of opposites as heat and cold, etc. At the same time his eyes are bound with the kerchief of illusion and he is fettered in the coils of lust after wife, son, friend, cattle, relations and many other visible and invisible objects of desire. "I am the son of NN. So and so are my relations. Happy am I, unhappy am I, a fool, a wise man am I, I am pious, I have relations, I am born, I die, I am old, I am a villain. My son is dead, my money lost, Ah woe is me, all is over. How shall I live, where is there a way of escape for me, where is my salvation?"

(Thus is he confused and blinded and) thus, he cries, caught in a hundredfold and monstrous net. Until in one way or another he meets one who—conscious of true being, of the Brahman-Atman, free from bondage and truly blessed—is also by reason of his abundant merit (in former births) full of deepest sympathy. He teaches the wanderer the way to knowledge, and the failure of worldly things and aims. Thereby he is freed from dependence on the things of the world. And he recognises immediately: thou art (according to thy true being) no wanderer (in Samsara). Limitations like desire cannot reach thee. Rather, what Being itself is, that art thou! So his eyes are freed from the bandage of illusion through Avidya, and he is like the man from Gandhara, reaching his own again, coming to the Atman full of joy and peace.

The text finishes:

To such an one the delay seems long (and weary) until—as he says—"Ultimately I shall be set free. Then I shall arrive."

This is a moving passage. The cold and abstract thinker Sankara here throws aside the mantle of the scholar. The heart that beats beneath his lifeless formulae throbs audibly and in a flow of living emotion the inner meaning of his whole speculative system breaks forth: a passionate search for salvation—for a good outside this miserable world—a home-sickness—a thirst for eternity.

3. But this desire has no trace of that thirst mentioned in Matthew 5:6:

Blessed are they that hunger and thirst after *righteousness,* for they shall be filled.

The evils which torment Sankara are the vexations of Samsara—wind, gall, slime, sickness, old age, endless rebirth, but not sin, unworthiness, unrighteousness. Yet these are the meaning of Eckhart's preaching and also of his mystical doctrine. True, Eckhart recognizes salvation also as of immeasurable subjective value, as the blessedness of being in God and with God, which only brings satisfaction if the seeker both has and is God's own bliss. This unquenchable thirst for blessedness is also one of the roots of his "blasphemous" teaching of the unity of the soul with God. "Not in creation, not in the gift," but only in the Creator Himself will this longing be satisfied and stilled. For Eckhart too, the creature, as it exists in itself, is an object of suffering. "Full of unrest and sorrow is the temporal." But right in the foreground of everything else, there is for him, something entirely different: namely, desire to win the "Esse" as *essential righteousness itself,* the absolute objective value in contrast to the worthlessness of the mere "creatura, sicut est in se." This objective element is so strongly emphasized by Eckhart, that it is unnecessary to multiply examples here:

The good man enters into all the qualities of goodness itself, which is God.
The righteous men take righteousness so earnestly that were God not righteous, they would not care a jot for Him.
If all the pain which is suffered on earth were bound up with righteousness, they would not care a brass button. So steadfastly do they cleave to God and to righteousness.

5

The Ethical Content. The Mystical Doctrine as a Doctrine of Justification

1. One might be tempted to take the whole of Eckhart's teaching as nothing more than a doctrine of justification interpreted mystically, a doctrine of justificatio impii, not achieved by the sacramental and miraculous offices of the church, but conceived as a transaction between the soul and God alone, and without mediation.

> Whoever understands God's ways shall always remember, that the faithful and gracious God has brought man out of a sinful into a godly life, and has made him from an enemy into a friend. *And that is more than creating a world,*

says Eckhart in the course of his simple preaching. But his boldest flights end always thus (which was also implied in his simpler utterances):

> May Thy boundless infinite Godhead fill my vile corrupt humanity.

Or:

> The righteous are like unto God, for God is righteousness. Therefore, whoever is in righteousness is in God and is himself God.

Or:

> Bonus homo inquantum bonus intrat omnem proprietatem bonitatis, quae Deus est in se ipso. (The good man, in so far as

192

he is good, enters into all the quality of goodness which God is in Himself.)

Or:

The soul now plunged in God and in divine nature, receives divine life and is of the order of God.

And what of his highest vision, that of the Godlikeness of the soul as Co-creator?

All that the good man does he does with the goodness in goodness: as God Father and God Son.

2. "The righteousness which is acceptable unto God," say the Scriptures. "The righteousness which is God Himself," says Eckhart. Both mean the same: the righteousness which is "greater than that of the Pharisees," as the New Testament has it, and which is higher and other than all civil righteousness, all that men call goodness or virtue: that which is essential, true, perfect, which cannot come from the creature, nor from works, nor from a created will, but as Luther says, "quae prospicit de coelo." This is the bond which joins Eckhart and Luther. For what Luther calls the righteousness which comes of faith, that is, the righteousness which is unattainable for all creatures, all flesh, all natural being, is God's own righteousness and can only flow from Him. This explains how Luther could love and publish the writings of the unknown Frankfurt mystic, the *Theologia Germanica,* which presents Eckhart's thought in a more diluted form; and why he was not offended by the supposedly pantheistic expressions of this theology, or that of Tauler, but on occasion used them himself.

In his commentary to the Epistle to the Romaus, Luther uses the words:

Sicut in naturalibus rebus quinque sunt gradus: non esse, fieri, esse, actio, passio, id est privatio, materia, forma, operatio, passio, secundum Aristotelem, ita et in spiritu. "Non esse," est res sine nomine et homo in peccatis. "Fieri" est justificatio, "Esse" est justitia. "Opus" est juste agere et vivere. "Pati" est perfici et consummari.

As there are five steps in natural things: not-being, becoming, being, acting, being passive, according to Aristotle, privation,

material, form, activity, passivity, so also in the spirit. Not-being
is the thing without name and is man in sin. To become is justification. To be is righteousness. "To work" is rightly to act and
to live. To be passive is to be perfected and consummated.

For Luther the categories of the doctrine of Being become here
merely repetitions of the doctrine of justification. But that is not
his invention, it was already an old theme and was taken for
granted at the time of Eckhart. We see therefore why Eckhart's
whole dealing with the categories and the passiones esse, which
is so strange to us, was familiar to his own age. They were often
accepted as a second dialect of the doctrine of justification and
were easily translated from the one to the other.

It remains for us to note that a mystical glamour touches
Luther's doctrine of justification also. It may indeed be said that
the terminology of the mystical teaching with regard to Being and
unity acquires in Luther's mind the meaning of the terms of justification by grace. The conferring of true Being, of unity with
God or Christ or the Word, unio substantialis (the union of substance) and substantialissima, to become "of one cake" with
Christ or God, that is nothing else than the outpouring of the
Holy Ghost—than to be revivified in the religious and ethical
sense, and to find consolation for the troubled conscience
through the word of the gracious promise. It is from this consolation that new motives are born in the heart, through which the
new and renewed life—the liberty of Christ—is constituted. True
as this is, it does not go far enough. For certainly Luther is not
referring to mere allegories, when he speaks of comfort through
the Word, and its effect on our emotional and volitional life, and
points the clear connection between comfort and experienced
love and an inner refreshening and strengthening of will. This
has for him the full majesty of the supernatural and the mystical,
and these experiences in their inmost aspect are for him a true
"bestowal of being," a sharing of the nature of the divine with
the creature. They are in all seriousness a unio substantialis and
the Spirit of God Himself in the hearts of men. So the Lutheran
idea of the "joyous exchange" between the soul and Christ (the
eternal righteousness of God) has something of that feeling of exaltation which we mentioned above as characteristic of Eckhart.
It is much more subdued, but can still be felt as the gladness of
the soul "to sit with Christ in equal possession."

3. The homo nobilis, the homo deo non unitus sed unus (the man who is not united to but one with God) is also for Eckhart in fact the homo justificatus (the man justified by faith). Approached from the standpoint of justification, the whole of his mysticism of being and suprabeing could be taken temporarily as merely a forma emphatice loquendi (a form of emphatic speech), which we might do all the more readily as Eckhart makes this claim himself in his apology when tried for heresy. It would mean that he uses his mystical expressions simply as a way of impressing upon the minds of his readers the truth of the doctrine of justication by daring words, striking pictures and unusual turns of speech. However, that would be to go too wide of the mark. He speaks indeed of "mystical things" and he means them. But he is right when he feels that justification, the new birth, the birth from God, the seed of God sown, the spikenard flowing from God, in short, the Pauline and Johannine teachings of justification, are in reality names for a mystical experience, inasmuch as all these terms imply a realistic possessing of God, a sharing of the self in the Zoe, or in the life of God. When we follow his earliest publications and his simpler writings, we are inclined to assume that it was this "realistic" view of the doctrine of justification with Paul and John, which gave the impetus to that experience which afterwards developed and was completed in his "mysticus intuitus." In any case, from the doctrine of justification, we can most readily understand how certain "Platonic" elements in speculation acquired a new importance for him. This is particularly true of his conception of participation, the Platonic "Methexis." In the Thomist system it had withered almost beyond recognition and was only carried along as an accepted part of the metaphysical dictionary. In Eckhart it regains its original meaning: a true participation in the eternal Idea, which is itself identical with the Eternal Reality and the nature of God, and is therefore a real participation in God Himself. In his doctrine of participation Eckhart does not even notice his own obvious departure from the Thomist theory. At the same time it is significant, that he develops his understanding of participation most clearly and decisively in regard to the idea of justitia and bonitas.

4. What we have said above applies particularly to that part of Eckhart's teaching which is most strongly colored with mysti-

cism: the teaching of the inborn God, the Eternal Word in the ground of the soul. Let us try to understand what simple facts of justification are thus indicated.

God speaks His Eternal Word from eternity. He speaks in a twofold way which is yet only one from the standpoint of God. He speaks it eternally in Himself, thereby He speaks it eternally in the soul. He begets His Son from everlasting within Himself and thus begets Him in us, and so begets us as His Eternal Son. But what is the Eternal Word or the Son when it is spoken into the ground of the soul? It is there what it is in God and for God Himself: God's very thought of Himself, i.e. God's knowledge of Himself which becomes the soul's through participation in the World. To have the Word in one's self is to have part in God's own knowledge and in that very knowledge of God, by which God knows Himself. This means further—to have the knowledge of God not as a mere accident, not as an empirical psychological fact, not in isolated concrete acts of perception, not as an idea or a theory, but as the very essence and super-empirical foundation of the soul itself. In Eckhart's expression: the soul does not *have* the Son, she *is* the Son. She does not *have* knowledge of God, but *is* fundamentally God's knowledge of Himself. What rises in us as a "thought" or a "conception" of God, is merely an outward function of the "faculties," not the essence of the matter. And so, says Eckhart, "God Himself knows and loves Himself in us."

This profound sentence may be gravely misunderstood, and then it becomes "Pantheism." For instance it may be interpreted as has been done by Eduard von Hartmann, according to whom God first comes to self-consciousness in human consciousness— which is for Eckhart sheer folly! For God eternally conceives His Son, His self-thought, in Himself. The "Godhead" is eternally determining itself as "God," who as the Father speaks the Word in Himself.[1] But God also eternally gives the soul all that He is and has. The soul participates in His Being, and thus she has being. She shares in His knowledge, and her knowledge is not

---

[1] "God the Father has perfect insight into Himself, profound and thorough knowledge of Himself, by means of Himself, not by means of any image. And thus God the Father gives Birth to His Son." (Evans 5)

therefore any deed or discovery of her own—this is the heart of the matter; but she only knows at all in so far as eternal Being, and consequently the eternal self-knowledge of God, is in her.[2]

5. As God speaks His Word eternally in the soul, so the soul gives birth to the Son again in the Father. This extraordinary pronouncement also has its very simple basis. It means the new obedience of the soul due to the experience of justification. The Son is essential righteousness, and the soul gives birth to the Son when the life of the homo justificatus bears fruit in good and perfect works of righteousness, in deed, temper, obedience, love and all virtue, which are then the "Son" reborn. "From every virtue of the just, God is born."

As a parallel to this rebirth of the Son in the Father, Eckhart, quite undisturbed by inconsistency or confusion of metaphor, expresses the further thought, that just as the Father in conjunction with the Son causes the spirit to go forth, so man having become the Son, in conjunction with the Father breathes the Spirit. These statements swing to and fro between metaphor and realism so that we must be careful not to take them only for the former.[3] That would certainly be a mistake, for undoubtedly Eckhart was trying to express the most real and mysterious relationship whose raritas astounded and excited him. But it would be still worse to divorce mysticism here from its ground of simple original Christian faith and thought, and to fail to understand that it is a mysticism colored by the Christian teaching of justification and permeated through and through by the influences of its origin, by Christian conceptions, without which it would be an almost empty contraption.

---

[2] Luther says precisely the same: "Solus Deus novit, et ci, qui oculis Dei vident, id est qui spiritum habent." ("God alone knows and they who see with the eyes of God, i.e. who have His spirit.")

[3] Compare such passages as the following:

"Conceptio enim verbi (a favorite word!) quae fit amore adhaerente et inhaerente rei, quam audimus aut cogitamus, aut cognoscimus, est ipsa proles mentis sive verbum natum."

"Adhaerens Deo concipit Deum, concipit bonum, florescit et in ipso flore fructus conceptionis est et perfectas est."

6

The Ethical Content. Mysticism As Experience of Grace

1. The preceding chapter brings us to the consideration of mysticism as experience of grace. Eckhart's peculiar teaching of the "deified man," the man of like being with God, eternally with God, creating with Him the world and all things, who is in truth "homo nobilis," embraces an extreme doctrine of grace:

> It is His, not thine at all, what is thus wrought by God, take thou as His and not thine own. (Evans 18)

> To be installed in God, this is not hard, seeing that God Himself must be working in us; for it is Godly work, man may acquiesce and make no resistance; he may be passive while allowing God to act in him.

True, in this teaching of Eckhart there is an occasional note of synergism, but that is not the meaning of his speculation. The complete annihilation of the creature, which in itself and of its own nature is absolutely nothing, is in line, as Luther found in Tauler and in the *Theologia Germanica,* with Luther's own teaching of the justitia passiva, sine omnibus propriis viribus, meritis aut operibus (passive justice without any strength, merit or works of its own), and had necessarily to end in this conception. That the man who is homo nobilis, not only united but one with God and this from all eternity and in the deepest ground of the silent Godhead, has yet absolute need of saving grace, without which he sinks into the abyss of hell, there to burn into the nothingness of the creature—this is so strange to our modern conception that we can well understand how people coming freshly to these things suppose that there is here some sort of compromise, or that we are dealing only with fragments of a traditional legacy. Nevertheless, it is in truth the meaning of Eckhart's fundamental intuition, however strange it may seem to us.

2. What has been said above of the twofold character of creation is not enough to solve the problem. There is only a single striking parallel which can be cited to throw light on the question, namely that of Paul. He will understand Eckhart who has followed the strange logic which Paul uses in the Epistle to the Philippians 2:12-13:

> Work out your *own* salvation with fear and trembling: for *it is God* which worketh in you both to will and to do of His good pleasure.

According to the rules of ordinary logic, these words are utterly contradictory. God according to His good pleasure (that means for Paul, according to His eternal foresight, before time or world were, unshakable, to be influenced and changed by nothing) elects and condemns and Himself effects everything, both the willing and the doing. What then is the meaning of the *exhortation* that man should work his own salvation with fear and trembling, i.e. exerting all his will power and straining every nerve? Paul believes that *we are* eternally in God's eyes what in time *we are to be:* eternally elected, eternally called and eternally justified by Him alone, prior to any choice of our own. This corresponds to Eckhart's homo nobilis, as he is eternally in God, sub ratione ydeali.

The man eternally elected and justified is surely for Paul also no more abstraction, but a mysterious reality. The election which is the same as justification (and in Eckhart one with "conferre esse") is for Paul too, no temporal act but an eternal act beyond space and time, beyond history and individual life, independent of our empirical birth, becoming, being and doing. Now this which with God is eternally fact and is determined by God's very decree (which doubtless for Paul is identical with the eternal and changeless nature of God) is also, according to his strange logic, for us a matter of *our* decision, creation, evolution, burdened with all the necessity of our own willing and working, and for that very reason, involving the risk of failure should we not will and work with fear and trembling. Even he, who is eternally saved and whom no devil can snatch from the hand of God, is a weak sinner, powerless and in need of saving grace.

3. It is quite impossible to make two such dual intuitions coincide or reduce them to a common denominator. But it is also clear that according to their own strange logic these two assertions are not simply contradictions. Indeed, it is not even correct to drag in the favorite word "paradox." Paul here knows no paradox. The passage quoted above from the Epistle to the Philippians without the least consciousness of saying anything bold or curious, passes on a note of simplest understanding from the one clause to the other, with the words "for it is God." So it never occurs to Eckhart, though he uses paradoxes boldly enough on occasion, that there is any contradiction between his homo nobilis, and the man in need of salvation. He says quietly and with complete naturalness:

> Our Lord teaches us here how nobly born man *is* by nature, and how divine is that to which he may *come* by grace.

Just because man *is* one with God, and *is* the eternal Son, it follows that he so urgently needs the collatio esse and therewith grace, repentance, penitence, forgiveness. He has also need of his own effort in devotion of will, in surrender, humility and that virtue which Eckhart calls poverty (thus spiritualizing the word) and which is in truth the keeping of an inward Sabbath, the "vacare Deo," that God may effect all in all. Compare the following passages:

> Nature makes the wood first warm and then hot and only then does she turn it into the *being* of fire. But God gives first being, and only then—within time—all that belongs to the temporal (such as becoming and doing). For God gives first the Holy Spirit and only then the fruits of the Spirit. The fire's process of becoming is with labor and travail, a restless striving *in time*. But the complete fire (in principio) is pleasure and joy *beyond time* and space.

Not only we but Eckhart himself recognizes the relation of his own thoughts to those of Paul:

Saint Paul says: We *are* eternally chosen in the Son. Therefore we *shall* never rest till we *become* that which we *have been* eternally in Him.

Or:

In God there is neither past nor future. He has loved the saints eternally as He foresaw them before the world was.[1]

4. The parallels to what has been said above (see p. 182) and the unity of Eckhart's fundamental conception, will have become clear. As the will which is completely composed and at rest has its immediate complement in fresh, untiring action; as the deepest inward unity of the soul is the vitalizing principle of its powers and its healthy activity, and as the simple void Godhead is the root of the possibility of God, person, creation, love, sympathy—so here the exalted terms of homo nobilis are the very ground upon which the nothingness of the creature and the need of grace must grow.

5. The relationship between the mystical thought of Eckhart and the doctrines of Justification and Grace can be summed up as follows: They run parallel and correspond almost point for point. Further: their terminology is interchangeable. As regards their meaning, they may be freely substituted for one another; often enough they even become synonymous. Finally, the thought-sequence of the first is so permeated and saturated by the content of the second that it cannot even be thought of as separated from it.

6. It must be added that apart from the doctrine of Justification,

---

[1] This throws light upon Eckhart's teaching of ratio ydealis. Here he accepts the Platonic tradition of the eternal idea of man from which the creaturely, empirical man is distinguished and in which, at the same time, he participates. But his real meaning is much simpler and has no need of this Scholastic speculation. It is simply this: One and the same man is beheld from two aspects. On the one hand as a creature of time and mortality, of becoming and of formation; on the other, as he, the same man, is eternally in and with God. This conception is similar to Kant's teaching of the intelligible character of man, who as a Noumenon is beyond space and time and natural law, and on the other hand, as a phenomenon, is subject to all these. The relationship is expressed by Eckhart in the words so often used by him "In as far as," "as truly as", "in quantum"—. One passage says: "Before the creation of the world, am I," "Before that am I,"

Eckhart, with his mystical ontology, theology, soul-doctrine and ethics, has in view religious and spiritual facts which stripped of their mystical clothing, prove to be fundamental facts of religious experience, and of the deeper life of the soul. These are recognized by him with a clarity and penetration which is rarely found. This is particularly true of his teaching with regard to the ground of the soul. What Eckhart means by the ground of the soul does indeed exist; if it is a "mystical factor" then mysticism is to some extent an essential and indestructible element of our being.

(a) Eckhart has seen that deep below the plane of our conscious spiritual life, occupied in individual, empirical acts of imagination, will and feeling, lies hidden the vast region of our unconscious life and being, into the ultimate depths of which the keenest self-contemplation seeks in vain to penetrate.

(b) Here at the core itself is the original being of man, the true center of all characteristic action and reaction. Here are the deeps which can remain unmoved and unchanged when at the surface the play of powers, thoughts, concepts, emotions, desires, cares and hopes of the moment is in full swing in time and place, changing like fleeting waves.

(c) Thither, the life of the soul can find retreat when it withdraws from the play of the outward faculties, from the divisions of discursive reflection, from the disruption of outward impulses: when, as we say also in our common speech, a man "comes to himself."

(d) Here independent of and deeper than all surface intellect, lies that power of knowledge, of intuition, of valuation and of higher judgment which enters our consciousness through the ver-

---

that means: "in so far as (in quantum) man is lifted above time, is in eternity, he works one work with God."

Just as Kant's "intelligible character" was not added to the empiric character, but is its eternal basis, so the ground of the soul is not added to the parts or the powers of the soul. It is homo sub specie aeterni (man in his eternal aspect) in distinction from homo sub specie temporis (man in his temporal aspect). Therefore Eckhart can answer the objection that he is teaching aliquid increatum in anima ut partem animae (an uncreated something in the soul as part of the soul).

Compare also: Si ponatur, aliqua particula animae sit increata et increabilis, error est. Si autem intelligatur sicut iam supra expositum est pulchra veritas. (If it is supposed that there is any particle of the soul which is uncreated and un-

dicts of conscience—the inner voice, the witness of the spirit within. Only here at the center springs the power and the unmediated certainty of all ideals, particularly of all religious convictions. Only what has penetrated to this ground of the soul and has here proved itself, becomes truth, unshakable truth for us. Only what comes unconsidered, unmade, unwilled from this ground of the soul, whether as an "image" in the imagination or as a decision in the power of the will, is genuine, is original, is rooted and essential, is true work and life. "From the ground of my heart"—sings the church choral.[2]

7. Eckhart's ground of the soul might be described in those metaphors which he himself uses for the Godhead: (a) as a wheel rolling out of itself, and a river flowing into itself. For it is on the one hand the possibility of the effectiveness of "the powers," and it gives to them of itself force, life and impulse. And on the other, all that is experienced and accepted only becomes life when it is taken up into this ground of the soul and is fused into the oneness and simplicity of the inward life, and stripped of its separateness and division. (b) Eckhart could also aptly describe this ground of the soul as potentiality and highest synthesis in his striking expressions: "becoming one," and "becoming nothing." For everything that enters into it by entering into the oneness of unmediated life[3] becomes "nothing," i.e. becomes free from all differentiation, "all accident."

These elements (a) and (b) throw a singular light upon Eckhart's speculation on the absolute Oneness of his "void modeless Godhead," and upon the motives of such thought. For him the

---

creatable that is an error. But if it is understood as it has been explained above, it is beautiful and is truth.)

This which is not a part but is the ground of the soul sub specie ydeali, is also occasionally called by Eckhart the intellect, and then he can say: *Falsum est quod aliqua petia vel pars animae sit increabilis. Sed verum est, quod . . . Si ipsa esset purus intellectus, qualis est Deus solus, esset increata nec esset anima.* (It is false that any section or part of the soul is uncreatable. But it is true that if it is itself pure intellect, as is God alone, it is uncreated and is not the soul.)

[2] What Eckhart says of the ground of the soul in the language of mysticism, Maeterlinck among moderns has in mind when he speaks of the "temple enseveli" within us, only he does not penetrate to the Master's depths.

[3] Cf. what Schleiermacher says in the second edition of his *Addresses:* ". . .to

soul is a counterpart and image of the Godhead. Now it is a question whether the original was not largely copied from the image, that is, whether the features which Eckhart beheld in the deepest essence of the soul, magnified into infinity, have not been objectified as qualities of his Godhead.

8. If we turn again to Sankara, we can measure in full the distance between the two masters. Sankara knows the atman in us, but this atman is not the soul in the Christian and Eckhartian sense: it is not "soul" as identical with "Gemut,"[4] infinitely rich in life and depth, a place of ever fuller experience and possession, an "inward man" with the characteristics of the biblical conception of this word. Least of all is his atman, "soul" in the sense of religious conscience, which "hungers and thirsts after righteousness," and for which "to be" is to be righteous with the very righteousness of God. Sankara's mysticism is certainly mysticism of the atman, but it is not soul-mysticism as Gemuts-mystik. Least of all is it a mystical form of justification and sanctification as Eckhart's is through and through. And Sankara's mysticism is none of these things because it springs not from the soil of Palestine, but from the soil of India.

take it up into the inmost part of the spirit and thus to fuse it into one, so that it casts off all that is temporal and dwells in him no more as something separate, but as one eternal, pure and at rest."

[4] An untranslatable word of the German language coined by Eckhart.

7

The Ethical Content. Mysticism and Ethics

1. It is because the background of Sankara's teaching is not Palestine but India that his mysticism has no ethic. It is not immoral, it is a-moral. The Mukta, the redeemed, who has attained ekata or unity with the eternal Brahman, is removed from all works, whether good or evil. Works bind man. He leaves all activity and reposes in oneness.

We have seen already how the Gita approves an ethic of strong and manly action, and how Sankara acknowledges the value of this "on the lower level." But as a mystic and from the point of view of his true ideal, all activity and all deeds disappear completely. With an almost appalling persistency and obduracy Sankara uses all the powers of his dialectic and his penetrating intellect to cloud and twist the clear meaning of the Gita which praises the deed dedicated to Isvara, and to reduce this action to a lower level than the stage of complete cessation of all willing and doing.

With Eckhart it is entirely different. "What we have gathered in contemplation we give out in love." His wonderfully liberating ethic develops with greater strength from the ground of his mysticism. Righteousness through unity with Being is for him, as little as for Luther, a mere imputed righteousness: it is an essential righteousness which blossoms in the living activity of the "new obedience." This arises from the fact that the divine Being is essential righteousness, for it has within itself the God of the Prophets and of the Gospels—-He who says of Himself "I am that I am." That text is the foundation of Eckhart's determination of God as pure Being. But this "I am" is, however, the God of all moral ideals in personal purity and perfection and of the social commandment regarding man and his fellow creatures. Thus this mysticism becomes voluntarist in the highest sense—a mysticism of the surrender of the personal will to the active and eternal will.

2. Almost every type of mystical experience demands surrender of the will, but in most cases it asks simply the submissive resignation of self-will, a denial of man's will before the will of God. This Eckhart knows well, but at the same time there is for him also something greater: the unifying of the will with the will of the Highest for fresh action. Thus Eckhart is the herald of the will, which united with the divine will, has become free, and no one has spoken more magnificently than he of the power of a liberated will. Will is joined with will. Into the eternal, active and unified will the created, individual and sundered will is merged, but in such a way that in the renewed will of the unified subject there now lives the eternal, holy and almighty will.

This idea runs through the whole gamut of religious and mystical experience and expression. It begins with the simplest form of ordinary Christian preaching and prayer,

> Speak, O Lord! that Thy eternal will may take form in me,

and rises to the highest levels of mystic union. At times it even overcomes the whole mysticism of Being which is lost sight of in the mysticism of the will. Or, rather, the attainment of Being becomes the attainment of the living will, and to be one with God is identical with being of one accord with God.

> Such a man is so much in accord with God, that he wills what God wills and as God wills.

Or:

> No man has this unless his will is completely one with the will of God. May God grant us this union. Amen.

3. It is here that Eckhart's seemingly cold speculation on Being acquires a special hue. Being precedes work. According to your being so is your work.

"Make the tree good and his fruit good." This comparison already points to something deeper than mere activity and even than disposition. It points back to a "being" which is the basis of all disposition. Eckhart would say similarly: "It is not a matter of mere disposition (Gesinnung), but of inward essence. Only from an inward essence can there come a disposition and my disposition depends upon my being. "Be essential and thy disposition and action will be right." Now God is essential Being and essential righteousness. It is not enough to have Him in thought, or in will or in disposition. Your very being itself must have essential righteousness: that is you must *be* God if you would be righteous.

> Totum suum esse, vivere, nosse, scire et amare est ex Deo et in Deo et Deus. (His whole being, living, knowing and loving is from God, and in God, and is God.)

8

The Ethical Content. Valuation of the World

Closely connected with what we have said in the foregoing chapter there is a further distinguishing element in the mysticism of the two masters. We can call it their attitude toward the world and toward the given reality of things.

For Sankara, the world remains world, painful and miserable, to be fled from, and denied. As we have already seen the result of this attitude is a peculiar art of painting the world in pessimistic colors. Samsara and Brahma-nirvana stand in sharp contrast to one another. Nirvana is a condition purely of the beyond: samsara could never be nirvana, and therefore salvation in Brahman is for Sankara realized only after death. It is first truly achieved when the mukta, he who has attained perfect knowledge, has tasted to the very end the fruits of his earlier karma, i.e. only with Sarira-nipat, the casting off of this mortal body. Till then he is in an attitude of expectation which for him lasts long and whose end he impatiently desires. The man from Gandhara and Sankara with him says: "It seems to him to be very long till he can say: I am free, I go to Him."

But Eckhart says: "I would gladly remain here until the last day." For him samsara is already nirvana, and both become one; he finds his joy in the world, radiant with God's light. It is characteristic that with him there are no mournful plaints or lamentations over the world and the body, which play so great a role in

Francis, occasionally disfigure[1] Luther's preaching, and are so frequent in Indian philosophy, both in Buddhism and in Hinduism. For Eckhart, so soon as a man has attained right knowledge, God shines through all creatures, and he wins the right to say that for him "all has become God."

> All things become to thee pure God, because in all things thou seest nothing but pure God. Like one who looks long into the sun—what he afterwards may see is seen full of the sun.

The world, which is for Eckhart also full of sorrow, as merely creature (sicut est in se) becomes, when it is found again in God, a place of joy and of joyous spontaneous action in all good works. Of course he would agree that what is begun here will later be fulfilled. But he is not impatient for it. He awaits no "surprises" of the beatific vision, in fact the whole idea of a "beatific vision" which was the eschatological ideal of his time—of Thomas and of Dante—is thoroughly alien to him. For Eckhart God is beheld not in visions but when He is known in essential knowledge, which is identical with Being and bears fruit in action.

> Many people imagine *here* to have creaturely being, and divine being *yonder*. That is not so. By that many are deceived. I have indeed said, that a man beholds God in this life in the same perfection, and is blessed in exactly the same way, as in the after life.

The difference between the "yonder" and the "here" when seen in God, is not qualitative, but is the difference between complete actuality there and its partial achievement here:

> After this life the potentiality and the partially realized shall be transformed into full reality. This transformation will not however perfect the experience of blessedness (in its essence) more than it now is.

---

[1] Compare: ". . . but while we still remain in this shameful sack of worms." From Luther's last sermon in Wittenberg, January 17, 1546. This style of preaching is entirely alien to Eckhart's mind.

9

The Ethical Content. Being and Love

1. Finally, following on all that we have said before, this herald of "knowledge" and of "Being" as the Most High is the glowing evangelist of Christian love, love of God and love of one's neighbor.

We spoke of the voluntarist mysticism of the Middle Ages and its parallel, the mystic Bhakti of the East, as a mysticism of exaggerated emotion where the "I" and the "Thou" flow together in a unity of intoxicated feeling. Eckhart knows nothing of such emotional orgies or such a "pathological" love (as Kant calls it). For him love is not eros but the Christian virtue of agape, strong as death but no paroxysm, inward but of deep humility, at once active in willing and doing as Kant's "practical" love.

2. Here again Eckhart differs completely from Plotinus though he is always represented as his pupil. Plotinus also is the publisher of a mystical love, but his love is throughout not the Christian agape but the Greek eros, which is enjoyment, and enjoyment of a sensual and supersensual beauty, arising from an aesthetic experience almost unknown to Eckhart. In its finest sublimation it still bears within it something of the eros of Plato's Symposium: that great Daemon, which is purified into a divine passion out of the ardor of procreation, yet even then still retains a sublimated element of the original passion.[1]

---

[1] Plotinus says: "The color flowering on that other height...is beauty: or rather all there is light and beauty through and through. ...But those drunken with

But Eckhart does not come like the emotional love mystics to an at-one-ment as an effect and as the summit of emotional conditions:

> Love does not unify; true, it unites in act but not in essence. (Evans 248)

Rather the at-one-ment is itself the condition and the first ground of the possibility of true agape.

Nor has his agape anything in common with the Platonic or Plotinian eros, but it is the pure Christian emotion in its elemental chastity and simplicity without exaggeration or admixture. The relationship of love to the moment of at-one-ment with Being can be described thus in Eckhart: unity and the oneness in Being and essence, expressed emotionally or having effect in the sphere of emotion, is love, and also confidence, faith, surrender of the will, and service. These are the forms in which the essential unity of the Godhead and the soul are represented in the regions of the "faculties" of emotion and will. Eckhart himself says:

> "This identity out of the One into the One and with the One is the source and fountainhead of forth-breaking glowing love."

Indeed, properly speaking, these forms are not the result of that unity nor is that unity the result of this love, but they are the Unity itself in expression.

Sankara also knows a unity of feeling based on a unity of being. The eternal Brahman is not only chit and sat, but also ananda, not only being and spirit but also joy, endless joy:

> Who knows the joy of it . . .

this wine, filled with the nectar, all their soul penetrated by this beauty [cannot remain mere gazers]. (Ennead, 5, 8, 10. McKenna)

"It is to be reached by those who (are) born with the nature of the lover . . . in pain of love toward beauty . . . until the uttermost is reached, the First, the principle whose beauty is self springing: this attained there is an end to the pain inassuageable before." (Ennead, 5, 9, 2. McKenna)

"That soul is an Aphrodite and longs for God to become one in love with Him, as a virgin of noble birth for a noble love."

And however far removed this Aphrodite uranios is from the Aphrodite pandemos, yet the rule holds that:

"He who does not understand that high passion ($\pi\alpha\theta\eta\mu\alpha$), should understand it from the analogy to the $\varepsilon\nu\tau\alpha\nu\theta\alpha$ $\varepsilon\rho\omega\tau\varepsilon\zeta$." (Ennead 6, 9, 9)

And it is self-evident also for Eckhart that the soul participating in God shares His blessedness. But it is again characteristic of him that he seldom makes use of this realization. The proper expression of the feeling of at-one-ness is not a mystical *pleasure*, but agape, a love of a kind which neither Plotinus nor Sankara mentions or knows.

10

The Ethical Content. Soul, Spirit, Conscience

Eckhart thus becomes necessarily what Sankara could never be: the profound discoverer of the rich indwelling life of the "soul" and a leader and physician of "souls," using that word in a sense which is only possible on a Christian basis. Upon Indian soil there could never have developed this inward unceasing preoccupation with the soul's life as a life of Gemüt and of conscience, and therewith the "cura animarum" in the sense which is characteristic of, and essential to, Christianity from the earliest days. It is upon this calling as a curator animarum (shepherd of souls) that finally everything which Eckhart has said or done as a schoolman or as a preacher, as a simple Christian or as a profound Mystic, depends.

Fichte and the Doctrine of Advaita

The experience of Eckhart is repeated in an astonishing way in the nineteenth century in the speculation of Johann Gottlieb Fichte. In him we have a twofold character. Firstly, in his teaching there arise currents of thought extraordinarily similar to those which sprang up far removed from German soil in India, and which there led to the doctrine of Advaita. Secondly, here also are to be found typical differences of Western experience as contrasted with Eastern. The whole speculation of advaita recurs in Fichte with a resemblance which at first sight appears simply astounding. One might be tempted to speak of a Renaissance of ancient Indian speculation, of a rebirth of this teaching in the spiritual life of a German thinker. It is seen in Fichte's treatise of 1806, *The Guide to the Blessed Life (Die Anweisung zum seeligen Leben)*.

As early as 1799, Schleiermacher had written prophetically:

> I see already a few significant figures initiated into these
> secrets, returning from the holy place, who have only to purify
> and adorn themselves before they come forth in priestly
> garments.

He had in view the figures of Fichte, Schelling, Schlegel, Novalis and others of his age, whom he anticipated would lead religion back again into the region of German culture in opposition to the rationalism of the time. Schleiermacher's prophecy was fulfilled. Religion very soon became a l'ordre du jour. Schelling, at first the opponent of Schleiermacher's *Addresses on Religion*, himself became a theosophist; Schlegel became a Catholic; Fichte wrote the above-named treatise in which the new religious impulse of the age breaks forth with overwhelming fire and force. He conceives a speculative system, far surpassing his former work, which brings a new revelation of the oldest mystical motives. Whence this came to Fichte, if the question is put in any historical sense, remains a real mystery.

We will begin with the analogies. They are so marked that one is tempted to add to Fichte's phraseology the corresponding terms from Sankara's Sanskrit, and even occasionally to repeat whole sentences and paragraphs from Fichte in the language of Sankara.

Anquetil du Perron had brought the Upanishads to the West through the medium of a Persian translation. Schopenhauer, later, was profoundly influenced by this work; Schelling knew it and spoke highly of it. But in Fichte there is not the slightest trace of direct relation with the East (just as he had no intimate knowledge of Eckhart). He illustrates the purest example of "convergence of types" imaginable; from the most widely divergent conditions and starting points there is here a convergence of thought, or rather of experience, which must be astonishing to one who is unacquainted with the more general occurrence of such examples. We will illustrate this resemblance in some of its fundamental features.

(1) Fichte himself says he proposes to present a speculative *ontology* (as a Guide to—the blessed life!).

> Being is absolutely single, not manifold; there are not several Beings but only one Being.—The obvious truth of this statement must be clear to anyone who can really think. Only Being is, on no account *is* anything which is not Being or which lies beyond Being.

> Tat sat ekam eva asti, ekarasam, avikaram avyayam aksharam. Na ca tasmin utpattipradhvamsau na ca murtinam paryayalile vidyete: kim tarhi sada sarvatraca samam santam svastham tad asti.

> Yad hi svayambhu eva, tad sanmatram eva sakrit-samstham anantaram purnam asti, na ea kincana tasmai upadhatum sakyate.

> This Being is simple, is like unto itself, unchangeable and unchanging; there is in it no becoming nor ceasing to be, no change, or play of forms, but only the same quiet Being and Remaining.

> For: what is of itself, that is and is whole, existing all at once, without interruption; and nothing can be added unto it.

2. This Being however has its "existence" (samsthana), and as existing it is consciousness (chaitanya, jnana). Consciousness is at the same time the only possible form and mode of existence of Being. (Sat is jnana.) Pure thinking is in itself divine existence, and vice versa, divine existence in its immediacy is nothing other than pure thought (chinmatra).

Likewise, it is comprehended only by thought. But this thought is distinct from the thinking of the mere discursive ratio (tarka), or reflection. In contrast to reflection it is what Eckhart called the intellectus, and Sankara the samyag-darsanam. It is the intuitus mysticus, the "real thinking" (satya-drishti) as opposed to the "ordinary mode of thinking" (vyavahara):

> "Real thinking" proceeds differently (from the common mode of thought) in filling out the supersensual region. It does not reason, but there comes to it (pratibhati) not the ordered arrangement of things nor their derivation and combination (by logical distinction and classification) but that which as One only is possible, real and necessary. And as such it is confirmed not by any logical proof (anumana) outside itself, but it brings its own proof (svasiddha) and is evident, as soon as it is thought, to thought itself as the only possible entire and absolute truth (satyasya satyam).

When this higher thought (para-vidya) has risen in us, from the strictly conceived idea of Being, it breaks down all objections of common reasoning and of the empirical viewpoint. There follow sentences which are to be found nearly word for word in the Mandukya Upanishad and in Sankara's Commentary. Fichte says:

> I say the real and true Being does not become, does not *originate,* does not come from the Not-Being. For . . . otherwise we should come to an unending regression, which cannot be.
> Unto that I add a second thing: also within this Being there can come nothing new, nothing can take on different forms, nor change. But as it is, so it is from all eternity, and remains unchanging to all eternity.

The Mandukya Upanishad says similarly:

> Whoever maintains that anything becomes out of that which is not, lacks proof. And to that which becomes out of something

Appendix 1

which became there is no end, i.e. we get the error of regressus in infinitum.

On which Sankara comments:

> If we accept the coming out of what itself became, this latter must again have come from something else which became, and that again from something else, etc. Thus we should arrive at a regressus in infinitum (anavastha).

3. Eternal Being therefore "is there" (avatishthati) as consciousness, as thought. And Fichte continues:

> Just as Being is One only and not several, as it is unchangeable and unchanging, whole and all at once, and internally, absolutely homogeneous (ekarasa)—so also its "being there" means consciousness, since this exists only through Being, and its "being there" means that consciousness also is an absolutely eternal, unchangeable and unchanging homogeneous One.

Observe that this divine thought is at the same time that "higher thought" of pure philosophic knowledge.

4. But now follows, as in Vedanta, the inexplicable fact:

> Yet there arises in contrast to this eternal unity of consciousness, an *apparent* multiplicity in thought, partly on account of various thinking *subjects,* whose existence is supposed, and partly on account of the endless array of *objects* which occupy the thought of those (apparent) subjects, eternally. This illusion is a condition of perpetual *change,* a constant swinging between becoming and perishing.

How does this illusion of multiplicity arise in that which is in truth One? Fichte answers:

> First and foremost: who raises this question as to the basis of multiplicity? It is certainly not a firm and unshakeable *faith,* for faith expresses itself briefly thus: there is only the One, unchanging and eternal, and nothing exists outside it; all that changes and is transitory therefore does not exist; its appearance is empty illusion; this I know. Whether I can explain this illusion or not my certainty is no more confirmed by explanation than it is weakened by my inability to explain.

(Sankara at one point answers this same question: "Who then is he, who is imprisoned in Avidya?" by replying simply and boldly, "He who asks," with the implied admonition: "Why do you ask?") Only the doubter is troubled by this question, and for him Fichte attempts to find an answer. He says:

> This light—left to itself—is dispersed and split up into manifold rays, and in this way is estranged from the one ray itself and its origin. But this same light can concentrate itself and gather itself again as One out of this divergence.

He also says:

> This Being is veiled (avarana) and obscured (tirodhana) in consciousness in many ways according to the indestructible laws of consciousness which are grounded in Being itself.

And again:

> The whole diversity is here revealed as existing only for us and as a result of our limitation, but in no way as existing in itself or immediately in the divine Being.

There occurs also in Fichte that peculiar "Inquantam," the "In-so-far-as" of Eckhart's expression:

> Since knowledge or we ourselves are this divine existence itself, so there can be in us, *in so far as* we are this existence, no change or turning, no plurality and multiplicity, no parting, differentiation, or cleavage. So must it be, it cannot be otherwise. Therefore it is so. In consideration however, of what we are in ourselves (cf. Eckhart's "quod creatura est per se"; and Sankara's "svatas") we are by no means that Absolute Being. Only *in so far as* we are Knowledge, are we at deepest the Divine Being. All else, which appears to us to have existence—things, bodies, souls, we ourselves (as single subjects) so far as we ascribe to ourselves an independent and self-sufficient existence—is not truly there, but is only existent in the (empirical consciousness) as something felt and thought.

Fichte asks of every true religion this concession:

> To go so far, that one is inwardly convinced of one's own Not-being, and one's Being solely in God and through God.

5. In more detail his teaching may be thus described. The true, absolute Knowledge conceives Being as the One (in that it is at the same time one with Being). This knowledge is also our

"Higher knowledge" and if we have achieved it, multiplicity has no longer any validity. But this Knowledge becomes "reflection" (why it does so, not even Fichte can say): it becomes "discursive, describing, characterizing, mediate knowing by means of differentiated predicates (bheda) and characters." It is consciousness as differentiation in concepts in which the original nature of divine Being and Existence undergo a change. Fichte says yet more expressly:

> The concept is the real creator of a (manifold) world.

This formula immediately proclaims what we are after. What we have said elsewhere of "the second way" is clearly repeated here: namely, the distinction between the intuitus mysticus of beholding Unity (of intellectual visualization), and secular perception. The former beholds the One and the Unity. But the latter sees in space and time, differentiates, divides one thing from another, breaks away from the original Unity, separates into classes, creates characteristics, asks not after "Being itself," but after "existence as this or that." All this it does by virtue of discursive understanding, using the instruments of conception. What for Sankara is "viveka"[1] is here reflection taking the place of immediate intuition, mediating discursively, distinguishing this and that, moving from one to another. For the Indian teacher, this differentiating knowledge creates the "prapancha." For Fichte, conceptual reflection creates "the world" as the static dead, objective being, opposed to the spirit, divided into this and that, in its multiplicity and contrast.

It is through reflection, says Fichte, that there arises:

> the opinion that it is this or that, bears this or that character. In reflection, knowledge is divided in itself. If there is no reflection, no apparition arises. But if the process is carried on from reflection to reflection incessantly, the world of each new act of reflection must appear in new form, and thus in an unending period of time it changes and forms and flows into an unending multiplicity.

Fichte now uses exactly the same symbol to describe the facts that we have used previously to illustrate our meaning (p. 112):

---

[1] Literally: the shaking asunder. For the Buddhists, "vikalpa."

Just as your physical eye is a *prism,* in which the ether, which is homogeneous, pure and colorless, breaks on the surfaces of things into manifold colors, so it is in the things of the spiritual world. You will not maintain that the ether in itself is colored, but only that in and through your eye and in counteraction with it, it breaks into colors, and though you are not capable of seeing the ether colorless, yet you can think of it as colorless, and you measure belief by that thought.

Though it be always God Himself that lives behind all these forms, we do not see Him, but only the veil which he draws about Himself (Maya!).

We see Him (through the eye of conception) as stone, plant, animal; we see Him when we pass beyond these, as the law of nature, as the moral law. Yet all this is still not He. Always the form hides the Being from us. Always our seeing itself covers up the object of our seeing, and our own eye stands in the way of our sight.

6. This doctrine of the clothing of the true object by the impositions of differentiating reflection is a most exact parallel to Sankara's teaching of Adhyaropa, the superimposing. Multiplicity in space and time is superimposed upon the one unique and by nature uniform Being, because of our seeing only in Avidya. There is here also another point of similarity, which first appears in this book of Fichte and is a completely new factor in his own thought. Schleiermacher had prophesied its arrival. In his *Addresses* Schleiermacher wrote five years before the appearance of Fichte's book:

What will happen to the triumph of speculative philosophy, to complete and finished idealism, if religion does not suffer a counterbalance and give some inkling of a higher realism than that to which idealism so boldly and so rightly objected?

Fichte does indeed become a "higher realist," and in the same sense in which the term applies to Sankara. He achieves this actuality by means of a religious impulse, now breaking through and coloring his speculation. Idealism is there where the object itself is perception, and is not there independently of perception (essepercipi). For a long time Fichte had held to this belief, but now things were entirely changed. The object of knowledge is here "Being itself," the eternal and indissoluble, and as such wholly independent of all our perception. It is the highest *Reality.* Only its limitation in "character, separation and multiplicity" the whole of this "prapancha" (i.e. the world as extended in multiplicity), exists through subjective perception.[2] Where there was no perception of difference, this multiplicity would be for all kinds of knowledge and all acts of knowledge, only one and the same object. There could also be only one and the same judgment, just as there is when an unbroken homogeneous presentation is the basis of judgment.

7. What is the meaning of this whole curious ontology? It is the same as that of Sankara and Eckhart—a doctrine of salvation. The very title—*Guide to the Blessed Life*—tells us that. The theme runs through the whole book.

> The impulse to become united with and dissolved into the immortal is the deepest root of all mortal existence.

And Fichte describes the condition of the painful search after this highest goal in words which read almost as a translation of Sankara's story of the man from Gandharaland:

> Thus the poor descendant of eternity, cast out of his paternal home, still always surrounded by his heavenly inheritance, toward which he dares not reach out his timid hand, wanders uncertainly from place to place in the desert, and is reminded by the speedy collapse of all his places of shelter that he can find rest nowhere but in his Father's house.

Again Fichte, even describes blessedness itself in Sankara's terms:

> Blessedness is to rest and remain in the One. Misery is to be dispersed into multiplicity and differentiation. Therefore the con-

---

[2] In the school of Sankara the argument runs thus: "Even perception experiences nothing manifold, because it cannot do so."

The opponent objects: "How is that possible! The object of perception is just the thing in its multiplicity. For we perceive forms and say: Here is a pot, here is a cloth."

Whereupon the pupil of Sankara answers: "Let us examine this matter. Take the proposition: Here is a pot. How is the being in general and the being of the particular thing posited? (Fichte's "Being" and "Being as. . . .") It is obviously a question of two quite distinct positions, which cannot both have the same ground of perception. Either the being of A or the Being-A of A is the object

dition of becoming blessed is the withdrawal of our love from the multiple *back to the One.*

So near does the German come to the Indian, yet they are infinitely far apart in deed and in depth; and they reveal anew the fact that mysticism even with an almost complete identity in speculation, can be divided by unbridgeable gulfs.

1. What is the meaning of God and Blessedness for Fichte? It is that of the Epistle of James in the New Testament: blessed *in his deeds.* He knows that he is called a mystic, but he answers:

> Real religion is distinguished by living activity from the fanaticism of mysticism.

He demands with every mystic "that the Divine Life be in us" and that wholly. But it must *live* and be active in us and complete its work as "living deed and power to act." This eternal one and undivided Being is for him, as for Eckhart "Life," and because it is life it is therefore blessed. To come to Being is therefore to come to "Life" out of the illusory life of divided and dissipated will and desire, which is really death. Fichte praises "Life" in words that recall Eckhart. The latter says:

> If one should ask life a thousand years, "Why do you live?" and it could answer it would say: "I live that I may live." That is because life lives out of its own ground and wells up out of itself. Therefore it lives without cause, living itself.

While Fichte puts it:

> Guide to a blessed life—in this expression, "blessed life" there is something superfluous. For life is in itself necessarily blessed; it *is blessedness.* Death only is unblessed.

---

of perception. It cannot be the latter, for the former is essential to its very possibility. Therefore only Being itself (and not being thus, being as this or that, being with peculiarity or special character, being as "seyn als—" as Fichte would say) is the object of perception. That means that perception does not perceive differences. Therefore judgments which posit differences must be based upon illusion."

We see that it is not an idealism of perception which is taught here, but rather a realism. For perception is held to perceive Being itself, the real. Only all *particular* being, in distinction from "Being itself," is dispelled. Compare with quotations given here R. Otto, *Siddhanta des Ramanuja,* 2nd. ed., pp. 34-35.

Now this "life" should be the "Being itself." This means that Fichte's ontology is the same as Eckhart's, a mask of the suprarational, which no rational ontology exhausts. He tries to indicate it, saying:

> It is common to think of Being as static and dead. Even the philosophers, almost without exception, have thought of it thus, and that because they pronounced it the Absolute. But this has happened simply because they bring with them to the thought of Being no living idea but only a dead concept.

Yet, in truth, the difference lies here, that Fichte cherishes not only a dynamic, but a wholly suprarational idea of Being, the same which we have met in the language of our two mystics, and that in particular he has within himself the mystical "vitality," which we recognized in Eckhart. Once more we are confronted with the problem, for which we as non-mystics, in spite of all our efforts, can find no completely satisfying solution—namely, as to why the mystics feel impelled to put the conception of "Being" at the foundation of their speculation. This cannot be explained merely by historical tradition; that is clear in the case of Fichte. For Fichte is entirely free from the accidental historical dependence upon Scholastic ontology under whose stimulus Eckhart labored. There must be a general inward necessity for mystics to express their experience in terms of ontology. And yet on the other hand, such terms rather fetter than expound it.

2. To the question: What is God really in His inward nature? Fichte replies with an answer which cannot be comprehended on the basis of "Pure Being":

> In that which the *holy* man *does, lives* and *loves,* God appears no more in vague ideas or as though cloaked by a veil, but in His own immediate and powerful life. And the question: What is God: unanswerable by empty ideas about God is thus answered here: He is that which the man devoted to Him and inspired by Him *does.* Wilt thou see God face to face? Seek Him not beyond the clouds. Behold the life of those given up to Him, and thou beholdest Him. Give thyself to Him, and thou findest Him in thine own bosom.

Doing and works presuppose object and multiplicity, and these are only possible through the reflective consciousness. But it lies in the nature of the Eternal-undivided-One, that, so soon as there is reflection, its own nature "comes forth" and issues in *deeds*. The following passage indicates this:

> God's inward and absolute nature (the One, Colorless, Matterless, Non-Multiple) issues as beauty, as man's complete mastery over the whole of nature issues as the perfect state, and the relationship of states issues as science.

3. This accounts for Fichte's entirely different relationship to salvation (as the removal of multiplicity and of the ego) from that which Sankara adopts toward mukti. True, Fichte like Eckhart says:

> So soon as the vain concept of individuality disappears, the former ego sinks into the divine existence, and it is strictly speaking no longer possible to say that then the affect, the love and the will of this divine existence becomes his own, since there are no longer two but only one. No longer two wills but one and the same will is all in all. So long as man desires to be something himself, God does not come to him, for no man (qua man and creature) can become God. But so soon as he destroys his own self purely, wholly and to the very root, God alone remains and is all in all.

This complete identity and the knowledge of it is Religion and the Blessed life. But here it should be noted:

(a) The higher knowledge of this Identity does not abolish the practical visualization of an outward and manifold world. I *know,* of course, when I have attained Knowledge, that this world of objects and its multiplicity, and the splitting of the eternal single consciousness into the manifoldness of egos, is false, but my *knowing* this does not dispel my empirical view of the world; just as, for example, my knowing that the sun stands still and the earth turns does not dispel my vision of the sun rising above the horizon, moving across the sky and sinking in the West.

(b) Now, except in the experience of samadhi, it is the same with Sankara. He who has attained Knowledge knows that all is only One and the One, and he himself is that One, but his senses still perceive differences, and he cannot dispel the vision of his senses before his Karma has been dissolved by death. But—and herein lies the difference—sensual vision of manifoldness through reflection, according to Fichte, *will* never be dispelled. For only in a world and in a multiplicity of egos is living action possible for us. Hence, the obvious attempt on Fichte's part, somehow or other, to anchor this world set up by reflection in the divine Knowledge.[3]

Thus the true relationship of the man who is saved, is for Fichte as it was for Eckhart: To know that he is one with the One, life with the Life, not united but absolutely unified, and *at the same time,* to stand in this world of multiplicity and division, not straining after its dissolution, but with Eckhart, working righteousness in it, and with Fichte, completing in it the living deed of ethical culture, and thus with both teachers bringing into this very world of non-being and of death, Being and Life. He must do this in such a way that his transcendental possession is itself the very source of power and the impelling force to moral and cultural activity. Fichte demands even of "simple" religion if it is to be religion at all:

> That man should feel the divine relationship continually and un-brokenly, and that the knowledge thereof, whether or not it can be clearly conceived and expressed, should be never-the-less the hidden source, the secret determining influence of all our thoughts, feelings, impulses and movements.

4. It will have become clear that what I have maintained with regard to Eckhart is true of Fichte: namely that their mysticism, though like Sankara's it makes an ontology the basis of its specu-lation, is yet fundamentally more nearly allied to that of the Mahayana, which rejects the ontology, than to that of Sankara. This closer relationship consists in what I have called "being open upwards" (page 187) in this speculation, and further in what I call their vitality and the dynamic of this "Being." It lies in Fichte's own express protest against the static, motionless, fixed and therefore dead conception of Being. It lies especially in the Mahayana ideal of the Bodhisattva, who renounces Nir-

---

[3] He says: "In the possibility of distinguishing Being itself from Being-as-Exis-tence there is given a principle on which is based the possibility of 'Being as this or that' in reflection."

vana, in order to remain in the unending activity of Samsara, and for which Nirvana becomes identical with Samsara.[4]

So Western thought, in spite of the closest similarities, is distinct from Indian thought. In the former, great impulses of mystical perception recur which the ancient and distant East has also known. But the German mystic Fichte is blessed in God when fellowship with God bears fruit in the "new righteousness" (as the German masters, Eckhart and Luther demanded before him). He is blessed when and because this new righteousness is the renewed will, resulting in work and action—the deed, which, with Fichte, passes beyond the border of mere individual ethics to creative, world-renewing, cultural activity.

[4]Fichte's *Guide to the Blessed Life* and his thought thereon culminate in a significant expression whose importance seems to me to have escaped the interpreters of his philosophy. What is blessedness? It is to be blessed in one's activity. But this blessedness is not merely the healthy feeling of power, or the pleasure of success, which the natural man also experiences, but it is as the word says *blessedness*. It is abounding joy and although wholly inexpressible, is in itself no negation but absolutely positive. Fichte crowns his teaching with the following words, which only the mystic can use:

"The concept can only express blessedness in negative terms, and that is true also of our description which falls into concepts. We can only show that the Blessed One is free from pain, from privation, from effort. But in what blessedness itself consists positively, cannot be described, it can only be directly experienced."

Like a flash of lightning this word illuminates also the situation in the East. If one asks about the content of Brahma-nirvana, of the Vedantin, or of the Paranirvana of the Buddhists, one generally receives for an answer the *negation* of the misery of Samsara. Questioned as to its positive content the teachers of Nirvana for the most part, shut their lips as an oyster closes its shell. Among them also the positive lies in the very accent, in the excitement with which Nirvana is mentioned, but not in "concepts" put forward about it. Many are misled by this and believe that millions of men in the East seek their salvation, and have sought it, in becoming nothing—Zero.

The Mysticism of the "Two Ways" in Schleiermacher

1. Mystical conceptions lie behind the higher speculation of more modern times—behind the thought of Descartes, the Occasionalists, Malebranche, Spinoza, Shaftesbury, Leibniz, and Kant. They form a background to the poetry of Goethe and of Herder. They were entangled with pietism, and in men like Poiret strove to become an element in general culture and to win considerable influence upon education and instruction. (Poiret: *De vera et falsa eruditione.*) Delekat has shown in his recent work on Pestalozzi,[1] how significant this background of mysticism was for the great Swiss educator.

2. Under the influence of Herder this movement became vital in romanticism; in Novalis it takes the form of strong nature mysticism, like that of the English romantics, Wordsworth and Shelley, though with a marked strain of eroticism. But in Schleiermacher, though it is outwardly akin to such romantic nature mysticism, it is in truth spiritual mysticism; and he is clearly at times in direct antagonism to the mystical nature-fanaticism of his own friends. In German romanticism and even in Herder, this movement is not mysticism in the strictest sense, but rather a diffuse emotional mysticism. As such however, it is clearly distinguishable. Although diffuse we can still, especially in Schleiermacher, trace our system outlined on page 48ff. It is clearly visible in his *Addresses on Religion* of 1799 and in his *Dogmatic* of 1821. The shifting of Schleiermacher's standpoint which has often been remarked, as between his *Addresses* in their

---

[1] It is easy to see for example how the fourth of Schleiermacher's *Addresses*, "On Education for Religion," is a link in a long chain of historical influences.

first form, and his *Dogmatic,* is related to our "Two Ways." It
is a change of standpoint from that of the "second way" to one
very near that of the first. Elements of the "first way" are by
no means lacking in the *Addresses,* but they are not outstanding,
while, vice versa, in the *Dogmatic* there are still elements of the
"second way" but it is essentially determined by the first.[2]

3. The *Addresses* contain two elements closely interwoven: the
protest of a profoundly religious man, arising out of the depths
of his piety, against the earlier Fichtianism; and, on the other
hand, a mystic attitude of soul breaking forth here for the first
time in Schleiermacher.

(a) Fichte in his first period had taken up the fight against the
slavery of "fatalism." Undoubtedly he was impelled thereto by
specific Christian impulses. The Determinism which limited
freedom and moral worth, or took away independence and nobility of spirit, the "Spinozism" which enslaved, and removed
freedom of action, responsibility and guilt, and ascendancy over
nature and the world—these were Fichte's enemies. Against
them he proclaimed freedom, and thereby protected the interests
of faith itself. He protested against the accusation of atheism. He
was convinced that he was himself an apologist, an apologist
against the enemy of belief—Spinozian determinism; and in his
eyes Spinoza was the real atheist. But since he had freed the ego
from fatalism, dragged the spirit of man out of the fetters of
nature, set him above the slavery and omnipotence of "things,"
and subjected nature to the sovereignty of man's spirit—where
was piety, or religion, conceived as piety? For it is piety which
Schleiermacher in the name of religion wishes to defend. But that
is the very opposite of the feeling of sovereignty. It is worship
and humility. This is the contrast of mood which I have called
anti-Fichtian in my edition of Schleiermacher's *Addresses.*[3]

All this has nothing to do with mysticism. It is simply devout.
But it is the first great characteristic of Schleiermacher's attitude

[2] Cf. R. Otto: *Religious Essays.* Essay No. VIII, "How Schleiermacher Re-
discovered the Sensus Numinus."

[3] I have edited the original form of the *Addresses on Religion* of 1799, and from
this edition I quote here. Schleiermacher's essays should be read in this original
form, because the following editions have lost much of the original power and
impulse of the first edition.

to his environment. This he had developed long before his romantic period and before he wrote his *Addresses*. It is maintained unchanged even when, as mentioned above, his standpoint shifts from that of the *Addresses* to that of his *Dogmatic*. In so far as "the feeling of absolute dependence" is identical with this contrast of moods, it is already present in the *Addresses,* and in this respect Schleiermacher is quite right, when he maintains that he has remained the same throughout. This feeling of humility is for him later the fundamental element in all religion.

This religious feeling had sprung up as a movement of his own spirit, and already in Schlobitten had freed itself from the confinement and spiritual aridness of rationalism. He had won through to it long before he came into touch with Schlegel and Novalis. It was this element in his *Addresses* which worked so strongly upon Harms and became for him the impulse toward "an eternal movement." When, in his *Dogmatic* he sets up this sense of dependence as a general and indispensable factor in human life, and maintains that this replaces and makes superfluous all "proofs of God's existence," he does at least speak from his own experience: to him it was the absolute a priori, the immovable and certain foundation of his consciousness. It is the fundamental element of his later dogmatic work. But it can be traced throughout the *Addresses,* as we have said. It was the service of the Fichte movement that it set free this humility by a sort of rebound in Schleiermacher and made it powerful for his age.

(b) Now, closely bound up with this in the *Addresses* is another entirely distinct element, that of the intuitus mysticus, "Vision and emotion," and this intuitus is predominantly that of "the second way":

> Beholding the universum; I beg you to make yourselves familiar with this idea. It is the fulcrum of my whole address; it is the most general and the highest formula of religion, wherein you will find the only point from which its essence and its bounds can be exactly defined.

The vision is of the universum; not inward, not of the soul, nor of the atman. This universum is the all of Being and of happening, wherever it takes place. First and foremost quite seriously the vision is of this All-being and event in nature, in history and in the soul, in its concrete reality and multiplicity. Yet at the same time this vision is more and something other than mere empirical comprehension. It is obviously a comprehension of significances and depths which the natural gaze and physical perception cannot achieve; it is an intuition, an intuitive apprehension of significance. This understanding is parallel to the stages of our system. That which is comprehended and beheld is:

(a) The Universum, i.e. not the mere sum of all things, even though never complete, but—and this lies in the very expression, universum—the essential whole, totally contrasted with chance addenda, Unity as offered to the manifold in being and happening:

> Religion lives its whole life...in the infinite nature of the whole, the One and the All.
>
> To accept every particular as part of the whole, everything limited as a representation of the infinite, that is religion. To see the infinite in men not less than in all other particular and finite beings.
>
> To know the same (sama-darsanam) everywhere under all disguises and rest nowhere but in the infinite and One (Ekatadarsanam).

(b) This whole and this unity is first of all a form of the manifold. At the same time it is perceived not sensually but intuitively. For it is neither the natural form of Being and happening, which the scientific glance comprehends, namely, space as the form of all that is perceived outwardly, and time as the form of all that is perceived inwardly, but it is beyond space and time: it is the infinite in the finite, the eternal in the temporal.

(c) To behold the universe and everything in the universe, in such a way means therefore also for Schleiermacher: to behold "in ratione ideali," to behold the idea.[4] Thus in Schleiermacher the universe becomes indeed more and more strange; finally it is a kind of mundus intelligibilis, a cosmos noëtos, a world or universe of idea, which is and remains ideal unity.

---

[4] "Lift yourselves higher with your contemplation on the wings of religion to infinite undivided humanity. Seek this in every individual. Eternal humanity is untiringly busy creating itself." "The genius of humanity." This is not empirical humanity, but humanity seen in its eternal and undivided idea.

(d) Soon that which was at first intelligible form ascends still higher. The "One," the "Whole," becomes an underlying *principle,* giving meaning and definition to Being and happening. Their relationship to this principle can only be described in expressions such as those we used above for relationships which lie beyond our categories of knowledge: "lying at the basis of a thing as its principle," "to comprise it." It was essential to the nature of the matter and not a question of compromise or rhetoric on the part of Schleiermacher, that he soon used as symbols for this One Principle of all being and happening the terms, "the high spirit of the universe," the eternal "Godhead":

> To love the spirit of the universe and behold his work with joy; that is the goal of our religion.

This One, behind and below the manifold, as we saw above in pages 52-54, is in the lowest stage only form, in the middle state essential form, and then "supporting and conditioning reality." This ascent from the stage of the universum (= form) to essential and conditioning form and then to conditioning reality is shown by certain expressions in the second edition of Schleiermacher's *Addresses.*

> God in whom alone is the particular One and All. Or is God not the sole and highest Unity? Is it not God alone before whom and in whom every particular disappears? And when you see the world as a whole and an All, can you do this other than in God?

This is not, as has been maintained, an adaptation to Christian theology; it is the advance of mystical vision itself from the first to the second stage which we have outlined in our system.

(e) These visions, these intuitions of the universum, can be described to a certain extent and Schleiermacher in his *Addresses* gives a whole series of terms as the verbal forms of such intuitions. He distinguishes them sharply from scientific comprehension. For here already, and that very distinctly, the view is propounded that religious expressions are not expressions of scientific knowledge, and are not to be classed with theoretical knowledge of the world. But they are not therefore for him false expressions; they are also not mere fantasies, nor a noble dream, but rest upon visions which comprehend something real.

Schleiermacher would have escaped misunderstanding on this point if he had clearly distinguished knowledge from scientific knowledge, and if, maintaining as he rightly did, that religious vision is not mere knowing, he had emphasized the comprehending character of these visions, which he undoubtedly felt them to contain.

4. Analogies with the mysticism of the "second way" are obvious from what has just been stated. Yet at one point Schleiermacher is clearly distinguished from the mysticism described earlier in this book: and this confirms our assertion that mysticism is not simply like unto mysticism. The consciousness of being borne up by this universum and of the innermost unity with it never causes in him those raptures of which we have spoken and which culminate in "creator-emotions." Though feelings of expansion are not unknown to him, the soul never becomes for him God, the part never becomes the whole; man is never that eternal, conditioning reality, which as the form of unity and totality bears and conditions all particulars, and into which the particular "silently fades."

5. If we pass now from the *Addresses* to the *Dogmatic,* we believe ourselves at first to be in an entirely different world. Here there is no vision of the universum, but the path of knowledge leads inward. According to the *Dogmatic,* I know by immediate inward experience that I am "absolutely dependent." In this teaching the divine is found in the depths of man's own being, in very close union with "immediate self-consciousness," or indeed through the highest self-consciousness itself.

6. There is no doubt that in Scheiermacher's true and deepest thought this sense of dependence is also an immediate experience of God. But this thought is veiled, if we take him strictly at his spoken word. For it is clear that in his terms he certainly distinguishes between that which is given without mediation, and that which is first seen after reflection upon it. The sense of absolute dependence is the immediate experience, and the thought of God is the first reflection upon that experience. This is the position which he takes up and defends strongly. In his opinion, dogmatic teaching has only to deal with the representation of the immediate religious feeling as such, and that is the feeling of dependence itself. What goes beyond that, it must be repeated, is not the im-

mediate experience but reflection upon it. Thus he writes in his second letter to Lücke on the occasion of the second edition of his *Dogmatic:*

> I have seriously considered whether the time has not already come with the second edition of my book to revise its form, so that the two forms of dogmatic propositions, those which express the qualities of God, and those which deal with the composition of the world, should only be called secondary forms. For, if it is true, that they express nothing, which is not already substantially contained in the propositions which bear the fundamental form, (i.e. mere description of the feeling of dependence as such) those two subordinate forms could be omitted. This is indeed my own personal conviction with which another is closely bound up, namely, that our dogmatic teaching will sometime learn to do without these two.

The reason for this apparently curious attitude is the same as that already dealt with in respect to his *Addresses*. The divine should not become a matter of theory and theoretical expression. The dogmatic object can only be the determination of the immediate feeling itself (as the sense of absolute dependence).

7. But Schleiermacher's feeling cannot be held in check by the self-erected limits of his theology. His "immediate self-consciousness" was truly mystical. Turning within, he finds in himself as direct experience something more than his "conditions." And therefore his "religious feeling" was indeed not simply a sense of self (which the sense of absolute dependence alone would be), but was undoubtedly immediate mystical experience of God. Only when filled by such content can that "self-consciousness" be called the highest and incomparable form of all self-consciousness: namely, when it is a knowledge of the depths in which the contact between the divine and the soul takes place and in which it is directly included in the consciousness of self. The expressions which Schleiermacher afterwards uses about God have none of them de facto, the stamp of mere secondary terms for others of the first rank, but they are concrete explications of a singular, direct and predetermined sense of God Himself. Expressions in later paragraphs, on occasion, entirely ignore the earlier pronouncement, that the thought of God is only a reflection upon the immediate experience, but is not that expe-

rience itself. They recognize simply and finely what the mystics of the "first way" of all ages have asserted, that the way into the depths of the soul is also the way to the divine. Thus in paragraph 30 he says:

> The sense of absolute dependence in and of itself is the sense of God set in the consciousness of the self.

In the freer language of the later editions of his *Addresses* he takes no account whatever of the confining concepts of his own theory:

> I have proclaimed nothing but the immediate and primal being of God in us through feeling.

8. Because of this it became necessary that the fulcrum of his addresses, namely vision of the universum, should disappear, and make way for feeling, which here is obviously used in an entirely different sense from that of the *Addresses*. In the latter, feeling was merely an accompanying emotion. Here in the *Dogmatic* it is a form of apprehension. Mystical experience and understanding are now entirely different. In the *Addresses* mystical vision was stirred by phenomena and particular events in the universe. It could be an individual act with its time and hour to which man could point, and which he could retain in his memory:

> If only I could and might express, or at least indicate, that first secret moment without profaning it! Swiftly and as if by magic an event or a phenomenon develops into a symbol of the Universum. I lie in the bosom of the eternal world. In this moment I am its soul, for I feel all its powers and its infinite life as my own. In this moment it is my body.[5] I feel its muscles and its limbs through and through as my own and its inmost nerves vibrate to my sense and thought.

It is quite otherwise in his *Dogmatic*. There it is not an individual act of intuition, here and now, but a feeling, which in the language of Kant, must be called a "transcendental apperception." It is a profound a priori, as the fundamental conditioning of the

---

[5] The identification of perceiver and perceived of the "second way."

spirit itself, a self-consciousness and God-consciousness that precedes all individual empirical consciousness. This in order to be realized and possessed in actu, needs and awaits redemption, namely that state in which taken up into the power and blessedness of the God-consciousness of Christ, it becomes an act and an abiding possession of our spiritual life.

9. Yet certain elements of the second way still remain also in the *Dogmatic*. This is obviously the case when Schleiermacher states that man in his sense of dependence knows himself at the same time as a "representative" of all created being.[6] He represents in himself the creature generally; and as we have seen, that is mystical and in line with the mysticism of the second way. The same is true when Schleiermacher in his *Dogmatic* asserts that religious feeling may be stirred by the love of nature. That is a final if faint analogy to the contemplation of nature sub specie universi. Finally, the mysticism of the second way is found in his conception of God Himself. For Schleiermacher is continually emphasizing the truth that God and the world may not be falsely separated.

God and the world retain for him the relationship of conditioning unity to conditioned multiplicity. Here there remains an element of the intuition of unity of the second way, whose fundamental conception was this: That which is, in so far as it is Unity, the Whole, and above space and time, is the Conditioning, Supporting, Forming, Comprising—the Divine, the Godhead. In the measure that it is multiple, individual, here and now, it is world and creature. They are related to one another as essential form to content, which indeed cannot be separated.[7]

10. The change from the faith of the *Addresses* to that of the *Dogmatic* together with the rejection of "vision" in favor of

---

[6] To find one's self, viewed as a finite being—and thus in the name of all finite beings—absolutely dependent.

[7] Cf. "The sense of absolute dependence includes knowledge of God, as the absolute, undivided Oneness."

Schleiermacher attempts to construct his conception of God as a necessary correlate to his absolute dependence. But he does not succeed. From this dependence one is more likely to arrive at a consistent theistic conception. It is clear, that in his doctrine of God the mystical intuition of the *Addresses* is still effective.

feeling, was a necessity arising from Schleiermacher's own nature. For however strongly he presents and upholds "vision" in his *Addresses,* he himself was no seer in the sense of the second way. Had he himself possessed this gift of the mystical vision of the Universum, we should have found traces of it in his life, in his testimonies to his friends, in his letters and in his sermons. But one seeks in vain for such spontaneous visions and experiences. Such experiences as he describes in his *Zwischenstück*[8] would have left their mark in his letters, and still more in the intimate personal confessions of the *Monologues.* Here he lays claim to the mystic sense. The inward contemplation and the ever deeper penetration within that he practices has in fact always been a quality of soul mysticism and of mysticism of the first way. In this sense the *Monologues* are strongly tinged with mysticism. For here we find the distinction between inward and outward; here is "the true being" as the real self, deep beneath the play of changing thoughts and emotions. Here is "Infinity." As I enter into this experience, as I no longer behold appearances or events, but "turn back into myself," I pass out of the sphere of time, to touch eternity and live within it. In these "hidden depths" "the light of God dawns." Here is "the hidden depth" as "the inner Being of the Spirit." Here I become conscious of "immediate relationship with the Eternal and Infinite." And "as often as I turn my gaze to the inner self I am forthwith in the kingdom of Eternity." "Here the spirit hovers above the world of time, and to behold Him is Eternity and immortal song of divine joy." Here is "Freedom," and this freedom is dominion over nature and natural law; it is to dwell in the true Being. Schleiermacher here has something quite different to say from the *Zwischenstuck* of the *Addresses.* The Eternal is not conceived whilst one is "lying in the bosom of nature," opening all the senses to her and becoming one with her, but rather:

> *From within came the great revelation.*
> *A moment of light crowned the long search.*

All this is mysticism of the first way. Of that of the second way there is scarcely a trace to be found in the Monologues, those

---

[8] Cf. R. Otto's edition of Schleiermacher's *Addresses,* p. 65.

true self-revelations of Schleiermacher. However much he attempts to describe and lay bare his own nature to his friends, he nowhere describes himself as a beholder of the Universum according to the second way.

Even in the second edition of the *Addresses,* six years after their first appearance, Schleiermacher radically alters the *Zwischenstück* so far as it speaks of mystical identification with the Universum, and allows only the self-evidence of feeling to remain, which is characteristic of the mystic of both ways. But such a correction would have done violence to himself, if those passages had really corresponded to his own experience. It would resemble a convert who later strikes out of his personal confession the description of the fundamental experience of conversion. If he really does this as Schleiermacher did, he would disavow the whole account. Schleiermacher did not discover the divine in beholding the Universum; he found it within.

Traces of the Unifying Vision in Kant and Fries

1. The basic conception of Meister Eckhart is reechoed in certain fundamental ideas of Kant. As, for Eckhart, intellectus and ratio, so for Kant pure reason and understanding are opposed to one another. Understanding is the capacity of forming distinct conceptions, and applies to the sphere of multiplicity in sense-experience. Indeed, the root conceptions of understanding, the twelve categories, as well as pure contemplation of space and time, form the faculty of synthesis, which is the capacity to see unity in contrast to the multiplicity and dissipation of sense-perception. But the highest principle of the unity of all is to him, beyond everything else, the idea of the Godhead, which, in the region of a theoretical and scientific knowledge of the world, is only used for regulative purposes, though even here, as such, it is of the utmost importance:

> The transcendental Ideas have a most excellent and indipensable regulative use, namely, to direct the understanding to a certain goal, whither the lines of direction supplied by their several rules, converge in a single point, which, though it is indeed only an idea (focus imaginarius)...yet serves to procure to them the greatest unity along with the greatest extension. *(Critique of Pure Reason)*
>
> Under the protection of such a fundamental ground to make possible the systematic unity...of the manifold in the whole of the world. *(Critique of Pure Reason)*
>
> ...The third idea of Pure Reason as that of the unified and all-sufficing cause of all cosmological series is the idea of God....To behold all cosmic connections according to the principle of systematic unity, as if they had sprung complete out of a sole, all-encompassing Being as the highest and all-sufficient cause.

The significance of Kant's dialectic, according to his own assertion, lies in the fact that though indeed on the one hand it proves the purely regulative value of these ideas in relation to our knowledge, nevertheless on the other it protects their objective validity in opposition to the objections of skepticism. The latter he tries to accomplish from the sphere of moral ideas in the form of his postulates. But he does not recur merely to a theory of moral postulates; in his third *Critique,* the *Critique of Pure Judgment,* he himself takes the path of the direct intuitus mysticus. It does indeed explicitly form the bridge between the *Critique of Pure Reason* and the *Critique of Practical Reason.* In the nonlogical judgments of mere feeling the echo of the "Idea" itself is conceived. And again it is here a peculiar form of unity which is perceived; not the unity conceived by the concepts of understanding, but an inexplicable unity of things and of the thing given in feeling, which is denied to all conceptual perception, and for which all theoretic questioning as to the "what" of the object is of no import.

But in so far as the pure capacity for knowledge in Kant is preconscious and subconscious, and all perceptions of unity, meaning and value rise from a depth of the mind which itself lies far below the level of the senses and of understanding, Kant also knows the "ground of the soul." Further, he knows in general "the treasure lying in the field of shadowy presentation which constitutes the deep abyss of human knowledge, and which we cannot plumb."

2. Fries has developed the last point further in his doctrine of Transcendental Apperception. Like the *Memoria* of Augustine, it is the self-enriching territory of the subconscious, held fast in dim conceptions, which forms the secret basis of all our empirical and individual consciousness. This transcendental apperception is formed through the unifying functions of "formal" apperception, and this in turn is a fundamental and primordial knowledge of eternal unity and fulfillment. This basic cognition of Fries' doctrine could not be otherwise or better described than by the mystical intuition of Eckhart, which is also not an individual act of empirical consciousness, but a fundamental element of the soul itself, independent of all here and now, and only in individual moments breaking forth out of its depth to actualize itself in empirical cousciousness.

3. Fries also took up the thought of Kant that the idea of the Godhead is "the unifying principle of all cosmic series," and gave it its assured place in Kant's conceptual scheme. Fries states that the idea of the Godhead arises for us in the third field of the category of relation, namely, within the range of the category of mutual causality. Through universal reciprocity of action and reaction the world of things becomes for us an ordered and unified whole. The very fact that the various cosmological series do not exist in isolation side by side, that their existence with one another is possible, and that they are possible as a whole of one cosmic system—this requires a principle, that, itself absolutely one, is the ground of the possibility of the world as one unified whole. Fries conceives this principle evidently by the category of "causality," that means, he conceives the relationship of the original principle of world unity to the world as "causa." But that would imply that the conceptually incomprehensible relationship of that which makes all things possible would itself be again comprehended by a category of knowledge. In this respect Kant had obviously both perceived and felt far more deeply. True, indeed, that he also uses for God such terms as "cause." But the groping synonyms by which he attempts to express this designation show that he deeply realized the insufficiency of this category and of all categories of understanding in regard to this original principle and its relationship to the world. He says, speaking in peculiarly vague terms which are clearly not conceptions but ideograms:

> ...the idea of *something* upon which all empirical reality *grounds* its highest and last essential unity.

Or:

> ...under the protection of such an original primal cause.

Or he uses the ideogram, which we mentioned above:

> ...out of one, sole, *all-encompassing* Being.

We said on page 54 that in order to fill in the conception of the conditioned being of the creature, which is not possible by any rational category but can only be completed by means of an ideogram, we have only such vague terms as "to lie at the ground of a thing as its principle" or "to comprise it." Such terms are no longer "categories" but mystical terms. For "category" means always a concept. But here we have no longer any concept, only the ideogram as a vessel of pure, inexplicable numinous feeling.

4. That Fries on the one hand, with his doctrine of premonition (Ahndung) and of religion as premonition of the divine teleology in the world clearly takes up the motive of Kant's *Third Critique,* and on the other is found to be as clearly in the line of mystical intuition of the second way, is palpable to every reader. His friend and pupil De Wette carries this still further for—and this signifies the most fateful change in the development of the intuitus mysticus—he relates the mystical intuition to an object to which it had never been applied by the old mystics, namely, to the *factual* in history.[1] Thereby he continues what Schleiermacher had already begun in his *Addresses,* but which in his later teaching he has rather suppressed than developed.

This mystical intuition in relation to the factual in history is the same as that which I called "Divination" in Chapter XVIII of my book *The Idea of the Holy.*

[1]Compare R. Otto: *The Philosophy of Religion.*

Luther on Method in Contemplation[1]

Because he was a monk, Eckhart of course knew and practiced doubtless regularly and methodically the art of contemplation, absorption, worship, or whatever other name we like to give it. Also, he knew moments when a man is "fixed with his mind in God"—is completely and inwardly gathered. But it is peculiar to the character of his mysticism that he recognizes no "method." There is with him no "methodus orandi." Luther is more "methodical" than Eckhart, and he expressly gives a methodus orandi in his book, *How Man Should Pray, for Meister Peter, the Barber*, 1534. Against the monotonous repetition of hourly prayers and the Rosary, he here sets forth the prayer of inward recollectedness as the true language of the heart, and at the same time as a clearly and methodically directed form of contemplation. As the object of such prayers of contemplation he gives no exercises in hallucinations of the terrors of Hell or the joys of Heaven, but he offers as a positive object of meditation the divine words of the Lord's Prayer, the Ten Commandments, the Psalms, or as he says, "a number of the sayings of Christ or Paul." He deals with these according to the old contemplative method.

(a) He expected that such prayers would be used in regular daily exercises:

> It is good that man in the early morning should make prayer his first and in the evening his last work.

(b) He would have men use them to conquer the well-known conditions of Acedia which are characteristic of all mystical life

---

[1] Cf. p. 33.

(in a heightened form) and are just as inevitable in the experience of simple piety:

> When I feel that through intruding occupations or thoughts I have become cold and lacking in zeal for prayer.

(c) He collects his thoughts and himself by means of an opening prayer and waits until

> by the words of the mouth the heart is warmed and has come to itself.

(d) With all the mystics he demands as preparation the vacare Deo—to empty and free the self from all distracting elements:

> Therefore the greatest emphasis lies therein, that the heart free itself and become joyous: as the Preacher says: Prepare thine heart before prayer, that thou tempt not God.

(e) To make the heart thus free he sets before the Paternoster as an object of contemplation, "when I have time and space," one or other of the Commandments:

> That I may thereby be made free for prayer.

He has also for this purpose created his own method of four stages. He makes of reflection on the Commandments "a fourfold twisted wreath," in taking the Commandment first as a doctrine (as something to be thought about: "I think what our Lord therein demands of me": cogitatio), secondly as a thanksgiving, thirdly as a confession, fourthly as a prayer. This scheme of the fourfold twisted wreath he applies to each individual Commandment.

(f) He thus reassures himself, before he begins his real prayer, by reflection on God's commands and promises, that he may then dare to pray. He then says the Lord's Prayer, and in silent meditation upon it repeats

> a portion of it, or as much as you like,

spending time in contemplation and consideration on each phrase. He does not intend that others should reflect upon and repeat these—his own thoughts, but that such exercises in contemplation shall be called forth in each, individually:

But I would thereby that the heart (of the reader) should be stimulated and instructed, as to what thoughts it should lay hold on in the Lord's Prayer. Such thoughts, when the heart is rightly warmed and eager for prayer, it can express in many different words, and with more or less words. As I also do not bind myself to such words and habits, but today thus, tomorrow quite otherwise I utter the words according as my heart warms toward them.

(g) What Luther so describes and recommends is the methodus "cogitationis et meditationis" of which Hugo of St. Victor speaks: First the definite attentive comprehension by thought of an intellectual content, and then meditation soaring freely above this conception. Above this rises for Hugo the "contemplatio" whence the Spirit itself enters, which teaches what man no longer thinks, contemplates or reflects upon, but what is thought in him. Similarly Luther continues:

It often happens that in a passage or a supplication (of the Lord's Prayer) I come into such richness of thought that I leave the other six (supplications) aside. And when such rich and good thoughts *come,* one should let other commandments slip away to give the thoughts room and to listen in silence (wordless prayer), and should take good care not to hinder them. For there the Holy Spirit itself speaks, and of its speech a word is better than a thousand prayers of ours. I have often learned more in one prayer than I could have got from much reading and considering.

Beyond the preparatory stages of reflection and meditation there lies for him the state of contemplation, where the spirit itself teaches men:

(See the end of the Meditation on the Second Commandment): And what I have said above in the Lord's Prayer I also exhort (here) once again: at the times when the Holy Spirit comes under cover of such thoughts and begins to speak in your heart in richly glowing ideas, do Him the honor of letting go your own preconceived notions (the merely personal cogitationes et meditationes). Be still, and hearken to Him who can better do than thou. And what He proclaims, that mark, and write it down. So wilt thou experience wonders.

What distinguishes Luther[2] from all "methodicalism" is not that

[2] For "The Mystical Element in Luther's Conception of Faith" see R. Otto's *Idea of the Holy,* p. 107 and the Appendix.

he had no methodus orandi, but that he repudiates the use of his method as the only lawful one, alone sufficing for all men, and that even for himself it is no law:

> Also I continue with the other Commandments as I have time and space or a desire thereto. For I will have no man bound to these my words or thoughts, but I have simply set forth my own example for him to follow who will, or to better as he can.

That each one has to find and to exercise his "way of prayer" is to him an obvious necessity. But if Peter the Barber cannot do this, one must at least give him an "example." In any case: Luther is more a stickler for "methods" than the "mystic" Eckhart.

A Search for Salvation, Not Scientific Knowledge[1]

Since the days of Lasson, Eckhart's speculative system has been the object of much caviling as regards his failure to deduct the manifoldness and multiplicity of the creature from the One Being, and so to explain it. In fact, in this respect, he holds a position very much lower than that of Plotinus, and this not only as regards the results which he obtains, but in his whole attitude toward the problem and his efforts for its solution.

But in truth we would go much further and say that a particular, isolated interest in this theoretical question as to the explanation of the world and its philosophy is not to be found at all in Eckhart. This clearly signifies that at bottom he is no disciple of Plotinus. Plotinus is indeed a theologian and a seeker after salvation. But it is not true that this is the sole object of his search. He seeks—and herein he remains a true Hellene—knowledge above all, and by no means only a knowledge of salvation. We should misunderstand him if we attached less importance to his strictly theoretic work, which he carried even to the subtle logical examination of the table of categories, than to his mystical rapture, or saw the former merely as the handmaid of his mysticism. But Eckhart could apply to himself the saying of the Buddha: "My teaching has but one savor, salvation."

In this respect he is also different from his teacher, Thomas Aquinas. Thomas is more "scientific" than Eckhart and has a more definite interest in wordly science. Eckhart differs still further from John Scotus Erigena, whose ideas he undoubtedly revived. Erigena developed in his writings a truly physicometa-

[1] See pp. 20, 94-95.

physical system which he called with justice: "De Divisione Naturae" (Concerning the Divisions of Nature). The very title puts his work into the ranks of the metaphysical physics of the old "physiologoi," and Erigena expressly claims to be such. The Christian idea of salvation is for him interwoven with the natural world-system, and has itself become theoretical metaphysics. Just as great is the cleft between Boehme and Eckhart. Boehme is more deeply moved by a speculative interest in nature and the significance of the world than is Eckhart. Thereby he is a true child of a new age of ferment in which, alongside religious interests and closely entwined with them, the modern search for an understanding of the universe to its very foundations, manifests itself. With the instrument of an unpracticed fantasy, with an entire lack of appreciation of his own limitations and quite unprepared for a full comprehension of the problem, Boehme flings himself into the tasks of a dawning age of whose coming he has strong forebodings.

In contrast to this, Eckhart is entirely and merely a seeker after salvation and a mystic. (a) It is characteristic of the mystic vision that it sees the manifoldness and multiplicity with which it is surrounded in the One. This and this alone is its distinguishing feature. It is no concern of the mystic to discover how the dispersive vision (i.e. the scientific vision) does its work, and so still more to exercise and strengthen it. (b) The seeker after salvation, as we have said above, finds the given empirical situation and seeks how this is to be overcome and not how it is to be explained.

Erigena, and still more Boehme, are typical theosophists, which neither Eckhart nor Sankara is in the least. Sankara, indeed, in explaining the ancient Upanishads, must deal with the whole of early cosmological speculation, but this does not constitute his real interest. And as soon as he gets into difficulties over it, he retreats to the position that the man who has known the One eternal Brahman is above this speculative system and can ignore it. "We do not explain the world, we explain it away."

The Mutual Intertwining of the "Two Ways" of Mysticism[1]

1. Abyssus invocat abyssum. Deep calls unto deep, say our mystics with the Psalmists. And they mean thereby that the depth of their own being cries out to the depth and abyss of the divine. But that saying also provides a good metaphor for the strange meeting, intertwining and running together of the "two ways" of mystical approach of which we have already spoken. Here also deep calls unto deep: the numinous depth of the eternal One in and behind all things (including the perceiver) calls to the numinous depth of the soul in its inmost being—where lies the marvel of God united with the soul. It was a meeting and mutual discovery of two primarily very different elements, when the old Ekam of the Vedas encountered the Atman. The words of the Chhandogya, "Sa atma," give expression to no self-evident experience and are no analytical judgment, but they reveal a most surprising synthesis. From that time onward in India, the two ways have been entangled with one another. Thus we find them in Sankara, and also in Eckhart, and in many another mystic of still other countries and races.

For those of us who are not mystics, this interpenetration of the two ways is always puzzling, and to those who misunderstand their fundamental difference it is very necessary to point out the enigma of their union, and to make clear the peculiarity of each in sharpest distinction. True, for the mystic himself there is here no riddle; to him the necessity of their combination is obvious. He knows nothing of the twofoldness of the ways, but from the peculiar quality of the objects he experiences both unfold clearly before him. He does not reflect on their difference. If he did so,

[1] See p. 56.

249

he would probably not be able to explain in clear-cut conceptions the necessity of their combining. It is to him an immediately felt necessity, and he has no need to analyze intellectually what is given a certainty in feeling.

We can neither recognize nor feel this necessity. The interlocking must always appear to us as an astonishing fact. It is particularly amazing when we view it from the starting point of the first way. We have nothing to do here with reflection upon outward things and their unity or non-unity. The root fact is quite other and is clearly presented to our gaze. It is obviously this: Casting the self free from all outward events, in an inward gathering, there breaks upon the mystic from the inward depths an experience, secret and wonderful, a foreshadowing of greater things not to be comprehended by thought. That which he neither knew nor felt before becomes living within him as the inconceivably strange and great, which he himself bears. It overflows and quickens within him, it lays hold on him and is his being. Is it the wonder of the soul itself which is revealed to him in its immeasurability? What can the things of the world trouble him then with their unity or multiplicity, with the query as to what lies behind them or at their base? Or, is it an oversoul, penetrating the soul of man, welling up and flowing through him, absorbing and uniting him within it—the Godhead? Then it is also the Godhead of the soul, her essence and her being, her life and her blessedness. But as to whether this Godhead is at the same time ''all things'' and the unity and being of all things—what does that matter to the soul!

2. To discover in the inwardness of the self the divine miracle in the soul, or the indwelling Atman, and on the other hand, behind and beyond the multiplicity of things to behold the One that is the essence of all things and of the self—these are, we say, two absolutely different experiences, and as non-mystics we cannot conceive how they can slip into one another and become indissolubly bound together. In India we see most clearly the entirely different starting points of each.

Here, the first is the discovery of the Ekam in and behind the world, which is recognized as the eternal Brahman.[2] The discov-

---

[2] Herein lies an insoluble problem for the rationalist and the ''evolutionist,'' namely: Why does the Ekam of mystical vision become one with the ancient, magical Brahman and why does this Brahman become the Ekam?

ery of the "inward atman," of the ascharyam in the inner self, is the second, and is completely independent of the first.

But the realization that this Ekam-Brahman is the "inward atman"—is the third discovery, and is again a new treasure trove in itself. How did it come to pass? Why do the Brahman and Atman meet one another? Our religious history simply relates the fact—that Brahman and Atman speculation "interpenetrate." But why did they do it? That it is "natural" is certainly not true and this is proven by the circumstance that atman-speculation in Sankhya and Yoga can arise not only without Brahman, but can definitely refuse to accept both Brahman mysticism and Advaitam. Did this happen by chance? and is it true that in certain directions Indian speculation forms a mere "syncretism" of the two and in others leaves them apart? Yet the doctrine of Sankara is certainly no syncretism, no chance flowing together and intermingling of previously existing streams. The inner uniting of these two ways and elements evidently takes place in Vedanta-mysticism under the compulsion of a strongly felt need. Such an inward compulsion toward this type of synthesis may also be induced historically: for the fact remains that not only once in India, but to the same extent in many totally different places, a corresponding synthesis is achieved, from essentially different starting points and under widely differing conditions. We find the same synthesis of the two ways in Eckhart and Plotinus and al-Hallaj. If this correspondence does not point to a hidden law of necessity, it at least indicates a powerfully constraining inward element.

The mystic himself would say: "Even that which was the Eternal-One and is in all things, that is the ground of my soul —that is my soul. This I know. He who does not know this has not yet seen, or has only partially seen." But the non-mystic will look about him for definite elements of reciprocal attraction, which must exist in any affinities between these two mysticisms. What the mystic perceives as the cogent root of the matter, appears to our secular vision only as a question of "similarity" or "relationship" between the intuitions of the two different ways, which gives us a mere psychological guide. What is for the mystic an essential and necessary connection of the two seems to us only a reciprocal attraction following the laws of psychology; e.g. the rule that in certain circumstances different, in other circumstances like experiences can intermingle in the soul under the compulsion of their resemblance, and can not only mix together but in certain events can also arouse one another—abyssus invocat abyssum—can be the occasion of the wakening of each other, and in interpenetration can mutually enhance each other.

3. Such moments can be cited. From them, we can explain at least "psychologically" that the vision of the Ekam carries with it (perhaps awakens and calls up) the vision of the atman, and that both coincide in close unity as in the example we have mentioned.

(a) "Sa atma: That—namely the One, Being Itself, the Brahman—that is the self." This formula in its first meaning does not yet say that Brahman speculation has combined with speculation of the *soul*. For the "self" which is spoken of here is not the "inner Atman," the indwelling in contrast to the outward, "the soul" in distinction from body, senses, powers, and so on. The contrast between inward and outward is not here referred to, but it is the "self" simply as the perceiving subject which is intended. Therefore, the "Great Word" continues, and says simply: "Tat tvam asi—That art thou." Thou thyself art this eternal-one-living Brahman. That does not mean you find the Sat indwelling in you, but you find yourself as the Sat and the Sat as yourself. This passage therefore refers only to the vision of the second way. But it is now indeed easily comprehensible from the standpoint of psychology, that when the "second discovery" of the "inner-atman," the ascharyam in us, has been made and we have gained the insight that we ourselves are not body nor senses, nor anything outward, but that our real "self" is something inward and indwelling—that then the formula "Tat tvam asi" which itself does not require this meaning at all, must at once and necessarily assume the meaning of the inner atman.

(b) The first and all-conditioning element lies not in those things mentioned under (a), but in the consistently numinous character of the object of experience. For however different it may be, on the one hand the discovery of the miraculous depths of the soul and God indwelling in the heart of men, and on the other the depth of the world in unity and oneness: both are above all experiences of *wonder*. And this is true, not in the modern emaciated sense of the word, but of wonder in the sense of the numinous quantity which we have tried to define in another passage. To express it roughly: Brahman and atman are both descended from a "numinous" sphere. So also, the vision of the Ekam, the One, is the vision of a "miraculous and magical nature."[3] For when we behold the "One" we are in the region of wonder and the element of unity therein, as we noticed above, is only the conceptually apprehended element of an inexpressible and wholly wondrous content.[4]

(c) Further, in both ways as we have seen, there is to a like extent the element of identification of the subject with the object. He who beholds Unity perceives himself as One with the One. But also he who looks inward knows his inner self as one and united with the divine. Thus, an original duality disappears for both lines of approach.

(d) The one who beholds Unity sees beyond space and time,[5] and the same is true of the inward vision. When the soul, turning in upon itself, sinking down into its own ground and depth, sees and feels itself in God and one with God, so, in equal measure, it beholds itself caught away from time and space, in the eternal Now.

(e) Similarly, the relationship of the many to the one so closely resembles that of the "outward" to the "inward," that they finally come to mean almost the same thing. For as the One is placed above the many as the "steadfast," the "essential," the "ground which bears the many," so the atman or the soul remains as that which is itself *one* beneath the multiplicity of powers, senses and capacities; as the unchanging element which is itself always the same behind the play of imagination and feeling, of thought and desire. The soul is at the same time the essential in contrast to the "accidental" of its outward periphery; the "truth" as opposed to the deception of the senses or of appearance. All the predicates of the Speculation on Being can therefore easily be transferred to the soul, or can arise simply out of its own nature. (This is very clearly seen in Eckhart.)

(f) On the other hand: the way of the intuition of unity is in a

---

[3] Only so could the Brahman and the "One" find themselves together.

[4] Only the pennon of the submerged submarine.

[5] Perhaps here there is the greatest possibility for the non-mystic to approach faintly to the experience of the mystic. For those great moments of experience, when, before the utter majesty or beauty of nature, or in the presence of some deeply significant event, the beholder catches his breath, the pulse ceases, and the sense of time disappears, are granted also to the uninitiated.

certain sense, also a "way inward." For what does the curious formula of the "inward" really mean? It comes in the first instance from the naïve conception of the soul "indwelling" in the body. The distinction between outward things and the inner soul was first understood in a crudely realistic sense. But very soon this meaning was spiritualized. We know that here as also in mysticism, the relation of the soul to the temporal body and temporal things is not itself a space-relationship, as it must have been if the early conception of the outward and the inward had endured. The "inner" sphere is not a question of space, it is the sphere of those objects which, wholly independent of and different from all palpable objects of sense-perception, are not the spatial concave to their convex, but are qualitatively opposed to them. To turn inward means then to make this qualitatively "other" the object of contemplation.

But it means still more: to win the knowledge which does not come from without but which the soul finds within herself. Here interpretation in terms of space is from the first meaningless. The paradox: "Knowledge not from without but from within the self" signifies knowledge, which I do not receive through the testimony of the senses, and so from without, but which I gain immediately and spontaneously through the soul itself, and in the strength of its own being. Now, of this nature is the vision of God and of the divine essence of the soul of the mystical "first way," but also the vision of the Unity behind the many, and of the unity of the subject with all and with the One. Not the "sensual" man, but the "rishi" of spiritual vision beholds the One and the Sat. The senses do not point me to that unity, or allow me to perceive in principio; they bind me to the disintegration, multiplicity and divisiveness of space and time. So, whoever beholds "unity," perceives it not through the senses, but through the "indwelling"—the soul itself. Atmani atmanam atmana; to behold the Atman in the atman through the atman, runs the maxim of the "First Way," and this perception through the Atman may be defined as the vision "indriyavyapara-anadhinatas": the vision independent of the function of the senses. Whoever "anyad na pasyati," who sees non-duality, who beholds all in one and himself in all, also perceives "indriya-vyapara-anadhinatas."[6] Where the capacity to perceive the self through the soul is awakened along the one line of approach, it follows that it swiftly and easily awakens upon the other.

In the language of secular speech we should have to say: "Knowledge of the (mystical) unity of the universe and of my own unity with it is Knowledge a priori." The senses provide the raw material for this. But what this "is," what it "is" in truth, wherein lies its depth, meaning and essence, the senses do not reveal. This is also discovered immediately by the soul "through itself," and that means that the soul finds it "indwelling" in itself.

This is what Eckhart had in mind in the following passage. A pupil asked him: What are angels? The master answered:

> "Go hence and withdraw into thyself until thou understandest; give thy whole self up to it, then look, refusing to see anything but what thou findest there. It will seem to thee at first as though thou art the angels with them and as thou dost surrender to their collective being thou shalt think thyself the angels as a whole with the whole company of angels."
>
> The pupil went away and withdrew into himself until he found all this in truth in his own ground. Then returning to his master, he gave him thanks and said: "It was as you foretold. On giving my whole mind to the subject of the angels and aspiring to their estate, at first it seemed to me that I was all the angels with the angels." (Evans, pp. 216, 217)

He does not inquire as to the being of the soul, but as to the being of "outward objects," in this instance of the angels. He finds this essence when he discovers in himself (a priori) what the angels themselves are. (Augustine has also affirmed such an "indwelling" knowledge with regard to outward objects: he himself brings it into play at the end of his Confessions, when he questions the witness of his inner knowledge as regards cosmological problems.) We have in Eckhart as a specially mystical element the fact that he "mystifies" not only as elsewhere knowledge a posteriori, but here also knowledge a priori. The

---

[6] The formula "indriya-vyapara-anadhinatas" and its positive correlate "atmana" practically correspond to the "Knowledge a priori" of pure Reason in contrast to the "Knowledge a posteriori" of sense-perception.

soul expands itself to the object, becomes the object—in this case becomes the angels. So it knows what an angel is.

(g) In support of his "angel-experiment" Eckhart could have called upon that sentence of Aristotle, which is also important for the latter's doctrine of knowledge: "The soul is itself all (namely δυναμει, so that it can take on any form)." This saying is only the Aristotelian interpretation of the assertion that "like is known through likeness," which, lifted into the sphere of mysticism means that knowledge comes only through identification. I must be what I know, and being and knowledge are identical (a purely mystical axiom). This is patently the maxim of knowledge of the first way: I know God in so far and because I "have my being from Him," i.e. inasmuch as I am what I know. But ultimately it is also the maxim of knowledge of the second way. For the all and the One, the Universum and the Unum know as such only because all with all, and I with all, and I in all, am one with the One.

4. We have found a whole series of analogies between experiences of very different content, which may explain to some extent how two revelations of different types but with frequent affinities can mutually flow into and penetrate one another. But there is no doubt that the mystic himself would declare such explanations unsatisfactory. Where we see mere connections and relationships of affinity he sees actual identity, where we make psychological assertions he makes theological, where we talk about religion, he speaks from religious experience.